Downhill from the Projects

Brian Shawn

Order this book online at www.trafford.com
or email orders@trafford.com

Most Trafford titles are also available at major online book retailers.

Printed in Victoria, BC, Canada.

ISBN: 978-1-4269-2130-8 (Soft)

*We at Trafford believe that it is the responsibility of us all, as both individuals
and corporations, to make choices that are environmentally and socially sound.
You, in turn, are supporting this responsible conduct each time you purchase a
Trafford book, or make use of our publishing services. To find out how you are
helping, please visit www.trafford.com/responsiblepublishing.html*

*Our mission is to efficiently provide the world's finest, most comprehensive
book publishing service, enabling every author to experience success.
To find out how to publish your book, your way, and have it available
worldwide, visit us online at www.trafford.com*

Trafford rev. 11/16/2009

 www.trafford.com

North America & international
toll-free: 1 888 232 4444 (USA & Canada)
phone: 250 383 6864 ♦ fax: 812 355 4082 ♦ email: info@trafford.com

Dedication

My sons: Matthew, Dylan and Noah….

The three most beautiful people I know.

Acknowledgements

First and Foremost My Sons Matthew, Dylan and Noah…Your Integrity, Honesty and Understanding are just a few of your natural talents. I find myself looking up to you everyday. My closest friends: Seth Curll and Matt Wright, Seth, truly an Angel on Earth when I needed one the most. Matt with your tough exterior you have an incredible heart. Our friends Carol O`Neil, Carol is the kindest person I know I am amazed to watch from the sidelines. Heather and Bill Sandgren Your Support and friendship are a gift to us. Dee Dee you are a beautiful human.Tom Krescholleck your heart is ten times your size. My family, John we kept on saying those were the days… Now we say that about last year….

Christen "Your equal to none"…

Jamie "See how Boston reflects off the water"…

January "don't start with me"…

Aunt Marion "You are a rare flower"

Becky thank you for seeing the *real* in me and thank you for letting me see it again

1

Take it all away

"OK boys lets go".

Like three little ducklings we followed Moms voice without even having to look up. We walked out the front door. I happened to look up and say "Hey what is this stuff?" Jimmy said "its fog" John added "yeah its froggy out". Instantly the humor and the experience we had with frogs gave me a sense of comfort,

(We like going to the brook to catch frogs. My fun was watching my brothers. It was a challenge, in the wild, watching, waiting one move and it was a free for all, the art of catching one without getting wet. Someone always ended up covered in the slimy green gunk, Or with some very wet sneakers, that was usually our cue to head home.)

We were headed down the hill on Magna Rd in *America Park,* the Lynn Projects. As far back as can I remember… that is my first clear memory. I was going to be five in a couple of days. The year was 1969. It was a troubled time… Mom was sick, we were told she was pregnant, she actually had cancer.

She passed away on my birthday. My father had a troubled past and he was serving time in State Prison. So we had to accept what ever arrangements he could make for us.

My cousin Stephanie, Aunt Ruth and Aunt Marion helped us move out. When I asked why we had to move, Stephanie and Aunt Marion let me know Mom was gone and she was not sick anymore, she is with the Angels in Heaven. So, we have to live with other people. They were giving me *a little comfort there.* Stephanie had long dark hair and big brown eyes; just a pleasant look about her. Her voice was soft and sweet and she spoke with sincerity. Without question she was a "Caring woman with angelic quality"

We were rounding up our belongings. Jimmy spotted **the** matchbox bat mobile and grabbed it. *I was looking for it!* Along with whatever else was to be taken with us "That's mine!" Mom gave it to me for my birthday" I spoke with panic. Jimmy shouted "You're a liar its mine! He was not going to give in to me, that's for sure.

Stephanie convinced me to take my Mothers perfume bottle; it was shaped like a cat and had a black soft velvet exterior. I accepted it, but I was not happy.

Jimmy and John went to live with Aunt Ruth and Uncle Ed, Stephanie, Ann, Joey and Gail were their kids. (Ed was actually Dads cousin and Ruth was his wife.) I went to Aunt Marion, Dads sister, she is a wonderful woman; married to Uncle Hank they had a great house on Norton St. and three boys of their own. The time I stayed at Norton St. was short, less than a year; I guess it felt comfortable and safe. What I remember most, is watching Underdog.

Oh, I was also a heavy sleeper or to put it another way, *I wet the bed*. Hank was not really happy about that. His anger grew and it was decided that I should not stay with them.

In the summer of 1971, I was sent to my Grandmother on my father's side, Grammy *Boober*, She married Walter Boober. Dad's father took off before he was born. And now Grammy and Walter were near seventy years old. My visit here was a trial visit. The only other alternative was (Aunt Ruth and Uncle Ed, they already had a houseful.) In the beginning, everything went smooth. Grammy had short curly hair, she wore thick glasses (which she would constantly adjust and then brush her hands across her sundress, it seemed as if one shoulder strap was always up and one down.)

The second you entered her house she stopped everything she was doing. And she would put all her focus on you. She loved everyone…

One Saturday, Dad had a twelve hour furlough, He was at Grammy Boober`s. Jimmy stopped in to visit and show me his *new* bike; He also wanted to teach me how to ride.

The first lesson was on the sidewalk and not so good. I got the thing going pretty fast (*I might say,*) an elderly woman stepped in front of me. I had no idea how to stop. *It was a direct hit.* I was terrified! She was crying in pain, I was screaming "OH MY GOD, I am sorry, I am so sorry" I was in complete panic! Jimmy ran in the house and got my father. They stayed with her until help arrived. I ran inside the house to hide. She was taken away by ambulance. It took over an hour to calm me down; Thank God my father was there. The woman received quite a few stitches in her leg.

The next day, I was able to tell her I was sorry, Soon, It would be forgiven. Grammy was her friend and well, *time is a healer*.

In September, I began the first grade and it was a rocky start, One day during the first week on my way home from school. I was crossing at the Square, just behind a pick up truck, suddenly; it rolled back and knocked me to the ground.

From the other side Walter watched in horror. I was alright, just a little bruised. However, that episode was (a sign that I could be a bit much for them 24/7) and it sent me right to Aunt Ruth and Uncle Ed. The move took place the next day which was another Saturday. I would have the weekend to adjust.

Uncle Ed was six feet four inches tall, somewhat stocky, his presence was intimidating. And in case *that* was not enough. He had a scar visible from the center of his forehead to the top of his left eye reshaping his eye lid. Later in life, I learned that it was due to an accident with a homemade circular saw. His demeanor was quiet and soft spoken (under "normal circumstances" Or in the presence of others,)

He loaded the station wagon with what little I had. And we headed over to Camden St.

The car had an unpleasant odor and all sorts of stuff throughout it. My mother was a clean freak; Aunt Marion and Grammy were too. I knew he was always fixing things, I figured that's "a working guy's car."

As we arrived, I noticed that they had a run down large red house with pealed paint, torn shades, overgrown weeds, and an old car with flat tires on the left side of the house (an area that had the potential of becoming a driveway) The debris on the ground was an exact match to the "stuff" in the car.

I stepped onto the porch and a similar yet stronger unpleasant odor filled my senses. (A gradual process to the climax I was about to reach) Jimmy ran past me and whipped open the door, disappearing into the darkness. It was dark enough inside that my eyes had to adjust. However, my nose was instantly aware of this unique atrocity.

(Saugus river at low tide has an odor much like human flatulence, The river was so close you could see the sun reflect the water off the kitchen ceiling, One half hour in the open air at low tide and I could faintly pick up the uniqueness of the river woven thru the uniqueness of the house)

"Wow" I thought, look at all of this stuff! Board games, books, piles of clothes, shoes, cups, tools, all sorts of paper, boxes, on chairs, on the floor, on counter tops and tables There was something everywhere! There was even dried poop on the floor. (Probably from the dog)

Then I thought to myself, "Is this where Stephanie comes from?" And there she was "Hi Brian, can I have a hug?" she said. I gave her a big hug and asked "Did your Mom die too? She said "No silly, Aunt Ruth is my Mom." I said "Then why do you live *here*?" as I cast my eyes over the filth and disgust… she was as out of place as we were. Uncle Ed interrupted and said "Jimmy, why don't you take your little brother in the back yard and play" "Ok Uncle Ed, C'mon Brian lets go" Jimmy replied

It was about 11am, the sun was bright and the sky was blue. The yard was thick with weeds on the right side, with bare dirt in the middle and sporadic growth to the left, it was spacious for a yard in this area. Just over the fence, I could hear kids jumping into a pool and laughing it sounded like lots of fun. "Hey lets see if we can play with them" I asked, Jimmy firmly replied "No!" I asked "why?" Jimmy said "they don't like us that's why!" why don't they like us? I asked. "Because they are rich kids and were not!" Jimmy shouted "But, I like them." I said. "You don't even know them!" He shouted "Yes I do," I replied "look they are laughing and having fun just like I do." I concluded

"Brian!" I heard a woman call out from the front of the house. Jimmy said "we better get in there quick; Aunt Ruth just called us to come in." I entered thru the front way taken by the now familiar odor, I could hear Uncle Ed yell out, (Rooty! did you holler out to that little one?) "He is right here!" She exclaimed

He called me over to the "sofa" Brian, *slight pause,* son, *another pause;* I want you to come here young man.(His voice became stronger; I was getting my first man to man talk) "Your Grandmother and your Aunt tell me you wet the bed, we don't do that here. You're going to sleep on the bottom bunk in the upstairs sun porch and Jimmy will sleep on the top. Your Aunt Ruth is going to check in the morning and if she finds piss in your bed. Well son, If she does, then I'm going to give you a good licking," He stated "What's a good licking?", I asked… He responded by saying "That's when I take off my belt, drop your draws and strap your ass over this coffee table, You got that young man?!", I said "yes," but no sound came out, He said " What's that? I didn't hear you" My voice squeaked "Yes" Jimmy realized this conversation had come to a close and asked "Can I take Brian down to the river?" Aunt Ruth replied "Yes, be back at 5 o'clock," We headed out the front way.

"Did Uncle Ed ever give you a licking? I wondered, Jimmy looked at me and said "It's not a licking, it's a beaten you'll see, He always does, Why do you think Johnny isn't here?" "Where is he?" I asked "He ran away!" Jimmy snapped back "well I hope I wake up dry, sometimes I do" When will Johnny be coming back?" "He's not" Jimmy said "Well your not going to run away are you?" I asked Jimmy said "No we have to live here!" "How long" I asked "until Dad gets out of jail" Jimmy replied, "were going to live with Dad again?" I asked with excitement "Yes someday, I don't know when, stop asking so many questions and lets just get down to the river. I might even show you the junk yard" he noted

As you approach the river the "beach" area is (a section covered with sand and dried reeds) and centered between a baseball field and a Junk Yard, The river covers many miles and out to the Atlantic, We were on the Lynn side looking out towards the Saugus yacht club (its about eight miles North of Boston, Mass) I was the youngest of three boys anything new was an adventure to me.(The river would prove to be a part of my being, in time a place from which I grew) Excited I said" Wow a baseball field, can I run around the bases?

"Nah c'mon its low tide lets "Jump rocks"
and try not to get wet. He spoke with an
instruction as if teaching a student. *Woo
yeah! Bam! Bam! Following his footsteps
from rock to rock bam! BAM! Not even a
near miss.* This was great; I could do it all
day

We went so far and turned and took
the same path back toward the beach. Jimmy
said "check this out" he turned over a rock,
there was a tiny crab about the size of a
dime, it ran sideways in search of a place to
hide. Jimmy reached down with a finger
and his thumb; he gently picked up the
angry looking, armor wearing, and weapon
holding, little creature. I said "hey does he
bite?" "Nah he's too small, here hold 'em"
Jimmy said, as he handed it forward, It's
pointed little legs touched my palm. I
quickly pulled my arm back sending the
creature on a short flight. Jimmy told me to
hold the sides and the crab couldn't hurt
you. I began lifting rocks and saw so many;
they all ran to hide as soon as the rock was
up. I asked why they ran sideways Jimmy
said "I don't know, enough stupid questions
lets go"

We walked down the beach in the direction of the junk yard. Jimmy warned me of the dangers "Be quiet, and follow me, keep your eyes open for junkyard dogs or cops, "Jimmy I'm scared" I said nervously "Just stay with me" he answered, we followed the length of fence until we found and opening. (I was amazed, seeing cars on top of cars, all smashed and busted up, set in rows, it was car heaven. I was not familiar with the term "graveyard" almost a year had past since Ma died and I was comforted with a less graphic terminology.) Jimmy said "stay on the outside edge near the water and we will go all the way to the end." Jimmy approached a VW bus he grabbed a door handle and looked all around "it's clear, c'mon" he opened the door and we jumped in. "What do you think? It's my clubhouse" he said "wow this is cool" I replied (this thing had carpeting, window blinds, benches and cabinets) "It's better than the sun porch" I added after a few minutes we headed back to the house it was near five o'clock

We missed lunch, and all that fun made me very hungry, as we ran into the house, I detected the scent of charred hamburger. It was somewhat less offending than the other odors

(Combine the following: Dog shit, dirty socks, dirty dog, human sweat, dirty laundry, piss, garbage, musty basement, mold, hundred year old lumber, and anything imagined not immediately visible to the human eye, mix well, inhale deeply, hold for ten seconds…And you may capture the flavor of this fragrantly robust uniqueness called home) Aunt Ruth said "Brian you sit over there, Jimmy, sit were you usually sit and Joey will sit in his usual seat." She dropped a "lump" of instant potatoes onto my plate. It had a few lumps of its own. I broke one open with my fork and powder puffed in the air. She poured cold green peas onto my plate from the can. I was about to indulge in my first *undesirable feast* and the best part was *a dry burnt hamburger*. I was used to *real* Potatoes, warm vegetables and a seasoned meat cooked to delight. Aunt Ruth, (She was *around five foot six inches tall, two hundred fifty pounds, coarse red shoulder length hair, and a face that resembled the skipper of Gilligan's Island*) enjoyed sitting, smoking cigarettes and chewing chopped ice. She put forth great effort holding that mountain of flesh so close to a working stove. I would really hate to seem ungrateful here. In fact, had it not been for the effort applied to the creation of that dry burnt burger. *I could have starved.* Kudos to her and lots of ketchup, (Or was it *cats up?*)

After we ate, we went into the living room and watched T.V. it was a much needed down time for me. I used more energy today than I could ever remember. (Not a good way to be. I am a *heavy sleeper* now compounded by exertion uh oh) around eight thirty we headed off to bed. Jimmy climbed into his bunk and I got cozy in mine. As I laid there recalling the days events.

Suddenly Jimmy sounded out in a melodious way (*Delta dawn what's that flower you have on could it be a faded rose from days gone by*) I listened close and when he finished I asked" what was that," he replied "It's a song, I sing myself to sleep at night and that song makes me think of Mom. It's about a girl that died and went to heaven." "Oh, I don't like what the song is about, but I like you singing can you sing more? I asked. And he did, in a short period of time I was out like a light.

I cannot remember being close to Jimmy prior to this, the sense of family was a comfort, which I was beginning to feel with him. He was four years older and the middle child. And for now, John was absent in anyone's life

The next morning as I awoke, I felt the coldness against my body it was not an unfamiliar feeling, I was soaked. I woke Jimmy up and told him. And said *" uh oh, I'm going to get a licking"* "No" he replied "your going to get a beaten, we have to get dressed for church so just change and maybe they wont check" We headed down stairs and got cereal. (Aunt Ruth was in the kitchen sitting at the table in her usual posture, open mouth breathing, while holding a cigarette, her finger yellow from pall mall non filtered, *it was a bit early for ice chips*, the chair she sat in was cornered in a way that she could observe all who entered. It was freed up at meal time for Joey to eat. If she had no other obligations she nested there.) Aunt Ruth said " when you finish at church go next door for Sunday school" "Ok" Jimmy replied "here's a quarter for the box" she added. The walk to church had a feel as if the previous day's adventure had not ended. Jimmy showed me various points of interest, "That's Veronicas house, she is nice, Aunt Ruth don't like her though and this is Georgians flowers, he lets us hang around and talk and stuff. I usually see him watering everything, Gail Kowalski lives here, she is Aunt Ruth's friend, and this is the lithe club we go here on Halloween for a party.

Sam is the guy that owns this building, it's a printing shop, he's old, but cool. Ill introduce ya" he was going on and on. Every place had a story. In no time we were at the church, "St. Mikes," we headed on past the church and over to the variety store. I said "Jimmy where are we going? We past the church" Jimmy said "relax were not going, Aunt Ruth gave us a quarter each were going to get some goodies, After that we will go back to the church and when it lets out we'll go to Sunday school, when you get there check the desk for money. The catholic school kids usually leave some behind" We went into "the smoke shop" it was the local variety. "Snell's" had better stuff but they weren't open" We got *sixlets, fireballs, wax whistles, dots, and watermelon stix,*

We sat between the church and school on the stairs. After we had our goodies we ran around and sang songs. Jimmy called out "Brian, church is getting out, go in with the other kids and don't forget to look for change, Just don't get caught! "See ya later" I replied

The sense of guilt and the excitement of more cash, made my head swim. I forgot about my sleeping habits, *what a rush. Ignorance, fear and guilt all wrapped up in a sugar high*

We were seated almost immediately, unlike regular school "God" was everywhere and we were in *his* classroom. (A young sweet woman, funny, she actually looked like *(The flying Nun)* from TV. Asked if we were ready to "blah blah)

I have my hands inside the desk. As I feel around, I am trying to identify the objects as they come in contact with my fingers. "I think it's a dime, it keeps slipping away, I have to lean down and look, yup it's a dime and there's a quarter, oh boy, I can't believe I'm doing this. I held the coins tightly for the duration of the class. *It never occurred to me to slip them into my pocket.*

When the class ended, I met Jimmy outside, "Did you get anything?" He asked, I reached out and opened my hand displaying today's catch. "Good, hang on to it, I can show you some good places to hide it when we get to Aunt Ruth's. He noted. Aren't we going back to the store? "I asked. " No, If we have stuff, there going to know we skipped church" He replied. "And they know how long it takes to get home." He added

We headed back to the house it's almost a mile from the church. We talked about the river and Jimmy told me about his friend Geo and his brother Freddy. They were our ages and we could hang around with each other. He told me things about Geo, He made jokes about him, making fun of the way he walked and talked, Jimmy grunted and said "hey um Geo" as he walked like an ape. I asked about Freddy, but Jimmy didn't know much about him, just the idea that he was my age.

Just before we approached the house, Jimmy stopped at a fence post with a loose cap on top. He removed it and showed me that on the inside was chewed up gum. "Just stick your coins on it and set it back on carefully, otherwise they'll fall, I lost a few that way" He noted. As you enter the house, you're in the "front room" and you head straight into the kitchen. If the light is on, your eyes adjust quickly about half the distance between Aunt Ruth and I lay a pile of bedding

The sight of bedding told me the whole story, I was about to embark on my first "licking" I was concerned, due to Jimmy's labeling this "a beaten", but without fear, prior to now, I had never endured any type of *physical* pain.

"Brian, come on over here son," Uncle Ed stated in an (as for a matter of fact, tone) As he sat on the *sofa,* holding on to a thick black belt, carefully folded in half. "You're going to have to drop your drawers and bend over the coffee table" I complied, "Your underwear too" he added. I was *frozen with fear and embarrassment for a solid five seconds.* Then, I complied, my underwear went down cautiously

And like a tornado, a series of events took place at seemingly the exact same moment.

Uncle Ed forced my body onto the coffee table, (I could hear a loud Crack! And a scream that could break the sound barrier, it was my own. All the while, Uncle Ed shouted with rage (Crack, scream and "YOU) thundered throughout me simultaneously, you want to piss the bed in my fucking house" he continued, Huh, you want to piss the bed? You'll never piss the bed again you son of a bitch!" My body tried to lunge forward as my hands covered my backside. I was shaking violently "Move you're fucking hands or Ill break your fucking fingers, Crack again and crack again Crack. My ass, my thigh, my testicles and my hand. Suddenly, it stopped; his physical and verbal abuse had halted. I cried uncontrollably bouncing with pain as my pants and underwear sat around my ankles.

"Pull up your draws and go kneel in the corner" he said calmly. I moved as quickly as I could, anything to be taken away from that very moment.

Aunt Ruth happened to be off of her chair and present in the doorway. Holding my sheets, she threw them in the corner and told me to make sure they were between my nose and the wall. I slipped as I feared a few hits from her direction; my head hit the door frame. "Get up and in the corner" she shouted in a less beastly manner than Uncle Ed

One by one I could feel people walking quietly past me. It was their kids; this ritual was indeed a spectator event. For the next fifteen or twenty minutes the only sound was my crying, this was in no way background music, it was a brand new song soon to become a number one on this play list drowning out the TV, wash machine and anything else within the area

The "corner" had a process of its own. (This punishment however, always came as the conclusion of the "Good licking" ritual.) You were on your knees with your forehead pressed firmly at the two walls *this explains the headache and knee pain, the back ache was from having to arch your back and be straight at all times.* In this particular instance, pissed sheets were added for good measure.

My whaling began to calm, (if you disregard the occasional sharp screech from the stinging sensations on various areas of my back and legs) "Can I get out now?" I pleaded. "No" Aunt Ruth answered firmly. Arch your back and put your face in the corner, Do you like the smell of them *pissy* sheets?" she added, my nose was stuffed from crying and prevented me from smelling anything. "No" I replied, it seemed like the correct answer. "Nobody else does either" she proclaimed. (I understood what she meant by offending odors, as I have been introduced to them recently.)

Awhile in the corner my sinus began to open and the smell of urine slowly took hold of my senses, It was offending yet familiar and far less uncomfortable than the rest of my surroundings. Pressing my face in that sheet was like having my own private fortress that hid me from the now sickening feeling (as the "other odors" that everyone seems to like) overcome me. After a few more prompts and friendly reminders I successfully filled my obligation. As "a good licking" had concluded. I was allowed to enjoy the remainder of a lovely Sunday afternoon.

For the first time I can recall, Jimmy was absolutely right it *was* "a beaten" I went upstairs to my room for a place to be alone.

"Did he get your nuts?" Jimmy asked from the top bunk. He was reading a comic book just waiting around for me. "Yes" I responded "and look at my leg, its red with a blue line and why is it hot there?" I asked Jimmy said "I don't know, but it will feel better later, just try not to get in trouble." Why did he give you a beaten?" I asked "Depends, it's always for different reasons. He said

"You had more than one?" I asked with surprise, "Yup, get used to it. Johnny got it before me its 'cause we're not his kids, Joey and Stephanie never get it, Anne got one and Gail is just a baby", he informed me.

Trying to justify a punishment that fits the crime gives me visions. Of myself standing on the headboard of their bed and pissing on their heads and faces prior to the beating Unfortunately, the beating was going to be sparked by an occurrence of any type that could be considered punishable behavior. It was unavoidable; it served as a need to an individual or individuals to be filled in some sick form of satisfaction.

"What do you want to be when you grow up?" A question that triggered thoughts of how I see myself as an adult, I visualize an understanding, thought out individual that could take a different approach to this problem. Something like this: Bed Wetting?

I have spent so much time concerned over this particular issue. There can be success in conquering this problem. Some things work for others and other things work for some. I know all sorts of head doctors have spent time and energy, along with medical doctors, experts and various professionals; And hopefully they have made some progress in some situations. Each situation is unique. **In my situation, I am alive with intensity, in a conscious and alert state of mind. You know, when I am awake. The cost of this great energy is to sleep with equal intensity.** *Without being carried away with the need of psychological repair as a solution. Or maybe even a medical evaluation relating to physical attributes causing some form of dysfunction.* **Let's be proactive,** *and maybe just a little compassionate. (Just imagine what it feels like to awake from a long night of rest and discover cold wet clothes and bedding.* **You do not want to move an inch, either direction** *that is insult added to injury. And if you have stress in your life, your body goes thru chemical changes altering your ph, creating very acidic urine. This product can actually burn your skin. Not to mention the cleaning and laundry you have just encountered) and of course the embarrassment! I could go on and on about* **the punishment that already exists** *without even a mention of the problem.*

*Like any changes you need to make
in your life or the life of someone you love.
Look at the entire situation and develop a
plan. Maybe cut back on after dinner
beverages and wake them a few times each
night. It may be rough in the beginning.
How long does a person's bladder take to
fill? Practice makes perfect. Just like
reaching any other goal you need to be
committed and stick with it no excuses. And
someone will gain a sense of self that may
move an entire life in a completely different
more positive direction*

Self indulgent daydreaming...   on
with the story

The Idea that you are in the filthiest
environment imaginable all the things a
growing child knew and would take for
granted are now a memory. Home sweet
home, A Mother a Father, Unconditional
love. Your eldest brother and all the basics
like regular bathing, tooth brushing, clean
clothes, your own toys, *Family fun and
laughter* The Wonder of Santa Clause the
Easter bunny, Meals you would look
forward to, the feeling of a full belly is gone.
Fresh whole milk is replaced by evaporated
canned milk to be watered down and used
for cereal only. Treats like cookies, cake,
chips and ice cream are replaced by a piece
of bread coated with sugar. To accept these
changes alone is difficult enough.

Energy used to grow at a normal pace like running and playing are now going to be used for hard labor. (*These sick mother fuckers are going to have us pull weeds by the root, shake out all the dirt in the hot sun for hours on a daily basis. The weeds are the actual greenery that is the back yard. My personal problem is, even though I am almost six years old. I have a solid foundation and do the job correctly and I won't stop until I am told.*) So why buy a lawn mower? I will work much harder than any machine

The discovery of favoritism….. and that is not on your side. *His kids had baseball practice, dance class and many other important projects like parties etc*

Money was not a problem here; Uncle Ed had a very good paying job at General Electric. Social Security provided financial support on behalf of my Mother for my brothers and I, The house was paid for "It was a gift from Uncle Ed's Grandmother"

Life itself can and will give all the growing pains a person needs. Who the fuck are these people?!

These circumstances will be accepted as the norm and are much better than (a good licking). I will piss the bed every night here. I may only be marked for a (good licking) on ten or twelve occurrences, for that specific reason. Jimmy and Johnny had almost a year of experience. *And to think Johnny is probably starving and sleeping in a cold hallway by choice.* He is twelve and the original pioneer of these (Good lickings) and all the other beautiful shades of grey. I guess the foundation of who your going to be is established by the time your five. Our mother had given us the greatest gift I can think *of a rock solid constitution,* Dad helped. The best part is… that if she were here or if he were not in prison. *We wouldn't even have a clue of who these fucking people were.* I met Stephanie and Aunt Ruth for the first time when Mom passed

Jimmy heard all he needed to hear and headed out.

Alone, I sat trying not to think about things. The dog strolled into the sun porch. "Don't poop Peppa!" I demanded, He wagged his tail and approached me. (He sure was a scruffy looking mutt, mostly Maltese I think. Tan, curly and dirty and he smelled like the junkyard.) He had a caring look in his eye. I could tell he was checking in on me, we were developing a friendship. *I could also tell he was one of us* (They say dogs have a sense a smell ten times greater than humans. *No wonder he lays in the middle of the street refusing to move when cars are coming*.) He barely spent any time in the house.

He would lay under cars or right in the center of the street. When he saw Jimmy or me, he would stroll along side, as If we all agreed to meet up at that time. If you called out "Peppa" he acknowledged. If you said "Go home Peppa" he acted like he had no idea who Peppa was and just continued on. For a little guy, that dog sure could eat. He had everyone's less desirables. If he wasn't around, the backside of the radiator had the rest. For a dog, he seemed to know a lot. Without saying a word he would just go along with things.

In the morning, he walked all the way to school with us. We went in without knowing what he would be doing or how he would be. He knew his way around. Every day when we got home, there he was just lying in the center of the street, flat on his stomach, with his legs straight back. *Looking like a turkey on Thanksgiving.*

In time, he would go on every adventure. He could do the rocks so much better than us and made a habit of taking the lead. The only *junkyard dog* I remember seeing was *him*. We should have called him *Poopa,* the way he left one everywhere we went. He left one on the front of a car in the junkyard once.

2
Protein and Adventure

The week was uneventful, we had school and after that we played around the river. Early the next Saturday Jimmy said "wake up, were going to Geo and Freddy's"

Aunt Ruth had made me some raisin bran, it was somewhat soggy, and one of the raisins had been "buzzing." In one spot, causing ripples in the milk. She asked "what's the matter?" I said "there's a fly in my cereal." She said "It's not a fly, it's a raisin! Just eat it!" I responded "but its buzzing" Just then Uncle Ed shouted from the "sofa" "What's the problem out there, She started to say "he wont eat his cereal" I stopped her and said "Ill eat it" I picked up a spoonful with the buzzing raisin and flakes as I bit down, I felt a tickle on the left side of my tongue. The next *crunch* was no raisin. Slowly eating the rest of the bowl proved to be a relief. *All the other raisins were soft and chewy. It had to be done.* I was going to hang out with Jimmy and his friend. I couldn't wait to meet Freddy he was my age.

Jimmy outlined the details of our plan "After we get Geo and Freddy were going to follow the river past the *dirt road* and over towards Barry Park" "Ok" I replied We got to their house; Freddy's mother answered the door. She was nice looking and very polite. As we went in, I noticed it was bright, clean and cozy. *Just like how we used to live.* I wanted to see more. Geo and Freddy came downstairs. Geo walked with his hands curled in towards his waist and grunted sort of like a small gorilla "Jimmy was right" I thought.

Freddy was a tough looking kid with curly long hair. They both smiled a lot. We headed out. The trip began in their yard. We had to *hop the fence* as Jimmy put it. Now we were on the *dirt road.* This was an area behind the houses that lead to green houses owned by Georgians flower shop. Drift wood and dried reeds found a resting place throughout the area. Now we are working our way up towards what looks like the beginning of the River. It came to a huge pipe with water rushing out of it with the strong odor of poop. *Jimmy kept blaming Peppa* "

I can't go any further" I said nervously. "Just hold the fence and turn your feet sideways and come towards me" He said. It was about five long minutes getting across the area. But I made it.

The pipe was for the release of raw sewerage to be sent out into the Atlantic so for a minute there… I really was up shits creek without a paddle

"Did you bring your money?" Jimmy asked. "I didn't know we needed it" I replied

"Well were going into Oakies" (a *variety store near the railroad tracks that lead to the park*) "Ill get ya something, try to remember it next time" He concluded, I got some wax cylinders filled with colored sugar water. *I think they were called wax sticks.* Jimmy got cupcakes, Geo and Freddy got ice cream sandwiches. Pepper had a Slim Jim we were sugared up and ready to go.

We headed down the tracks and we came upon a huge rock cliff. (Probably fifty feet at its highest point) Jimmy and Geo ran to the center and just started climbing, Peppa ran around and past it. Freddy waited until he had my attention and began showing me the right rock edges to use for support. As I approached the top, I could see Peppa looking down, He knew a short cut. At the top there were various heights that could be used to jump back and forth. Some requiring more skill than others, since this was my first time, I stuck with the short jump. It was great place to start.

I discovered the back side was covered with grass. It was simply a downgrade to the tracks. (Peppa's short cut) Jimmy led the way; the park was just up ahead. Jimmy said "Hey Brian remember the frogs we used to get at Magna rd?" "Yup" I replied "Well look here" He said, just then, I saw one at the edge of the water, "Wow I'm going to get one this time." I said with excitement. (I know how this is done; I have seen it many times before) I went to the edge quietly looking, "he" had his back to me, slowly and steady, and with both of my arms fully extended closer to him I go "Gotcha" Ha I got him, now what? I wondered.

Jimmy said "We should start getting back" Well, I guess we should head on back with our new found friend.

I had to be extra careful now as I pass thru *shits creek*. I am taking a passenger. It was surprisingly easier this time. I was starting to lag behind with too much focus on the frog. I had to jog a little to catch up. I began picking up the pace; jumping over scatter pieces of drift wood and through weeds all of a sudden I fell. I had pain in my left knee and lost the frog. I tried to get up, but a board was stuck to my leg. "Help" I called in panic. They stopped and ran back to me. "Oh Shit" Jimmy said, Geo had a crazed look on his face. Freddy tried to help me up. "Geo go get Uncle Ed"

Jimmy shouted. "Hurry!" He took off running.

"Oh no Uncle Ed's going to kill me" I cried "I am in big trouble, Ouch it hurts. I cried" Jimmy said "try to calm down your going to be alright, I just wish Uncle Ed would get here." (The board laid flat on the ground. A three inch common nail pointed upward through the board. My knee landed on it, the nail was imbedded about a half inch deep. Movement in any direction caused serious pain.) "Good here he comes" Jimmy noticed
Uncle Ed skidded to a stop and quickly got out of the car. "How the hell did you do that?" Uncle Ed said. "I fell," I said, as I cried.

"Ok Jimmy, hold his leg, Freddy and Geo just hold under his arms" Ill be right back." He said, as He went to the car and got a tool.

He placed the (pliers) just under the head of the nail and pulled sharply.

I did not see any blood… but at the end of the nail was a white piece of flesh. It was so much pain and so much relief. I wasn't sure if my leg could not bend or, if I would not let it bend, but it was as straight as a pole.

"Were going to have to get you a tetanus shot so you don't get lockjaw" Uncle Ed noted. I said "I didn't hurt my jaw, it's my knee" and I continued to whimper.

I was really not sure how to feel about Uncle Ed at this point. I was grateful for this act of heroism on his part. But his existence in my life will continue to be an unnecessary evil

In fact his existence is the reason I am at shits creek, However, Not without that paddle now

(I never actually got a shot or an X-ray. The comment Uncle Ed made was most likely for Geo and Freddy to include in their version of the incident providing they tell their parents, which they most likely would.) I held my leg stiffly for many hours. The morning after the incident, my knee would not bend, even with all my efforts. After a while I was able to work it to a point where it would. It seems like it had to go past a *lock* of some sort.

3
Miss Understandings

(My father and Mother instilled a strong "respect for your elder's factor". I am proud of that and I feel it's a great method in parenting. Respect everybody Even though adults can make mistakes just like anyone, they are only human. If a child is able to pick up on one of those human errors, it's a treat.

Taking that Icon out of character for a second (A blooper) I guess

Miss Fitzgerald was my teacher, she was nice and professional. She wore a white blouse, long blue skirt, black shoes, short, curly hair. If you saw her on the street you might say 'oh yeah, she… is a teacher'. You could tell just by looking. Freddy and I began spending time together, one form of pleasure, was to watch people and find all the humor we could through their actions, and then deliver a repeat performance of what we saw. It was even funnier that way. He was in the next classroom. I would look in the window and gesture some hello and how are you from time to time.

Miss Fitzgerald was teaching us math, while holding a piece of chalk. She counted moving her fingers, maintaining a firm hold, on the chalk. A process that placed her middle finger straight up, "Wow" I thought, Freddy has to see this. Staring at her and glancing down to my hand. Back and forth I focus; I wanted to get it just right! Then, I could show him through the window.

Her voice broke my concentration. Suddenly a high pitched screech as she shouted my name. She had the attention of the entire class. There I was in the echo of silence for a second. Standing up, firmly holding out my middle finger in her direction.

"Go to the office and see Mr. Dickson" she ordered. He will want to speak with your father." She added (I last saw my father "Dad" when I was four. *He is known to me as "Dad" maybe "Daddy" here or there but for the most part "Dad".*)

Mr. Dickson was a large figure, balding with graying hair on the sides. His voice always very loud and very clear, on this day, it became much louder and clearer. (*Miss Fitzgerald is his fiancée.*) "I have to speak with your father, I can't find his information.

What is his name?" he asked. "Dad"
I replied. "What? Don't be funny with me
kid! I want to know his name!" He shouted.
Worried and confused, I figured maybe the
name "Dad" no longer applied "Ah Daddy?"
I guessed. His face flushed quickly,
reddened with rage,
"OK Daddy - O" I shouted! Having no
more Ideas of what he was looking for.
Threatening to slap my ass with his three
foot ruler, he smacked the table with a loud
crack.

All the excitement got the attention
of the office secretary. She knocked loudly
on his door. He opened it. She came in and
said; " He lives with his Aunt and Uncle, I
found the number here." She handed a piece
of paper to him. He made the call, informing
them of this violation. (I am not having a lot
of confidence in the intelligence level of
adults at this point. Stephanie couldn't
figure the bat mobile was a new gift for my
birthday? Any moron could tell that was a
fly! This huge idiot had no idea my father
was in fact Dad! Even the sign in front of
the church: Posted: 2 hour parking 8am to
6pm *that one troubled me for years.*)

I seem to have violated this mans
wife to be, he was adamant over the phone.
This problem will be corrected immediately!
This was the feel of the situation.

Uncle Ed knew just how to handle it.

Later… while lying on my bed, after a good licking and the corner. I was cooling down as the stinging sensations began to subside, an all familiar feeling. I wondered when *they changed* Dads name. And what is it? Ill ask Jimmy or Stephanie.

A while later Stephanie had come by to check in and see how I was." Hey little guy, you ok honey?" She asked "Yeah" I said unenthusiastically. "What's Dads name now? I asked curiously. "Your Dad?" she questioned,

Impatiently I said "Yeah!" Your fathers name is John "Why"? She asked. I told her what had happened (my side of things.) "Oh Brian, Dad is what you call your father. That's why I call Uncle Eddie Dad, He's my Dad. My Uncle John is your Dad you see? She explained "And someday you might be Dad to someone." She added

"Well, I wish somebody would have told me that before." I stated "That's why he got mad at me" I added, (Figuring, He could relate to my sense of humor, if he had a bit of smarts. *The finger thing was simply silly, and not meant to cause such trouble.)*

"Well now you know and you can say "John is my fathers name" she declared "Keep calling him Dad though, only big people can call him John" She added

I wonder if that yard stick would be worst than the strap? He was so pissed off; veins were bulging from his head. The sad part here is Mr. & soon to be Mrs. Dickson are most likely beautiful humans. Talk about being driven by passion.

"Brian, you're going to sit next to Ronnie from now on, he's a very good boy, and he should keep you out of trouble" Miss Fitzgerald stated. (I noticed he was drawing a picture of a house with a yard and a tree. Very much like one of my frequent doodles) "Hey, I like that house," I said, I like to make the tree branches move up and out from the tree trunk" I noted We got along very well; He continued to be my doodle partner in school. He was too clean and shiny to hop fences, travel the tracks and river banks. *And the junkyard?*
Forget it! I went over his house a few times after school. His influence was fine, (if *I needed a behavioral example. My perception of the finger incident was not the same as the teacher*.) Ronnie and I could have been best friends, had the circumstances been different. His home life was very much like mine used to be. I was a very good boy once too!

It was Saturday morning, "Jimmy can we go back to Barry Park?" I asked. "Sure, Just don't forget your money this time" He added "Ok Ill get it now" I replied I went to the house next door and slowly pulled off the cap. *What the heck?* The quarter was there, but the dime was gone. "That's dumb! Why would someone just take the dime?" I figured, oh well, At least I have the quarter! After the first "take", I never got change again. I was too afraid of getting caught and what "God" would think.

"I got the quarter but someone took the dime", I said, to Jimmy as he walked over to me. He paused for a second and began shaking his head, back and forth. He smiled, and said "no one took the dime; it fell down, now c'mon we should get going.

For all the times we went to *Barry Park*, the closest we ever got to the park was the outer fenced area. *At that time* There were too many sandlots, Rock ledges and tracks to explore. The river and Junkyard are worlds of their own. In summer, around the first week of July you could find a bonfire at almost every stop. ("*Lynn, Lynn, the city of sin. You never go out the way you come in*")

"Grampy McGee" was the image in my head, the first time I ever heard that one.

He's my Moms father, *one tough old Irishman.* Grampy stood about 5'9" He wore a hat, it was tipped just off to the side and the brim could almost cover his left eye. When he talked he would lean towards you and spoke from one side of his mouth. What ever he said, it always seemed like it was (just between you and him.) It felt like you were with *James Cagney* or *Al Capone.*

He always had a good joke with horrible endings too *"A little ant with a little head sat upon the foot of my bead, I coaxed him close with a piece of bread, then I crushed his fuckin head"* He liked going from cute to shocking. He came to Aunt Ruth's house for my birthday. That was his only visit there. When Mom was alive, he came to our house a few days a week. This time he brought me some presents. A warm winter coat, and G.I. Joe the 12" tall original with all the supplies. Complete with a real beard. Aunt Ruth's son Joey was not very happy about that. He wasn't going to be happy until it was his.

After Grampy left and was out of sight. The deal was made. Aunt Ruth convinced me that this was more *Joey's style of a toy.* I should get a plastic machine gun that made a sound like baseball cards in bicycle spokes. In time he ended up owning that as well.

4
Continued Education

Report cards were going to be distributed in a couple weeks. Jimmy wanted to change things to improve his marks.

"Brian c'mon, I have an Idea" He said ", "Ok" I replied "What do you feel like doing?" I Asked "Well I'm not sure if I can pull it off, but were going to check something out." He stated. We headed off in the direction of the school.

We went to the side of the school *an area that separated the Elementary from the Jr High.* It was the boiler room and it was lower than the other buildings. They were all connected. The only car in the lot belonged to the custodian. *He was a tired old man.* According to Jimmy and as long as we were quiet we would be fine.

Jimmy got a metal garbage can and flipped it over. He climbed up and was able to place his foot on a window ledge and his hand on barbed wire just between the "barbs" this was on the outer edge of the roof. Then he went over and before you knew it, He was standing on the roof.

"Knock the barrel on its side and bring it over there, if you see anyone, kick it hard so it rolls. And if they ask what you're doing, tell them you're playing with your dog. Ill go around and open a door for you" He said quietly

I was pretty worried at this point. If I messed up we were doomed, Peppa better not run off now. For Jimmy this s a B&E! For me, I was invited in as a guest right through the door

I met Jimmy at the side door "Be quiet, I am not sure where the custodian is" He said as Peppa ran ahead. He had some *snooping* to do of his own. We looked around and grabbed some colored markers, note pads and Jimmy got some money and a watch from a desk. Jimmy peeked out a window *"looking out' from time to time.* Then he saw the custodian on the 3rd floor in the next building repairing a window. Now we knew we had plenty of time.

Jimmy was doing something at the teachers' desk and said "I'm all A s and B s now. "Good want to leave?" I asked "Soon, I'm still checking things out" He replied

Peppa got a good scent, and began sniffing around near a desk. He got into a squatting position and took a huge dump right on the floor!

"Jimmy Peppa just took a crap!" I said with excitement "Good" Jimmy said then he got a metal dust pan and some construction paper. He scooped it up and said "follow me"

We went into a classroom, Jimmy said "open that drawer" he pointed to the center of the large wooden desk. *He dropped the shiny wet pile into the drawer and closed it..*

"The Teacher from this room is a real Bitch; she laughed at me when some kid said I had big ears!" He said "That will teach her to laugh at me!" He stated with great satisfaction, we got out and headed home. No one ever knew a thing. I ended up sitting near the window in the classroom just above the boiler room the next year and I could see how he got in. I told Freddy, He told everyone else, that shocked me. Nobody believed him though.

5
That's using my head

Our next adventure brought us on the other side of the river. It was the view we looked at from the baseball field. It was a sandlot with broken up hot top and Tractor Trailers were all around. Jimmy and Geo were snooping around in the trucks, Freddy and I were playing. We would take long weeds, (Jimmy would refer to it as rabbit grass. It sounded like a whip and could do some damage if you pulled the leaves off of it and began swinging it around) we pretended to be attacking things with swords. Then go in for the kill and make a whip sound.

The pieces of hot top are also called black top and who knows what else. Ideally its broken chunks of the road material that streets are made from

I was kneeling down next to a trailer, looking down at my new piece of rabbit grass. (You have to change them often; this type of play causes the ends break apart.) I got up all ready to begin the next battle. I felt as though I bumped my head.

Freddy's eyes opened wide. I wiped away an itch from my forehead and saw blood. Somehow, Jimmy knew what had happened. He ran over and said "Oh my god! I'm sorry don't tell Aunt Ruth!" We have to get help. We went to Oakies; blood was everywhere, Head wounds can bleed like crazy. "Call an ambulance Please hurry!" Jimmy shouted to the store owner. Soon the ambulance arrived. The Paramedic wrapped my head and helped me onto the stretcher,

He asked "what happened? Freddy said with great excitement! "We were playing, Brian was on one side of the truck and Jimmy was on the other. Jimmy threw a big piece of hot top right over the truck and it hit Brian in the head!" (Freddy was holding the weed whip and he talks with usage of his hands. The whip was his pointer in this situation, his display allowed the whip to slam across my eyebrows with enough force to slice my forehead) as I lay on there on the stretcher.

After some stitches and the promise of ice cream, I was all fixed up. The ice cream promise was Aunt Ruth's display of good parenting to appease the Doctor.

On the way back to the house; "Are we going to get that ice cream?" I asked

"No! You're lucky you're not going to get the belt!" She replied with the usual care. *Knowing she was right* and I was ok. It really did seem like I was going to get that ice cream a short while back, the way she talked around the doctor. Jimmy was too.

The story Aunt Ruth and the doctor got pointed the blame at some other kids and they took off. I was sad, this was deserving of an ice cream for sure.

(Heartless Bitch! *No wonder I steal change and find my own treasures.* If I had a GI Joe, I could be safe at her house playing with it in the yard. Just like a fucking normal six or seven year old.)

Freddy was a little tough and he liked to wrestle around and he liked to tell on other people. I wrestled enough with Uncle Ed so, I am beginning to view Freddy differently now. And the river, no matter what side I am on "shits creek" Stinks if you ask me. I am thinking of new areas to explore.

6
Keeping change

"There's plenty of water to drink, right from that tap!" The most common group of words Aunt Ruth ever said to me. No matter what I would ask for to quench my thirst or to remove distaste from my mouth. Or even to ingest a non solid, As if this were to be a concentrated solution of great mathematical proportion, how, why, front ways, back ways it was always. The exact and final answer

And to watch her kids chug down milk from a glass and eat cookies, Juices of different varieties, soda. Don't ask! The answer is as plain as the nose on your face (which is also serving a punishment for some horrible things done in a previous existence) " *Can I have some juice*?" If asked the answer was simply.........

"There's plenty of water to drink, right from that tap!" Let's add to the equation, "Brian, walk up to the store and get a half gallon of milk and a loaf of bread. And don't crush the bread this time!" Aunt Ruth added (Maybe the guy at the store should not put them in a bag)

Or maybe you should put some clothes on that pile of stinking flesh and take your fucking car you lazy lowlife skipper looking fuck. And take the mile ride yourself. So your kids could have milk and peanut butter sandwiches.

I may get lucky and have sugar bread. Cereal is a *weekend* food. School has lunch that will hold me. Jimmy has the right idea, when you see what the world can offer you need to seek out and provide for yourself. He was always thinking and was very bright; he needed to feed his mind, even more than his belly. His smarts not only allowed him to get "A" and "B" grades in school. He could *win the hearts* of others. Jimmy would jump at the opportunity to get milk. On the walk to the store, he knocked on doors and offered to get them whatever they needed. "Just keep the change" they would tell him. I found that out by accident.

A woman called the house and asked if Jimmy could run an errand. He wasn't around and, I was given a chance to "keep the change" I was so excited; this was one change I wanted to keep. I *racked up* enough to buy a Pepsi, Yankee doodles and chips all in one score. And it was *legit*. Jimmy found out and he put a damper on it. This was his idea. I hope it doesn't create a *life long rivalry* he is my brother.

7
A Giant adventure

"Can we go somewhere different?" I asked. Jimmy had an idea, we were going to explore beyond the school. We would go down Boston Street; we were going to strawberry brook. We could smell potato chips cooking from time to time. The walk was very long we remained "street side" the entire time.

No back roads, tracks or rivers. The aroma of fresh chips was so pleasing; I could have sat back and eaten 1000 bags. We were getting closer to the brook; it traveled behind Boyd's Potato chips. As we arrive intoxicated by the aroma, we had to find a treat. "Hey want some chips or M&Ms"? Jimmy asked "Yeah" I said "We can come back to the brook later" He noted. We still had a bit of a walk to go. We were going to *Giants,*

It was a large store, with purple and white stripes up and down the building. It was past manning bowl and before the MDC rink. "Wow, Boston is huge Jimmy." I said He just laughed and said "it's Boston St not the actual city. " Boston is further than this?"

I asked "Yup" much further" He said

"Let's look around, and see what we want. We can grab it, and head back to this staircase and sort it out" He said "ok" I replied

Toys, treats, people, this place had it all… Wow GI Joes, matchbox cars, chips, M&Ms, every candy you can imagine. Jimmy had an extra pocket inside his coat. I had a snorkel Jacket with many pockets. "Take what you want and hurry" He whispered to me. I loaded up. We met at the staircase. M&Ms big bag, Chips, and my very own GI Joe. "Yeah, now that's shopping. I emptied out my treasures; Jimmy threw his in the pile. He also had soda, hostess cup cakes, Twinkies and Mad magazine. "Alright, we have to find a place to hide this stuff" Jimmy said.

We went to manning bowl. "Stay here, Ill find an opening and lead you in" Jimmy said. A few minutes went by and he ran back to where I was, He was on the inside though, talking to me through the fence. "Follow me there's an opening around the other side" He said. We got to a little area that seemed like a good place to rest and eat.

We have struck it rich! "Our very own source of goodness and a taste of sweet success." Why didn't we think of this before?

After a well-deserved break, It was probably a good idea to milk this cow some more.

The feeling was somehow different this time. The happy feeling had changed to a hint of fear. I was going after the matchbox bat mobile. That was *all* I wanted. Jimmy had a couple of cars and for whatever reason, some kid we had never seen before walked out with us. The guy next to him *was probably his Dad*. "Hold it right there boys!" His Dad said "He held a shiny gold badge and showed it to us. "Store detective, you're going to have to come with me!" He stated.

This kid was not with his Dad, He was actually stealing! (This fucking Moron had the game of monopoly under his coat. It was sticking out top and bottom. Store security
figured we were together. Well, given the fact that we were stealing too.)

This will at least give us a ride back to the house. My feet and legs were tired and sore. And my ass is going to join in on the feeling. "Come on over here boys" Uncle Ed said "Which one of you want to go first?" he asked

I thought about volunteering and I'm sure Jimmy did too. The only sound was *silence*. Uncle Ed had to make the decision for us. "Drop your draws" He said, with full knowledge of the routine *underwear* were automatically included. Those familiar sounds *"Crack", screaming and "you!"* thundered through the room as Uncle Ed shouted the reasons for this particular "Licking". It had an entirely *different* feel this time. I am taking a spectators view of the situation. The fear that ran through me was stronger than anything I could imagine. It was from the sight of my big brother, being as helpless as can be. I wanted to save him. I wanted to tell him, he will be ok, if this monster would just stop! Stop he did. Jimmy ran to the corner, it was my turn; I felt the blows to my back and legs. I could not hear a sound. In my mind, all I could see was what Jimmy went through. I felt so sorry for him. To me this was the worst beating I could have imagined. Or was it?

We were very bad boys and got no sympathy from this one. Stephanie usually bandaged up our feelings. Not this time. She was also spending time with her boyfriend. Danny, he was about 6' 4" and had dark skin and long hair, he was an American Indian. He was really nice to everyone.

In our room we bandaged up our own feelings, we quietly talked about the "olden" days when we were a family without fear and beatings. And about Mom, Dad and Johnny we were in bed without supper! That was a much appreciated gesture on Aunt Ruth's part. *She showed us.* I probably had more in my belly now than I ever did from her house at one time… Just being away from that group of people with the knowledge that the storm had passed having memories to share without wonder, was a very comforting way to close the day.

We never returned to manning bowl for our goods. In time we were back there, but the stuff was gone. Looks like GI Joe could be having quite an adventure of his own. I hope it's a good one and that we are not forgotten. I mean hey we helped him escape.

8
A beautiful sound

About one week after that Dad got another twelve hour furlough "Brian, Dads coming over." Jimmy said with excitement. "Right now?" I asked, "Yup" c'mon down stairs, He stated. "My Dad's coming?" I asked Aunt Ruth as she sat in the corner chewing crushed ice. "He will be here in a while" she said, I waited in the kitchen asking Aunt Ruth all sorts of questions about anything and everything. "Why do you ask so many questions?" she asked,

Stephanie intervened "Ma, How's he supposed to learn anything if he doesn't ask questions?" "He doesn't have to ask so many" She stated

"Is anybody home?" I heard the most beautiful sound in the world. It was Dad! I had the biggest smile on my face. "Hey Bri" He said, the look on his face, said to me that he was not to happy about the surroundings. "You want some coffee John?" Uncle Ed asked

"No I am good Eddie" Dad said, as he made a gesture with his hand. "I hear you and Jimmy were in Giants stealing" My father said to me.

Instead of darting my eyes at Aunt Ruth and saying "*You disgusting piece of shit, Rat fuck, miserable snake in the grass, zoo creature, you pull shit stained bed sheets from your ass when exiting the bed, you made me eat a fly and watched while your dirty, creepy looking, sick fuck husband beat me. Should I tell him all that or do my father and I deserve a simple fucking moment?!*"

I said "I am sorry, and I won't do it again". "Well just try to be a good boy" He said

"When can we live with you again?" I asked, "Pretty soon Bri" he answered We spent about an hour together and he had to get going.

9
Shopping?

Back to the old routine, wondering when we could be a family again.
We went to a couple of Joeys Cub Scout meetings, the watered down Cub Scout juice was actually good with chocolate chip cookies; It was well worth the wait. We got to see a police dog display put on by local law enforcement.

With the holidays coming, Aunt Ruth was doing a lot of shopping. Most of the time, this was done around "dinner" Or "suppa" as she said. *What she was getting, was beyond me.* For two birthdays, I got a hard plastic football bright orange the first year and a lime green exact match the next. I was not the sports type and it hurt to catch. Come to think of it, anything Joey or Uncle Ed "threw" while teaching me sports was thrown with fury. As the hurt was more of a focus than the fun. Great sportsmanship

10
A Christmas Roast

Between Stephanie and Ann, dinner was usually served. Aunt Ruth was often late returning from various stores looking for sales. This Christmas season has the typical feel to it. Dark colored socks for your hands, so the other kids thought you had mittens. The best way to find them was in Joey's room. Stained white socks were noticed right away.

Jimmy and I would make our lists and never see them again. This probably helped, when we were left empty handed, we weren't aware that we were missing anything. Ann was a frequent run away just like John. She would cut our hair from time to time. The barber asked me not to come by anymore, as the odor and head lice were not hazards he could deal with. The school nurse also sent me home once, for the same reason, well the odor. We counted on Stephanie to feed us. Her cooking was a holiday treat. Gail is getting old enough to become involved and aware of the world around her.

With about a week or so until Christmas, things were a bit out of the norm and eating became less frequent. School lunch was removed from the agenda. Sugar bread made you hungry later. Uncle Ed changed shift, he was working just days and now added early evening. He wouldn't cook anyway. His thing was to lay on the "sofa", with his right arm behind his head, and his left arm in his pants. As he was positioned, he would watch, black and white movies, usually about soldiers or cowboys and Indians. This particular evening Aunt Ruth took Gail and Stephanie. We were left to wait. I didn't see much of Jimmy or Joey. My stomach began to make the usual noises. I ate a piece of bread, "the heal" that's all that was there. The feeling came back so I had some water. That helped for a few minutes.

It was becoming very late; my stomach was beginning to hurt from being empty. The noises began to work with pains. Finally Aunt Ruth came through the door, she was holding bags. She noticed I was in pain and firmly said "What's the matter?" I told her "my belly hurts because, I am hungry" She was *not* in the mood for *hungry*. "Wait a minute!" she demanded. "Ok" I said weakly, as a cramp came on, I moaned in pain

She ripped open the freezer door and opened a box of hotdogs. She took one out and threw it at me. It hit my face and fell to the floor. I picked it up and I Said "aren't you going to cook it?" She shouted "It's just like bologna so eat it!" I picked it up and saw floor debris on the very cold hotdog. I wiped it with my shirt now whimpering. "Go to your room!" she shouted.

My room is the front sun porch. To get there you go upstairs and through Aunt Ruth and Uncle Ed's bedroom. Figuring, I will have to eat this frozen relative of bologna. I imagined going to the river, at the river, I would often sit at the beach and make tiny campfires. I would start with matches that were always available. Then, I would gather dried reeds and light it up. You could blow air into it to increase the flame or smother it with debris if it got out of hand. I became quite an expert.

Jimmy and kids from the neighborhood constantly made me aware of the danger. I could hear Uncle Ed's loud voice now, Stephanie and Danny are laughing. Sounds like fun. Wait a minute, Uncle Ed leaves a Zippo lighter on the dresser, I just walked by it. I went back to get the lighter.

I got an old pan from under the bathroom sink. I filled it with water, in case it got out of control. I gathered up Lincoln log roof pieces. Paper and whatever else looked good for kindling. I cleared an area on my bed and constructed a teepee of combustibles. Armed with a hotdog in my left hand and a Zippo in the right, I was ready. Without wind, it started rather nicely. "Wow, now it's cooking," I thought. I must have been so involved, I couldn't hear Jimmy come in. I looked over and saw the look on his face. It basically said HOLY SHIT! "Jimmy wait, don't tell, I have water, see its out!" I pleaded, as I dumped the water pan over it. Too late he was gone.
I have no idea how everyone in the house could fill big buckets, pans and little buckets and get up here so quickly. Well with the fire out, the spectators already in place, Why wait? Uncle Ed came at me with RAGE he grabbed my shirt. I pulled my body back, causing the shirt to come off. "YOU WANT TO BURN DOWN MY FUCKING HOUSE! YOU COCKSUCKER, YOU SON OF A BITCH!" his Belt came off, I was cornered, and I covered my head and turned my back to him. "YOU MISERABLE PIECE OF SHIT,"
The hits were coming on fast and furious! "YOU WANT TO BURN DOWN MY FUCKNG HOUSE? HUH? ILL FUCKNG KILL YOU, YOU FUCK!"

The hits came left and right, ENOUGH! Danny screamed as loud as Uncle Ed,

Danny pulled him off and said" You are going to kill him if you don't STOP!!!" My ear was hot and ringing. My back felt like it was on fire. It felt like the skin split apart from the center. The show is over; everyone went down stairs except Stephanie and Danny. She was extremely upset and crying

Danny said "Brian, I'm a 21 year old man and I couldn't imagine what you just went through. You are very brave. Stephanie and I are going to take you to the hospital. Cover yourself with this sheet." I couldn't move my arms. Stephanie helped we headed out the door it was total silence.

11
Clean Linen

In the hospital, I was lying on my stomach, with my arms out to the sides. My face was on a pillow. "Oh this pillow smells so clean" I thought. I spent Dec 23rd through Dec 27th here. Nurses and a Doctor came by looking at my back and washing me up and using creams and lotions on my back and neck. Stephanie and Danny came in too. She didn't talk much now, she just looked sad. Danny did. He made me feel, like I was his best friend and a man he could admire. I liked the cleanliness here. I didn't think I wanted to smell a clean pillow so bad. I would take that kind a punishment for it.

Danny and Stephanie took me back to the house. I was much better now. They told me Uncle Ed *was really worried*, that the whole house would burn down. And I can't blame him for being so angry. They also said he was wrong, to give me such a beating. They let me know, if I want help for anything, always ask them. And they will take care of me.

I got back to the house, everyone seemed to just watch me and how I acted. I guess they were feeling me out. Christmas is past. There was a package with my name on it. I opened it and found a box with a bunch of cars, not matchbox, but steel colored car frames with wheels. I was happy that Santa remembered me.

Jimmy was distant from me for the week. He spent time with Joey. I played with my cars most of the time until we headed back to school. For the winter months Jimmy and I found most of our adventures were at a large pile a snow just outside of the house in an empty lot for General Electric employee parking.

Soon spring and summer came around. Jimmy and I were sent out to the back yard to pull weeds. "Joey had baseball, otherwise he would help too" She would always (yell) say.

I have no idea what was said to the hospital staff. Or even what the rules on abuse were back then. It was 1972 Uncle Ed, almost lost his free house and someone could have been hurt. To this date, I believe I was in complete control of the fire. I wonder if he had homeowners insurance.

12
A free trip to Ohio

"Brian come in here" Aunt Ruth called out to me. "This is your older sister Amy" Aunt Ruth said. I looked at her and then at Jimmy (he already heard a car pull up and he became nosey)

"When did I get a sister?" I asked. "Your Dad was married before and he had three girls"

Amy, Linda and Debbie "Hi Brian how are you?" She said. She talked funny I thought and mentioned it. "She is from Ohio" someone said. We got to know each other for an hour or so. "How would you and Jimmy like to stay with me for the summer?" She asked

I looked at Aunt Ruth and Jimmy and I asked if Dad knew about it. Aunt Ruth said "Amy went to visit Dad in Jail and he thought it was a good idea." I said "Yeah, when can we go"? "Right now" Amy replied. Aunt Ruth got some clothes; we packed up and headed out.

I had all kind of questions. Amy didn't seem to mind, as she patiently answered them all. We stopped at restaurants; we saw the aquarium. We stopped at a hotel, it had a shower.

I took a long hot shower and sang songs so loud; I could here laughing in the other room. (Every time I hit a high note) The next day we got to Garfield Heights just outside of Cleveland.

Her place was very modern, with large windows and a built in pool. It was a complex with other residents it had a feeling like a hotel or something I saw on TV

It was very nice; we had all sorts of food, drinks, anything you wanted… just go get it. At trash time, you could open a door in the hall and throw it down a chute. We spent the summer swimming a lot and going to the park. (*We were like regular kids or the rich kids. Jimmy told me about.*) The park was new and it had slides, swings, monkey bars, and a merry go round. This is the best summer fun a kid could have. We spent July and August there. *Nobody shouted. No one had to steal, or head on adventures to escape real life. And nobody got a beating.* I saw fireflies for the first time and ate a plum from the tree.

I met my other sisters and their mom. My Mom was much prettier! *Well, being eight, I told the woman.*

I just call 'em, the way I see 'em. "*My* face feels funny" I said to Jimmy one evening as we sat in the Amy's living room on the couch. "That's from smiling too much" He said "I like it" I responded

All good things must come to an end. We took a greyhound bus back to Boston. Somewhere along the route a woman gave me a stuffed animal. After she left Jimmy made me trade it for a green Jell-O with whipped cream. I was not too happy about that. Reality is creeping in.

13
Back to reality

Aunt Ruth met us at the bus station, she was quiet, and it was a very hot day. I became more aware of just how hot it was as we approached the car. I picked up the scent that I had all but forgotten. It was warmed by the sun.

" Hi Aunt Ruth, I said " Yeah Hi" she grunted "This fuckin' traffic sucks!" she complained " And the fuckin' weeds are out of control, your going straight to the back yard when you get home!" She demanded (*Hey Guys life's great just jump right in*!)

It was not too bad when the car was moving, but the stop and go traffic forced the odor into my sinuses. I was looking forward to smell of greenery by now. Aunt Ruth had to get a soda at McDonalds. She went through the drive thru. The transaction was made. She carefully poured the soda out leaving just the ice. We have been here before, don't ask for anything! She will chomp her ice the rest of the way *home*

By now, I felt nausea and wanted to throw up. We pulled up to the house. Jimmy and I jumped out and ran to the yard. The weeds were taller than me, Rabbit grass, elephant ears, and an occasional patch of grass. We worked harder than ever; *apparently our absence is the cause of this disaster*

It was *our* responsibility to correct it. We began around noon and tired around 5pm. We had such a big pile of weeds, it resembled a small hill. It looked like we had so much more to go.

Uncle Ed built a fenced in, squared off area in the front yard. It had baby toys and a chair. Aunt Ruth shouted "Brian, Jimmy can do that!" I want you to play with Gail in the front yard." She added It was here, I spent the remainder of nice days. (*Even when Gail fell asleep.*) "Just stay out there and watch her!" I was told

From hard labor to a cage which is worst right? People walking by, had me feeling like I was a monkey at the zoo. I was bored and at times, anxious other times. Well, it's better than a black belt.

A short time later… Aunt Ruth
stated "Your father got out of jail, and he
will come by today"

'To take us back!?" I interfered excitedly.

"No! Aunt Ruth said "He has to get a job
and a place to live first:

"Oh how long is that going to take?" I asked

"Awhile" She said

*I have a sense of ("Ill believe it, when I see
it") the only sure thing in my life at this
point are the beatings. And constant
punishment for any fucking reason*

*The beatings were so routine, that
we were beaten once for a dumpster fire (we
went to see, because we heard fire trucks.)
So it must have been Jimmy and I that lit it*

14
Meatballs

Dad was out, And he got work right away. He knew a lot of people in construction. One of the jobs placed him in McDonough square. (Working with Aluminum siding)

Jimmy and I would walk past the sight on our way to school. Dad talked with us, for a minute or two every morning. He also gave us each a quarter for the store. I liked the idea of seeing him and the quarter was nice too. Just feeling like I was important to someone, felt best. We started leaving earlier than before, just to get to the square.

A couple of months later, Jimmy and I, were going to have dinner with Dad and his new girlfriend. "Elaine" She was an Italian woman with three girls of her own Tammy, Grace and Leeann. Grammy Boober introduced Dad to Elaine. I remember the first thing I thought when I met Elaine was that she smiled when she saw me and she could cook real homemade Italian food Just like the *Latin Villa* on Western Ave.

"Oh boy what's that smell?" I said, as I entered her kitchen. It was delightful. "Italian sauce with meatballs and sausage, were going to have it over ziti." She said.

(*Her place was very small. It had one bedroom, her kids slept on couches and sleeping bags. It would be too small for us to move in.*)

"Why can't we live here with you guys?" I asked. "We plan on getting married, and after the wedding, we will all move into a bigger place" My father said. *A short time later they were married.*

The wedding was great, Music, food, fun, what a way to start. People were all happy and dancing. At the end of the ceremony, I was ready to leave with Dad and Elaine. It was tough; they were going on a honeymoon for a week. (*Come on already; let's get me out of Camden St, please, what's the hold up?*) I thought

During the final week at Aunt Ruth's house, It seems like I was just sitting in a chair with my things in hand waiting to leave. No hugs, no tears. I didn't even look behind me as we headed out.

Dad got out months ago, Jimmy and I, were *released* together. We went to live with Dad, Elaine and her kids, in a rented house on South Street. The street had a "good end" and a "bad end". We lived exactly in the middle section.

"Tammy, Elaine's oldest was on her own at this point, she was a young adult. Grace was close to being on her own. Leeann was my age and loud like Jimmy

My father got us new clothes and a membership to the boys club. I will also start little league baseball soon, I would finish the school year at Breed. Next year, I will start at Connery. The merging of families was strange. Nobody actually connected.

Jimmy and I met up with a kid named CJ. He was funny and very confident.

CJ was also a *kleptomaniac*, truly an *illness*. Watching this kid work was fascinating! Bikes were his favorite.

One day a man, was walking through the schoolyard. He had gloves on; and his hands were down at his sides.

CJ squatted down and walked behind the man in the same pattern. When he had the timing just right, he snatched the gloves right off the guy's hands! He turned and took off running the other way. The man stood there staring at his hands and looked back and forth and all around maybe thinking he had some sort of magical intervention.

The time I spent with Jimmy when CJ around was a bit nerving. You never knew what he was going to do next. The humorous aspects were not as frequent as the fear

15
Different roads

Jimmy and I had, what seemed like the same routine as before. We were usually together. Until One day, when we headed out as usual. Jimmy pointed to the right and said "You go that way, I'm going this way" *(I was confused. Why? I wondered where we are going to meet up.)*

"Then what"? I asked

"Then, you find your own friends, and Ill find my own!" He shouted. "What's the matter?" I asked. He walked away without saying a word. He *is* four years *older* than me.

I probably stood at that corner for a solid minute feeling somehow betrayed

I went back to the house and listened to my radio. I wondered what had happened in Jimmy's mind to react the way he did. Otherwise, I was fine. The house was clean, and free of fear. The food was good and plentiful.

The next day, I would have to formulate a plan. I started hanging around with kids from the same street. The things they like to do, like playing hide and seek, kickball and street hockey. It was fine for now.

We continued to go to church and Sunday school. We actually sat thru the Mass. and contributed to the *offering* box. *Giving a little back*. I thought the Priest was the next thing to *God*. I began to think I should consider becoming a Priest someday. Jimmy had ideas of his own. Jimmy and CJ have moved on to fist fights and stealing cars. Jimmy jokes around and says "I'm fuckin nuts" ha! "Problem here is, he was well on his way to becoming nuts or a little crazy… I should say

Jimmy got arrested for assault. The report stated that Jimmy had walked up to an individual and punched him in the face, *breaking the kids' nose*. And then began shouting at the kid, asking if the kid wanted more. When a Police officer asked what provoked the incident. Jimmy said "He was a big bastard, I wanted him to know, I'm not afraid of anyone!" "Why did you believe he thought *you* would be afraid? I may not be big, but dynamite comes in small packages! (Jimmy provoked the entire thing in his own mind. *He had never even seen the kid before that moment.)*

Trouble with the law was becoming more frequent with Jimmy and a big problem for Dad. I also gave Dad some grief. I was still a *heavy sleeper*. Elaine was losing patience. I was taken to a Doctor and a decision was made to perform surgery to correct the problem. *Enlarge my urethra*, (in theory, I would pee more during the day.)

Health care in the sixties and seventies!

Mom was *not pregnant*, my injuries were from a *violent assault*, and my dick works fine.

I have more concerns regarding the intelligence level of adults here. Jimmy is waving a huge red flag. He has proven that his reality is somewhat distorted. A bladder to me is a bag that empties when full. The size of the escape route should not really matter. The timing and amount of fluid intake may have some bearing on the situation, but hey, I'm no Doctor.

Funny, the time away from Jimmy… has freed up so much mind space that I am able to focus on how much Elaine resents me. At least with Jimmy, I had a sense of self worth. However, that can diminish quickly given the right circumstances…

16
Relax, get cozy

"You're going to feel some pain the first few times you pee, and you have to drink plenty of fluids." The Doctor said as we left the hospital after my surgery.

Dad took me home and went to work. I was told to take it easy So, I got a folding chair to use as a table. And set it up at the recliner. Home alone with soup and TV. Not a bad deal.

Well that first pee was AHHHH! HOLY SHIT!!! Some pain? Some incredible pain when you release at full force. I got over it and went to rest. A while later... I heard the phone ring and tried to get up quickly.

The folding chair was propped over the recliner foot pad. I pushed very hard with my feet and the folding chair folded forward and catapulted towards me. I moved my hand to cover my face and busted my finger and my nose. I never liked folding chairs or recliners after that... I continued to be a heavy sleeper. It has created some serious disharmony.

Elaine became very vocal about it. "Did you piss the bed again?" She said often, and she didn't care who was around. (I was beginning to see a few other things in her that I didn't like. She spent a lot of time with her boss. He was an Italian guy. I saw him tap his hand on her ass.) I tried to stop all fluids after dinner. It didn't help. Maybe, it's because, I have a huge piss tube now?

I thought about church and God. One day after church I flipped over my hamper and placed assorted towels over the top, pretending to administer my own sermon at Mass. Elaine walked in and said firmly "What the hell are you doing?!" I was embarrassed and said "Nothing ah I don't know". That was it!

She sent me to a head Doctor. The findings were *I was a normal, bright young man*. She was *pissed.* Forget what I said about doctors. I guess they *are* quite intelligent
Jimmy could use a few minutes in this office.

17
Ouch that's different

Leeann was spoiled. Elaine is beginning to create a bit of rivalry. Girls are great!
Boys suck and so on. I *tried to avoid* the both of them. Elaine always altered her facial expressions anytime we interacted. In case her words were not powerful enough she always added a hateful and angry look to emphasize what was said. Elaine had two things I like; her meatballs, and her nephew Dave. He and I became best friends. Dave was a big kid, tall and chunky. I was average height and thin.

Our friendship began at another wedding. I heard him making fun of the guests. They were all *his* relatives, Elaine talks through her nose, (Dave squelched up his face and said "*so anyway*", one of Elaine's favorite things to say in gossip or conversation.)

That got my attention. He pointed out that his Uncle looks like a chipmunk; His Aunt is sneaking drinks behind the coat rack. Dave's Grandmother likes to drink Monday nights and sing loudly out the window. This type of humor is the beginning of a good friendship. Now, is a good time for such a bond.

Jimmy continues to impress the world with his *creativity*. "I don't know *who* he is anymore." I Hope he does because this young man has so much knowledge. And the way he thinks is at a level above your average person. He can do so much, and has the stamina, not to give up. No matter *what* he is focusing on.

18
Role models

Johnny started coming in and out of our lives for a while. We have not really had a chance to "reunite" He spends his time with Dad and young adults. I am still considered a little kid

He had too much time on the street. Any time he had a chance to *settle*, he went back to street life. He was doing drugs; "heroin" was a favorite. I sat in the kitchen one night. I was drawing pictures. Dad found him and brought him home. He seemed very tired or very drunk, a minute later he seemed normal and back again, to tired or drunk.

He said "Hey Bri, Shhh! Hey, don't talk. Shhh! I want to, I wanna shhh, don't talk" he was nodding out again. On an *up* moment, he saw the butcher knife on the table, *dinner wasn't cleaned up yet*. He slowly took the knife, "Shhh" he would gesture a finger to his lips, and slowly slid the butcher knife in his coat, and then nodded off.

Dad got him up and they began to
head down the stairs, He was going to Detox
Johnny fell down the stairs head over heals.
I Shouted "He's got a knife!" Luckily, the
knife fell out and no one was hurt.

He went to a rehab; I won't be seeing
him for awhile. He will be in and out of jail
a lot too. If Mom was still here, would
things be this fucked up? What the fuck is
wrong with my brothers, I should be looking
up to them. How?

Jimmy and I share a bedroom;
Jimmy uses his mind to create things that are
pretty cool to have as an average person.
Our ceiling has eye hooks, wires and twine
all engineered to perform various functions.
You could open the door; turn off the light,
Turn the radio on or off, even open blinds,
all from the comfort of your bed. We had a
car stereo with eight speakers in our room,
along with flashing lights, all running from a
car battery. He made an extra wall in the
closet that appeared to be the very back side
of the closet. It was for hiding things.

(Whenever he did talk to me, he
would brag about something he did, that he
wasn't supposed to.)

He also gave details, of how he got away with it. Like when he put an (M-80) *quarter stick of dynamite* in a woman's mailbox. He taped a cigarette to it, so he would delay the timing of ignition, enabling him to far away and not involved in the incident.

One time he was with my father during the explosion. My father knew he was with him and backed him up and nearly fist fought the police officer.

Jimmy had a way of *kissing* the right *ass* too. Elaine earned a likeness for him *in this way*. For the most part, she could give a shit less for him or me. Jimmy is kissing her ass all the time. I think its part of his plan. Maybe she will cover his ass for kissing hers?

Jimmy puts his nose into every ones business. If you do something wrong and he finds out he will run right to her and tell on you. I always wondered what he got for his efforts. Maybe she would gently pet him like a dog. I cannot visualize anything else. Every time he told on you he would smile with great satisfaction. A satisfaction a dog would have from the personal petting time.

Growing up, Dad was a small time criminal. That is certainly not the case now. In fact, just having done his time, gave him a feel for his responsibilities. He developed such a strong character. He is slowly becoming an establishment of sorts. *An Icon.* Everyone that would meet him knew he is solid and has a high degree of values. That small time "shit" was a very big mistake. And far behind him, He believes in himself.

He wants us, to be better than even we think we can be. My brothers are creating some difficult work for this to happen with them. I have a pretty clean slate. He will stop me in my tracks if he even *thinks;* I'm becoming less than a great person. One, with respect, integrity, consideration, compassion and so on and so forth…

At this point my Father was really on his own trying to parent kids that he had already lost in a sense. Elaine needed her ass kissed and refused to be "Motherly" to Jimmy and me. Dad had his hands full with her and work. I was feeling alone and hoping to have some sort of importance in someone's life. I took an interest in an organized activity

19
Self Discovering

I always show respect and try not to speak out. It's not always the best Idea. During selection for baseball, I quietly waited to be picked and I ended up at right field. *First year* little league kids *never* hit the ball to right field. There I sat... on the grass.... with my glove on.... popping the heads off daisies with my free hand waiting to change sides.

I was *not good* at all at batting. *Hopefully,* I would get hit by the ball or walk. It was the only way for me to get on base. I wasn't discouraged, I really like this game. Hopefully, I will get better. Practice makes perfect.

(The next year, I knew, I liked the game and I would like to be the pitcher. *He throws the ball like it's an art.* All the focus is on him he could be the reason we win or lose.

Luck was on my side we had all new kids and a new coach. The new coach looked in my direction and said "What position did you play last year?"

"Pitcher" I said. There was not a sound from anyone to contest it they were all new kids. I had to lie. "Ok" Show me what you got. I headed to the mound and fired the ball down there like a cannon!

"Nice…. try not to throw sidearm you will waste your arm in no time." He said "What" I wondered. I have no clue what he's talking about. But what a throw! I practiced against the wall at the oil company near the tracks all year. My fast ball even scares me!

In time he was able to straighten my arm out. I pitched my way to the city series (East vs. West) I helped us get 1st place in the west; Even though we lost the series in the last game. My *batting* did not help.) It was worth all my efforts.

I played the game and did what I thought that could make the game better for me. This has given me a better feeling about myself and a sense of individual accomplishment. *I realize as a person I am ok*. Jimmy on the other hand….

20
Criminal and insane

"Brian, check this out" Jimmy said, While holding a key with a box that had wires coming off of it. "What is it?" I asked "It's an ignition; I can start any Chrysler with it" He replied, "what do you need that for?' I asked, figuring he was making a new contraption. "To steal a car you fucking idiot" He said sarcastically. "What? No Jimmy, throw it away!" I said with panic. Jimmy looked at me with a look of surprise. "We'll see" He said cautiously as his eyes reacted in a way I never saw before. Then he left the room; I sat back and had a terrible feeling. Hopefully, he will do the right thing. He is so smart and seems so stupid at times. Jimmy knew he was clever. He has to constantly show off his smarts and how he *gets one over* on people.

He used it alright… and my terrible feeling was correct. He was caught!

There are two kinds of people in Jimmy`s eyes good guys and bad guys.

Jimmy is a *good guy* and so is everyone else that agrees with him.

If you are on the side that agrees he has wronged you have now plotting against him! And you're like the rest of those bad guys!

Jimmy has been brought home by police so *many* times now. However, enough is enough! This time even Elaine is fed up

"Say goodbye to your other brother" Elaine said with sarcasm, as if I caused him to fuck up. "Why" I asked "The police just called, they chased him in a stolen car and on foot through Barry Park. They saw him, and he is known to them, he got away. When he gets home he's going to jail!

Jimmy went through the legal system and was given a break. He received counseling for being a troubled child. But has he learned anything from this? Of course he has. Now he can apply this new knowledge to his creativity

Jimmy is getting too wild for me. "Check this out" Jimmy said He was wearing a cast up past his forearm. "How did you break your arm?" I asked "I didn't, I stole some cast paper from the hospital and wrapped it myself, Looks good though huh?" "Ah yeah" I said nervously. He continued "I wanted Roxanne (*a girl he liked*) to think, I broke it, and she would feel bad for me and give me lots of attention." "Ok" I replied "I have to cut it off before Dad sees it." He said,

Jimmy then proceeded to slice the cast away at the forearm and down to his wrist, His eyes widened as blood, began to pour out from the cast.

(He just got out of the hospital for a blender incident! He was using the blender to make a frappe and the settings are 1-8. He pushed 1, 2, and 3 and as he hit 4, he didn't push hard enough so figuring the spinning blades jammed. He put his hand inside, and pushed 5; the blender kicked on and almost took 4 fingers.)

Jimmy seems to feel he is right no matter what! "Hey want to see me knock that kid out?" Jimmy said, he noticed a kid walking towards us. What?! I replied. "Then he wont *fuck* with us" Jimmy answered.

Feeling like I had to rationalize I said "Jimmy, Just don't look at him, and maybe he wont *fuck* with us anyway" He turned to me "YOU'RE A PUSSY!" He shouted. "AND THAT'S ALL YOUR EVER GOING TO BE, A BIG FUCKIN PUSSY!

I am a pussy? At six years old, I took massive beatings from an unusually large man. I stood ready for them as I knew they were coming. I had no other choice; I am sure grown men wouldn't stand before a six foot four inch monster ready to take a beating especially if they knew exactly what the beating consisted of. And I am a pussy?

(I am just happy not to get beatings anymore.) *Dad* may get loud, but *he* is a teddy bear.

Maybe Jimmy forgot when I wasn't a big fuckin' pussy. I was a little punching bag. I am an inch taller than Jimmy now. I am wondering if size matters. He is the one in need of a role model. I would try but I am too big a pussy for him to take direction from me. And I am his (little) brother

Jimmy has learned he can yell very loud and he likes the SOUND OF HIS OWN VOICE and everyone is starting to hear it. "PRACTICE WHAT YOU PREACH YOU FUCKING ASSHOLE", is a favorite.

If he is in a good mood, he will turn to you and say "that fuggin azzol", after the initial "fucking asshole".

It also seems he has some sort of (mission) He can remember something someone did 20 years ago and pull it right into now. Some form of manipulation. He compares *that* to *this*. He is a real tricky one. *"I am Jimmy! I'm right and everyone's wrong!"*

Jimmy and CJ became the bad asses of South Street.

I hang around with "the other pussies" from the good end. It is peace and quiet that I enjoy and I cannot have that in the presence of Jimmy. I feel grounded… especially when I visit relatives: *Grampy McGee, Grammy Boober, Aunt Marion, My mothers Grand mother, Nana Perry… she is in her 90s and very sharp.*

When Dave could come from the eastside we usually earned money. In winter we would shovel snow all other seasons we pulled weeds, cleaned yards, washed cars, we even cleaned houses. The money gave us freedom to do things

We always had cash and it was still *legit*. I never had an urge to fight with my fists. I steered clear of obvious trouble. I guess that made me a pussy. But being from Lynn should I be a pussy? Hmm who developed this derogatory category and is being a pussy going to mess up my entire life? I never ran from a fight and never really had confrontations maybe one or two.

How do I live with myself being a pussy? Who else knows about this? The act of being a pussy and the fact that I have now become one Will I be able to look at myself again? Will I be able to look my family in the eye? I don't feel like a pussy

21
I want to fit in

Out of one school and into another can give you a chance to be viewed in a better light. In the old school, I had been the *stinky kid* in class. Other kids had shiny hair, bright clean clothes and most of these kids had a normal family and home life that gave them a great deal of self esteem. Your hair and clothes are the latest fashion

Dressing that way allows you to be *Individua*l and *fit in*; you had a sense of *pride*. I had no concept of this thought process.

I am aware that the kids in this new neighborhood view me as a good looking nice kid. Now, I have new clothes and I am clean and shiny. My hair is beginning to look like the style. I can go to this new school as an equal. I would like to fit in. All the cards are in my favor, my ducks are lined up. So I thought

Just a few days before school…. Elaine sent me to a barber to have all my hair cut off. A "wiffle." This is just above a shaved head. I pleaded with her "I will be the only kid in school that looks like that!"

First she became agitated then showed a smirk of delight. Great, from one form of *abuse* to another, *what is wrong with people*?

It looks terrible on *anyone*. Everyone at school has long hair, it defines style. Boys and girls, first impressions say it all.

Now, thanks to Elaine, I can look forward to a few ear flicks, a slap to my head, being called baldheaded prick, dickhead, loser, and whatever else served the moment. *I am where I wanted to be now.* NOT!

I could constantly *feel* so much anger directly from Elaine when she was present. I had no Idea the word "hate" existed. When I first heard it spoken, an image of how *she treated me* flashed into my head.

She slowly let it seep out when Dad was out of sight.

Once she charged toward me with gritted teeth she was holding up her fist and she said "I want to punch you right in the face!" I can't stand you! All because *her daughter had started running her mouth and I told her to be quiet.* She was a very bitchy girl, it gets tiring. Another time she pushed my face into a radiator causing my tooth to chip.

My feeling was correct; the woman just hated me. I have to deal with this instead of planned beatings. I am not allowed to be present or have an opinion. Her spoiled little daughter has the same attitude now. I have great intentions, I don't get it. I think real assholes deserve to be treated this way. I wonder if I look like some kind of asshole

It has to be *jealousy* I am told from older relatives.

"Jealous now there's a shocker Jealous of what?" I wonder

That they were unable to be spectators at Uncle Eds? Well I forgot, no one knows about that. Yet

The new stigma that surrounds me at school has turned violent.

Ray and Bobby were punks at school. They decided to hold me down and tie my hands behind my back then they proceeded to beat my ass. A police officer walked past minutes later and found me behind a bush. I said "two bigger kids did it." And that I never saw them before.

I knew, I was going to see these guys everyday and feared more beatings. *I guess Jimmy is right, I am a big pussy. If I was allowed to blend in with the rest of the kids maybe the entire school wouldn't see me as such a pussy. I am beginning to feel like I just won't fit in anywhere. When Mom was here, I was very happy and developing at a pace that would probably have lead to wonderful future. She is gone and well, Dad tries but he just doesn't have the love for me like she did. I was her baby.*

Months later my hair grew in and I could blend in a little better, First impressions always seem to have the greatest impact. I have already been labeled as some sort of outcast. Its not like many people in the school are knocking themselves out to be near me.
In my heart and mind, I feel great about myself. I just wish all these adults weren't creating so much difficulty for me. On my own… I socialize quiet well. And I seem to be liked by people when I can create my own first impressions.

22
Not all women are bad

I am discovering some girls aren't *so bad*. Some of these young ladies are finding an interest in me. I notice a lovely young woman, I saw her as a *beautiful princess*, long dark hair, tan skin, brown eyes; she has a soft smile that never seems to go away. She waits for the bus in front of the church every day. I pass by and try not to stare. It's not easy.

One day, as I approached her. I noticed she was looking right at me. And when I looked into her eyes her smile widened. A surge of warmth had come over me. "Hi, I'm Brian" I said.

Hi I'm Sarita, I see you come by every day, do you live near here? She asked. "Yes, right down the street" I replied. We talked enough to exchange numbers.

In just a week or two, we grew to like each other very much; her school had often gone to Barry Park for outside activities and one day. I decided, I would like to see her, so I cut class, and headed over.

She told me a kid named Robert was taunting her. I felt a need to defend her honor. I walked up to him. I slapped his face so hard my hand was burning. He went down to the ground and then got up running. I felt good, for I had defended a princess.

She was in complete shock. *Where's Jimmy to call me pussy now*?
Barry Park is a place I would often see Sarita, You could set the time, I would be there.

Robert's brother Steve decided to be there to surprise me. I showed up at the usual time nobody was around. A larger kid walked towards me, He stared in my eyes without saying a word, and he began to throw my body around the park, like a rag doll. He continued picking me up, and throwing me down. Finally, I had the distance to get up and run. Again *where's, Jimmy to call me pussy now*?

I called her later and gave her the details. She felt bad and invited me over her house. I knocked on the door, her father answered. He was a very dark Spanish guy.

He must have known I was coming over. He introduced me to his son. The kid was a bit larger than I am.

They made it clear that they objected to a white boy trying to see his daughter. It seems like they talked about it and expected me

I could see Sarita just past the door. She looked worried. I had to know how she felt, so I called the house, her younger sister answered and told me never to call again.

I stayed away in hopes that I would hear from her. I saw her sister after that, but the conversation was nothing more than "hi how are you." I wondered if she still felt something for me. She expressed the same feelings I had *before the incident at the park*. I wonder if that changed things. I did it for her. I didn't believe their story about race.

There were many more interests to come my way. I wasn't thinking about races or anything; to me people are **whatever their hearts say they are**, and a good deal of that is seen in the eyes. I looked into a lot of eyes after that.

(Not too many shitbags want to let people know that right away, so they can put on a wonderful show, but that's a tough act to play all the time. Elaine & Leeann put on a show for months, before I caught on. Uncle Ed and Aunt Ruth didn't even try to pretend.)

23
Looking for love

I began to spend some time with a few different girls and I was getting a chance to look into their hearts, hoping to find what I am looking for. Even though I haven't developed an understanding of what exactly that is. However, I know that when I was younger, and my Mother passed. I lost the *unconditional love between her and me*.

I have a need to get a *sense of that* back. My step mother is not the person to help me here. As I get to know these young ladies, I am not acting very curious about sexuality. I am acting very curious about commitment.

Dad is the type of guy that will put *all* women on a pedestal. He says *"there's no such thing as an ugly woman."* His *views on respect* for woman feel right to me. His choice of a woman doesn't

I am beginning to spend a lot of time with Lois. She is petite, with shoulder length light brown hair, brown eyes and pout lips. The time was short… One day at school a girl named Lynne walked over to me and said "Lois doesn't want to see you anymore" I said 'Why?" (*I could see Lois standing across the lot watching.*) Lynne said "because you didn't try anything and you were together awhile" So, I responded "I wanted to show her respect"

Lynne said "Oh well, you should have shown her that you wanted her, because now someone else is, don't call her or bother her!"

I was very surprised; I thought about it, for a couple of days too, I wasn't hurt. I really wanted to have her as my girlfriend. I missed the boat and maybe it's for the best. I talk to a few girls, I got some numbers, It's really not a big deal for now. Lois seemed very sweet and I read it all wrong. If sex was that important why didn't she initiate the task?

I spent some time with a girl named Dawn for awhile. She was very pretty, she had long wavy blonde hair, blue eyes, and it didn't last because Dad thought she wore too much makeup. He said "she looked like a tramp."

I usually took the city bus to school... the bus stop is close to the school, but you still have a ten minute walk. In that time, I walk and talk with plenty of girls to feel connected.

Some mornings I walk alone and think... constantly wondering why I'm here. What's life about? And where am I going? School, to me was a place parents sent you *teenage daycare*. Why is Mom gone? Why was I beaten so badly? And why does Elaine hate me? Is something wrong with me? Why are my brothers so fucked up?

I have a lot on my mind. I have no place, I *want* to be. I just heard Johnny is out of jail and he has changed, should I care? I am still the same guy I was when I was five. However, I still have some nights when I sleep heavy, and some nights I don't.

My birthday was coming up in a week. I saw a *brand new* bike in the basement at our house. Wow, I thought my very own brand new bike... finally maybe *life's good*.

The day after my birthday the bike was still there. I figured they forgot. I waited and hinted about the bike. A week later, I heard Elaine on the phone, she mentioned that she got some *assholes kid* a bike for his birthday. Sure enough it was gone, along with my smile. That's ok I took it out once... while she was at work.... what a ride!

24
Don't talk to strangers?

"Hey Bri, you're looking good"
Johnny said as he approached me. He was
coming down the street… to stop by the
house for a visit. "Hey Johnny" I replied.
"It's John" He stated "How are you?" "I
continued. He went on to say "Excellent, I
started a job; all my criminal shit is behind
me now. So what have you been doing with
yourself?' He asked, "Just school and stuff"
I replied. We did some "getting to know"
each other. He gets out of work at this time
everyday, we can meet at the sub shop and
hang out. Gradually we began to develop a
routine. John and I have the same sense of
humor; we enjoy making fun of people we
don't like. Uncle Ed and Aunt Ruth are the
basis of much of that humor All he said was
"You know who Aunt Ruth looks like, I
replied The *Skipper*! We burst out laughing.
It seems we both spent some time thinking
of that. . I talk in the same insulting way
about Elaine and her kids too. John doesn't
know them at all. They aren't *very* stupid,
but they like to act cute and like *they don't
get it*. It's disgusting; pretending to be naive.
Their just such *phony people...*

John and I began to meet up every night after dinner; we usually sat in the super sub, and talk about anything like my passion for the 1980 Monte Carlo, black with the square headlights. The previous year, had round ones and made the car look cheesy. I think we had a complete night of conversation just about that. John gave me the run down on his day to day progress.

We were establishing a relationship. We were becoming brothers again. Jimmy is still so out of control the courts are offering him jail or military, He is joining the Navy.

John is really happy about his new found freedom, and he is working very hard. Dad is feeling great about all of his kids right now. Everything looks good. Dad feels people should be given as many chances as they need.

You never know when they will *come around.* Look at Dad; He was a small time punk. Now his integrity shines through.

He seems to have more trust in Elaine than anyone else does. She lies very often, She buys second hand shit for me. She goes above and beyond for total strangers. The ones she wants to impress. It's always 'name brand' and top of the line. It's all about *taste you know*. She says. *Oh please.*

My opinion is, go outside and play hide and go *fuck yourself*!

She has proven to be a manipulative spiteful *C word*. I never thought that word applied to anyone, until I thought about her. Not even the skipper. *Maybe* Ann, but definitely Elaine. She did her best to impress *anyone who's anyone*. I was nothing. She showed me that in everyway she could.

I bitch about my home life to John a lot. I think he feels that I am talking like a child and that can be annoying. He firmly tells me how *happy I should be* to live at home and have free room and board.

He works and provides everything for himself. I think I would choose that over the bullshit at home. He tells me I wouldn't like Jail and Living with her is better than Jail.

I would have to go to jail and see that one to believe it. We have different opinions on some things.

25
I want answers

I get off the bus at the same place each morning and start my ten minute walk across the field to the school. Today the sun is shining; *an early spring morning* is a little cool. I find myself thinking the usual things, *what's it all about?...*

BAM! Like lightening striking, something hit me and it hit me hard *in the mind!* A lot like one of Uncle Ed's beatings. *Holy shit I'm going to die someday. I can't avoid it. I can't hide; I can't buy a way out! It's really going to happen, Oh please help, what the do I do? In complete panic, I ran as fast as I could, I ran right to the bathroom. I have scared the shit out of me. Literally!* This is clearly something I never felt before...... a conscious nightmare

The experience I just had, will occupy my thoughts for some time to come. Even to the point, where I bring myself back into the same moment and do it all over again.

Now, I have an attitude that says who gives a fuck about anything? I try to look past it. Am I becoming *mentally ill*? I know my brothers are fucked up. And we have had the same trouble. I wonder if they went through the same thing. Or am I alone? The only one in the world who knows, with this much certainty? The "*maybe it won't happen to me*" Attitude is very naive however, everyone I know, acts like they are protected. Jimmy turned me on to music. And a lot of songs that helped me to express how I feel and I got direction from other songs For awhile… I let music give me both. *Self medicating through song.* School was here and there; I would sign in at homeroom and take off for the day. That way I wasn't absent. I just wasn't there. (No phone call home) I figured it was "my time" and I should try to enjoy some of it. Eventually someone caught on when Dad found out, He was furious! I got him so upset, he shouted at me, until *he* was almost in tears. I figured, I should *try* for respect to him. I still thought of it as a *daycare*.

I sat beside the school and spent so many hours just watching other people and looking at all the life around me. I would take in as much sunshine and blue sky as I could. I would feel balanced this way. As long as it was warm, clear and sunny I felt everything was the way it should be

26
Step into another world

"Ok class, we have a new student *Gil* from Georgia", announced the Math teacher. Nobody was impressed. Gil was a thin scruffy looking kid. No one in class really seemed to care. I just thought for a minute that maybe the kid came off of some farm or something

The next morning on my walk across the field, I noticed he was walking just ahead and he was smoking a cigarette. "Hey little kids aren't supposed to smoke" I said.

I was about 5'7 he was about 5'3. He turned around and laughed. "Hey I'm Gil" he said. I told him, I knew, I was in Math when he was introduced to everyone. "Brian" I replied. We talked shit for awhile. We were both smokers, so I let him know the good spots he could sneak one without getting caught.

Another thing we had in common was a love for dirt bikes. He had one that needs repairs and I built one out of junk parts. "You want to come and see that bike?" Gil asked. "Sure, I'll walk home with you. I replied and asked Where do you live?" "Deer Park" He said. After school Gil and I met at the *smokestack*. That's the hiding place for smokers. "So how come you don't talk funny if you're from Georgia? I asked. He said "My father is a trucker, and we move a lot depending on where he works the most. He added "We were born and raised in Chelsea, Mass", "Oh cool" I replied "I'm one of seven kids, I got my fathers name." he said. We went to his house, He was right there are lots of kids running around. There were two older girls around my age, they were quiet and average looking, Marie and Terri. The only difference was Terri wore glasses and looked a lot more like the mother. I was there to see a dirt bike. It had some rust and needed a little work. But, I let Gil know we could fix it this weekend. We began to meet on the ten minute stroll across the field at school. Gil and I would talk a little each day. He said his sister Marie, thought I was nice looking and she may want to get to know me. I thought about it, and at the time I had no *real interest*. I felt good knowing I was being checked out.

After school we headed over to his house. I began working on the bike. Marie came out and poked her nose around. *I had my hand on a part while, I was trying to hold the bike in position. The wrench I needed was just beyond my reach. "Marie can you grab that for me?" I asked. She tipped her head back and made a sound like "hmm".* Then she walked away (striding like a show pony) I was pissed, what an asshole! useless bitch! I thought.

That solves that; she could think I am the best looking guy in the world now. *Who cares?* (Asshole) I told Gil he just laughed, and said "Yeah she can be a bitch sometimes, she's just playing with you, and you'll like her if you get to know her"

I had no use for that. Gil and I started spending a lot of time riding the tracks. He brought a kid named Pete along one day. *Pete and I didn't seem to click at all.* I began feeling like a third wheel when the kid was around. I met Gil's father and Mother, His father was your average beer drinking American Dad. He was in his 50s like my father. His Mother looked like a "bag of nerves." Gil met my father and Elaine, he knew my Dad was cool, but he also thought Elaine was phony.

That Friday he stayed at my house for a sleepover. We were going to head out first thing. The tracks started at my back yard and go past his house, to donkey hill in Saugus. The hill has small jumps and climbs it's a lot of fun. We stopped at his house with the rest of his parts and headed out. We spent the day riding the tracks and hill. We probably put 110 miles on the bikes. We decided to stay over his house Saturday night. We got in around 11pm. His sister Marie was watching TV; we just hung out and watched with her.

After about a half hour Gil headed off to bed. Marie sat in a chair wearing very small shorts. I glanced over once or twice. On my final glance, I noticed she had no underwear and she opened her leg just a touch more. *I saw all I needed to see.*

I said "Marie take off your shorts" *she slipped right out of them.* We quietly went to her room.

The next morning I had a *disturbing feeling* just hoping I did the *right thing.* I had to talk to her alone. I knew she was *no virgin* and she was a year *older* than me. She also liked to *play games.* I became pretty worried, but I wanted to play it cool. I'm in new territory now.

I was close many times before. *She just took something from me* and I need her to do the *right thing*.

I am not as tough inside as I look outside. She has taken a *tender heart*. I wasn't in love. *But I wasn't so strong now*. I go with an idea of "I take what God gives me." And good or bad I accept. Until now, I had *no say*. Now it's my choices that will determine what path I follow. This is the second life changing feeling I have had in weeks. For the next few weeks, I spent all my time trying to learn her behavior. I'm looking for *who* she really is. I guess, *I already knew, just from the bike incident*. My father always said "*go with your first instinct*." My first instinct was not so good.

Over the next few weeks.. I thought she was doing the right thing. It seems we are an item. She does have some male friends and she played the jealous card a few times once she skipped school with a kid she knew. His name is Ted. I am really starting to worry. What I am learning is that I wanted "someone I could trust with my entire life." It's not just a childish thing; *I have a real need in this life*. I want to make up for what I lost over the years, most fifteen year old kids don't have this idea… I am sure of that.

I left school early and went to her house, only to see her with Ted. They were smoking on the porch. "What's up?" I asked she said "We skipped and hung out" *like it was no big deal.* I asked "why didn't you call me?" "It was a last minute decision" she said. This isn't making me feel any better. Ted took off. I quizzed her but she had all the answers. As she saw the panic begin to set in… she would rub my arm and say "Hon" and then tell me anything that would calm things for that moment. A few days later, I introduced her to Dad. He was fine while she was present. When he got me alone He went through the roof. *"I've known a lot of Maries in my time! Stay away from that douche bag!" She's nothing but trouble, and if you knock her up, you'll have bigger trouble with me!"*

I began thinking; the last girl I brought over had too much makeup. However, she was a *nice* girl. He didn't know. I guess he won't ever like who I bring home. Now Marie and I are going to have to be careful. Her father took off to Georgia. He left his wife,

Terri is his step daughter. He took her with him. From what Gil said The mother is too old and her head is messed up. But Terri looks like the mother did when they met.

I guess he traded one for the other. *I can't see these red flags*? "So your telling me *your father is banging your sister*?!" I said with surprise. Gil said "Terri is not his daughter so more power to him." "But she's 17 and he's 50" I said,
Gil responded "If it makes him happy"

27
You asked for it

"Brian I have to tell you something" Marie said. "I'm pregnant" I just stared into her eyes, wondering if she was telling me the truth or not. She seemed to be serious at this moment. (I became somewhat *happy*, and then *concerned*. I am only fifteen and she is only sixteen. What should we do "I *take what God gives me*") I responded by saying "what do you want to do?" She said "What?! You're not suggesting an abortion!" I said "no but, I don't know what you want" I'm with you" She said "I am having this baby, and I will tell him all his life, *you wanted to get rid of him*!" I shouted "I never said that! I am with you! Holy shit, I never said it. We decided to tell her mother... I can't tell Dad. I am going to wait for some ideas on how to adapt to this revelation.

Marie's mother is somewhat slow, and she has a speech issue. Marie makes fun of her behind her back. The woman has a lot of integrity, considering her mental health status is an obstacle. She is also a nervous wreck. The news has given her a bright outlook on things. She seems very happy

She will soon have a grandchild. I went home each day as if all was great in the world. I got a part time job at Boyd's Potato chips. It was pretty cool watching the actual production. From dirt covered potato to delicious snack food. Off the production line they taste even better than they smell from outside. *The very smell I followed years before.*

I started saving a little money and skipping a lot of school. Marie quit entirely. She just stayed home "barefoot and pregnant" One day she had morning sickness And I secreted a *smell* that made her *vomit* whenever I went near her. Not like when I was a kid. It was probably stale chips this time. I was so amazed. I would purposely go near her, to see if it really worked *it did*. I felt bad doing that but it was so amazing to see

Dad found out I was skipping school, and he figured I was at Maries. He came over with the Police. I was returned to school and Dad came down very hard. I began going back and forth often sort of running away.

Dad got a CHINS warrant (Child *in need of service*) Jimmy also got discharged from the Navy dishonorably. Dad was pissed off at us.

John met a girl named Cheryl and they are becoming quite an Item. John and Dad were bonding. I was in a *deceitful* situation and I didn't think I could trust John. So I avoided him

Gil had been present when Jimmy was home and they began bonding. Gil and that kid Pete that I didn't like started smoking weed with Jimmy they had a common interest.

Jimmy had no idea Marie was pregnant. But soon, she will show. I waited for answers. One day while at Maries, Her father called He wanted to talk to me.

(" Brian, I know you were hanging around with your friend yesterday and you were at white hen pantry at 6pm, I know everything you do, I also know my daughter is pregnant, Your going to be a man, and do the right thing and your not going to hurt my little girl. I have two tickets at the bus station in Boston. You'll both get on the bus tomorrow, and hightail it down here I got you a job and you can stay with Terri and I, until you get on your feet.")

I had no idea he had me watched.. I paused a moment... "Ok" I replied

Marie seems happy and I found this to be a way out. I am sure in time; I can show my father I am man enough to take on this responsibility. This is my time. I have to take control of my life, because, I don't hate me and I will not hurt me. If I have to tell Dad and Elaine I will be hurt and most likely sent to reform school. If Elaine has her way

28
Southern fried Brian

We headed out the next day. I knew I had to go. Dad was going to be very pissed and very hurt. I have what I was waiting for. A family, I will be a father; I will be there for my child. I'm taking what God gave me. Even though Marie seems to be much less of the person I had hoped for.

She is about to become "Mother of my child" maybe that's what's needed to help her grow. We took the MBTA to Boston and got a Greyhound from South Station. With a little walking in town between the bus rides.

One last look at the common and Beacon Hill, I may never see this again. From Boston to New York was straight forward, It was like a little day trip.

At Port Authority a couple of junkies took the seat in front of us. We nervously watched them shoot up. They tripped out in a *down mode*, No problem, As soon as I could get the *needle images* out of my head. They kept to themselves

We took I 95 all the way to Savanna Ga. It was cool to see a new world coming my way. Red dirt replacing the brown dirt, smells of Georgia pulp and pecan trees.

Go figure, we have 'Lil Peach' in Massachusetts, A *quick talking Yankee town.* In Georgia the *peach* state they have 'Kwickie' food store instead… that is backwards. Now, I have the sounds of the locusts buzzing in my ears all day. Everyone seems to have an air conditioner down here.

After a layover in Savanna, We got a bus right into Macon, Georgia. If the United States were an actual being, this felt like its *rectum.* People had hubcaps hanging off the porch with *for sale* written on tape across it. Racism was horribly open. I saw the sign on the Barber shop it read:

"Boy's hair cut $4.00
Men's $6.50
Woman cut and style $ 9.00
Black kinky hair $ 9,999.00 "

We're going to stay at *Samson trailer park.* The entrance is ½ a mile long; it's a winding road with an old pick up truck, which has flat tires and weeds growing from the debris on the bed of the truck. Just off Pio Nono ave.

I would say to Marie "pi o no no" kitty cat. *With a higher pitch in my voice.* Every time the sign came up.

And Signs like Piggly Wiggly, what happened to Stop and Shop? When I hear the name, I picture short fat naked women with curly tails pushing along troughs to load up on grub.

Oink, squeal, Oink my goodness yawl a sale! Wow, You getting all this Marie? "Hey look at this place. Its years behind" I said. I looked at her and realized she had been here before. She just smiled I think she was just enjoying watching me freak out.

Terri and Gil were very welcoming. Gil put on some friendly charm. I have been waiting to be accepted for what I am as an individual. This is a good start. The thought of a "Motive" had never entered my mind.

Gil said "Hey you're looking good" He has a touch of southern drawl in his accent. When did that happen? He's only been here a few months. I laughed and said "thanks this place is weird huh?" He laughed and said picture the "United States is here" as he held his hand up. "And Macon is here" he moved his other hand a great distance away.

"*They are ass backwards here.*" He added. ("What *are we doing here* then? I wondered.) I responded with "hmm" I see what you mean." "Well you're going to be a Daddy. (He made it sound like I hit the big league I am a man now and the child has been broken the secret to life was to transform from child to Dad with no in between.)

He even said "No *girl is a woman, until she has a baby*." I guess that's equal for men. It seems to me, I am a man. I am *important* now.

I wanted to be worth something to someone, ever since I was five. I am something to Dad, but he was gone for a great deal of my life. He also has his wife and she has instant credibility

Elaine is his partner. She makes half of his decisions in life. *His darker half* She has only known me four and a half years. And she stopped acting as if she liked me three months into that.

It sucks so bad knowing someone that hates you. Living with it is much worse; always on guard and afraid to be yourself. My opinion is… *Dad I had to go.*

Your wife didn't help with your credibility and the impact you had on me. I wish it were different. That wife of yours has changed my destination more than once. I could be more religious who knows? I would *never* say these things to him. It's a respect thing.

"Take a week or so to get comfortable and you will start working at the trucking Company. You can change light bulbs, patch holes in trailers, and grease the landing gear. You can handle that right?" Gil stated. "Sure" I replied. He threw me a Beer and said "Let me show you around"

We drove out to the "Sunset *grill*" A car made popular from TV was on a trailer outside the bar. "Wow see that?" I said. As if I am having a brush with greatness. "Yup, I think they film the show around here." He noted. We walked past dirty picnic tables covered in beer bottles and ashtrays. We walked in the door.

Inside, I noticed a bar and a pool table there is not any seating other than the bar and the picnic tables outside." Hey Granny Get me a beer and get my *son in law* one too" He said to a very tiny woman that had to be in her 70s.

"Now stop that Henry or I'm gonna kick your ass out again, this time ill bust your head on the way out!" she shouted to a customer. I have no idea what he was doing but she is one tough old broad. *Son in law* wow, I am somebody, Will I *marry Marie*? I don't see her as my *wife* yet. I get a feeling, and I "know" certain things that *may happen* and I don't "Know" that yet. For now, I am just waiting. Most of the time, I get assistance from *someplace else*. It's a course of direction or an opportunity. But it is, usually what determines things for me. Right now, I am over 1000 miles away from what I know and I am thinking about a baby.

I woke up to a chill in the trailer. And I could hear the ac running. I went over and shut it off. I made coffee and got a smoke. I wanted to sit outside and wake up. I opened the door and the heat blasted in and gave me the feel of being submerged into a hot bath. I was taken for a minute. I began to think about the ride to the sunset grill. Gil informed me of concerns he had. *"Terri has been fucking around with a couple boys I know one, his names Roy. I put a stop to it, but, when I am on the road, I can't keep an eye on her. That's what I want you and Marie to do. She won't fuck around with Marie here."*

Now I see… He took advantage of our situation for his needs

Is he going to tell Marie or do I? Well I will tell her anyway. Later

The Sunset grill was pretty cool, *a real shanty.* Granny*, She* didn't even card me. Do I look 18? I guess so, and the Car. I should have gone closer to it and looked inside, maybe another time. It was awesome and in real life I could touch it

"Hi, wow, it's hot out" *Marie broke into my daydream.* "How ya feeling?" I asked. "Good, we have to get an appointment at the health clinic, so I can get checked and they will give me some vitamins." She replied "Ok I said. " My father is going to have you drive him to work, He won't need the car when he's over the road, and he's usually gone a week at a time." She added. "

Nice, I can drive; I only drove a car once in a parking lot. Seems like I'm going to like this

The car was a station wagon with an automatic transmission. It wasn't a big deal. I didn't have a license and wasn't worried I'm not stealing the fucking thing. Gil always left a full tank of gas.

Later that morning, Gil and I headed out to the trucking company. So he could show me where it was and to let me "see *my new employer*" We arrived and he told me to *wait in the car a minute* he had to get an Itinerary and logs and things. He was gone about ten minutes. When he returned, he informed me that the job was no longer available. But since I have the car, I can find one on my own. Take all the time I need.

He headed out in the truck and I headed back to the trailer park. As I arrived Marie was sitting outside with Terri. It was a break from cooking and cleaning for them.

I think Marie was taking charge and setting the rules. Terri wasn't real happy. Marie was bossy with her, and as long as Marie wasn't making fun of her, she would try to fit as an equal. Terri *took what she wanted* and was smart enough to keep it quietly within herself. For the most part she was a little slow and childlike in front of Marie. Marie's appointment was for the next day. The Clinic It was across from the Medical Center down town... across from a large bright red "*Jesus Saves*" neon sign. I wasn't sure what motivated Marie's next act. However it was a childish maneuver that will fuel my concerns or my jealousy. I noticed a piece of paper entitled "In Sex"

The paper had a list of Guys names and * star ratings after each of them. The list was about 12 names long "Brian" was in the center and had a 2 star rating meanwhile a few names had 3 and 4 stars. It was left in the open intentionally the stars caught my eye.

Marie saw me viewing the list and smiled fiendishly. "What is this?" I asked. She said "It's nothing just a joke" "Bullshit!" I replied, (I recognized some of the names. Her Brother Gil had mentioned them… as old boyfriends at times when we talked. The guy Ted I was worried about was listed and Pete the neighbor from Deer Park. Ted had 4 stars.) "Relax hon. I was joking you're the best, and I wasn't with all those guys so don't be mad." She said, as if she were talking to a child. My mind is racing. (*Don't be mad? what do you think I'm slow? of course you were with those guys! Thinking about Terri's activity triggered your thinking about your own activities. Yes you have a pussy and you like to know it's in demand. Great! Get a personality to go with it moron. You just wanted to get a charge out of watching me worry.*) I watched TV alone for the night. It was a wonderful boost for my self esteem. Do I even have any yet? This is what I get to deal with the rest of my life?

I'm only fifteen years old. I want the family and it is developing now, why is she messing with me? Does she know something I don't know? Is she making fun of my kindness? She knows I will do anything to have a place in life with my own family. I have poured my heart onto this girl. Shit! She told me her first time was when she was 13 and she's had 11 guys other than me. What am I doing? The next morning we got up and had coffee and a smoke. Then we showered up and headed out. I wake up with a wonderful feel and I am always happy once the day begins. It's usually the events of the day that chip away at my smile. We got to the clinic

Marie is beginning to show now. We got all the paper work and she was getting checked and instructed. "Are you the father?" the nurse asked "Yes" I responded "Ok then you can be with Mom for the ultrasound". She added. (Wow, there's the fingers and a leg. that head is huge) *My thoughts as I view the images*. "Oh and it's a boy" the technician noted we had asked if they could tell.

Well, I guess Marie was right, when she found out she was pregnant she mentioned "he" and "him" My entire life is now wrapped in this moment that's why I am here. The images I see are my future now. Marie's father had said "A happy mother makes a healthy baby" Oh boy… well I am going to work hard.

Gil has a *gift* for making *you* feel *special,* like the only place anyone wants to be is with YOU!

I see him *charm* others *as needed.* I am sure his magic gift, has calmed Terri for awhile. I've seen him *brag* about his *"son in law."* To other people as we try to develop friends around the area. I have *"Nothing but good things to say about him. That boy is a hard worker and a real nice guy."*

(Was he trying to sell me or was he selling himself through me? Who was he to them, having instant credibility anyway?) *Now, I feel great! I am a hard worker and a real nice guy.* He lifted "you" up often and he would take you down enough to adjust his strings like a puppeteer. You eventually hung on his every word. He could have formed a cult. "You *see you have to sell yourself and be positive let these people know you're the best, because you never know when you need one of them."*

"Oh *yeah*" Was my response. I was thinking I should just be myself and not try to *sell anything*. I know I am a great guy and a hard worker. If the situation arises it will show. Whatever, it's not my game; it's his, so fuck it.

As we head home, I am in tune to all of her needs. She is going to be the mother of my child, and in time, we will most likely marry. I focus on the mothering aspects of this young lady. I suggest stopping for ice cream or something to eat. We had money from when I worked in Massachusetts. Gil, her father had left money with Terri.

Cash on hand in case we needed anything or if she needed anything. With Marie being pregnant the focus of attention is on her. Terri is a bit resentful. It seems they have had issues most of their lives anyway. Step sisters, I had one and I think it sucks. Now Terri is more than a step sister she is Gil's woman. *(Oh daddy, yes Oh daddy)* What the fuck?

He was Daddy at some point. Come to think of it he is Daddy to Marie, Was his name on that list? No, I wouldn't think it would be even if he celebrated her 13th birthday with a bang. Or even a good spanking who knows?

At this point Marie is a *Mother to be*. That's how I want to view her. Our thoughts are focused on a "baby." Were looking at baby clothes and cribs and going to the clinic. Gil and Terri get very involved now too. We had a focus together now. The only distraction is an occasional "water bug" a *cockroach on steroids*. Gil usually comes home by the weekend. Saturdays Gil and I run errands we usually end up at the sunset grill for some beers watching granny get beat up or give a beating up to hairy rebel. I asked a local what the trick was to getting a job, I can't seem to find one. He looked down and said "*its them tennis shoes, real men wear boots*." I can't get a job because I wear sneakers?

Oh fuck me! Oh yeah, I'm in another world. The next day, I bought some boots.

Sundays, we take the girls around to shops or to the lake for relaxation. Marie is *showing* much more she wears the pants that stretch with her. And the cute little tops that puff out like a boob skirt. I am starting to get some heat about not working from Gil. I haven't been able to find anything. I have no experience and I am a *fast talking Yankee*.

I built a lawn mower out of spare parts; I found in my travels I cut lawns at $5 -$10 a lawn. It's worth about $20- $30 a day. That included walking from house to house with the machine in 90 degree temps. That's not enough to make it on our own. "We" are working towards being independent from "them" Terri must be giving Gil some grief, she feels like an outsider at her own "home"

Gil informed me, that he was going to help her get her license. I should not stay too cozy with the car. And he gave me some information on rents, so I will know what to expect. I need to make over $140.00 a week I was able to get a part time job at Days Inn as a dishwasher. That gave me solid income of eighty bucks a week and the lawns gave me the rest. The schedule worked out well too. We started saving and Marie was close to having that baby boy.

Throughout the pregnancy we took many trips to the Clinic eventually Marie was spending a lot of time in bed. I would use my free time to sit in the ac and watch TV All I could find was "tv13" the station that came in without cable. Cable wasn't available in that trailer Park yet. I would often think about Dad.

I hope he is ok. After the baby is born, I will call him. The routine continued with the same chores of cutting lawns, washing dishes and weekend errands during the day and beer at night. Gil began taking the car more often.

One night around 10pm I was ready for bed. Marie informed me that she was in labor we had to call a cab. We got to the Medical Center with plenty of time. She was checked in and ready. Hospital staff waited for her to get to 10cm. Just as she did the Doctor was "where he needed to be" in seconds the water and baby came rushing out.

The Doctor was in shock he said "*I have to call my wife about this one she aint gonna believe it!*" It was a boy 8lbs 4oz with a full head of hair. Marie was happy and tired. Terri and I were like *little kids giggling over this tiny human.* We stayed until daylight. We would come back later in the day with Gil, He got the call and couldn't wait to see his grandson.

On the ride back to the trailer, I talked with Terri as if she were my equal and she really felt great. As if we had a bond of real friendship. Usually when Marie is around Terri is very quiet. And she appeared to feel like a misfit.

My mind was everywhere my first thought when I saw the baby, was that he resembled that kid Ted from Lynn. How could I think such a thing? Shouldn't I feel a bond with this child?

I had trouble sleeping as these things went through my mind. Maybe I was too tired I was up over 20hrs. I have worried about this before. So it was always in the back of my mind.

Gil got home and wanted to rush up to the hospital. So Terri, Gil and I got in the car and headed up. Terri couldn't stop talking about the baby. We stopped to check on Marie she had rested and has her energy. Her father gave her a kiss and a card. And told her he was proud and the usual things a father would say. We all were excited together.
I looked at the baby some more and had difficulty getting Ted's image out of my head. I signed the birth certificate so nothing else should matter any way.

Gil and I stared at the baby through the glass as I tried to think more about this baby being mine. And that I am being an asshole.

Gil shook his head and said "**Well, I had my doubts, but that boy is yours**" What *did he just say? He knew his little girl had been screwing someone at the same time I was*? "You had doubts? Who's did you think it was?" I asked. "**Pete, But that's your baby boy**" He replied. I didn't like Pete on his own merit, and this guy Gil just acted like it is common knowledge that she was screwing him and the baby was most likely Pete's?

Wait a minute it must be true, Gil talked with her on the phone when we were in Lynn, that's how he knew she was pregnant. What else did she tell him? When I asked about Pete she said she *never slept with him*. I am fucking furious! I want to tear that birth certificate into pieces, *spit the biggest chunk of lung butter right in her face*! And get on the next bus home.

I told Gil, I was not feeling too good and I will take the city bus to the trailer park. He was fine with that. I couldn't even look at Marie. I still think were both wrong, and Its Ted's kid. *Fuck the bunch of them.*

A couple of days went by… I stewed in my thoughts and tried to keep my composer around "them". When Marie came home I told her what I was thinking and what her father said.

She gave me the usual "He's just kidding hon. it's only you, you're the best, she rubbed my arm and talked to me like I'm a child. *She does this exactly the same, anytime I seem to have tapped into the real truth.* When I come up with a bullshit guess, she acts entirely differently knowing that she's not lying. She responds with more attitude and less nurturing. Well, I will shut the fuck up for now and let her mother this child. I am ready to call Dad though.

The timing was good for what takes place now without injury to anyone. Gil sat me down for a "man to man" He simply said "Well its time for you to start thinking about yourself." I responded by asking "What? I don't know what you mean? (*I thought I was building up for the big game and here it is and I am ready*) "Its time to think about what Brian wants, that's all I'm saying" He replied. (I really think he has another father in mind for this child) What the fuck is going on? Who are these people?

29
Child in Crisis

I am calling Dad. I went to the bus station and called from there. Elaine answered; she said "Where the hell are you? Jimmy said you're in Alabama or Georgia or something? I want you to know your killing your father! He cries sometimes over you. Your 16 years old and he doesn't know whether you're living or dead! *She was not out of line she was right.* "He isn't home from work. He will be in an hour call him then!" She added and hung up.

"Hello" Dad answered, a surge of happiness ran though me hearing Dads voice again. "Dad" I said. His voice was calm and quiet he said "Are you calling because you want to come home?" "Yes" I answered. "I have to make some calls and borrow the money but I will buy you a ticket. Call me back in a couple of hours" He stated "Ok Ill call at 8pm" I replied.

I wasn't leaving the bus station, at this moment, I had one family and one home, and it was over 1000 miles from here. I hung around the bus station smoking and pacing.

"Y'all waitin' for a ticket to Boston?" a voice called out. "Yes" I answered "Ok its here someone just called it in" he replied. I called Dad and let him know, he said "Call me when you get to Boston Ill pick you up" "Ok I love you" I said "You too Bri" He replied. The bus was heading out at 9:20pm; I went and got some food. Then I called Marie and said "I am going to Lynn to see if I can get a real job and get us a place.

She was happy because together we had bitched about Georgia and the knowledge that her father wanted us out on our own anyway. I have time to think….. I wonder if that's my baby, She swears he is, aside of my concerns regarding trust in her, we do get along. I can have the family I have waited for. Dad knows everything now and he is ready to accept my secrets. No more hiding. My mind is racing. I don't feel like I'm abandoning a mother and child. I feel like I need *my family* and they need to accept my life now.

I sat on the bus for a few hours alone. A pretty blonde girl boarded the bus in South Carolina and sat next to me, she was around my age, we didn't talk too much but, the interaction was genuine and warm. She could tell I was tired, Eventually, I put my head on her lap and closed my eyes it was innocent and very sweet. She stroked my hair and shoulders. I felt, like I was just where I wanted to be. Somewhere in Virginia she got off the bus. I wanted to ask her if I should go with her. But the words just wouldn't come out. *I wonder if she thought the same thing*? I saw in her eyes she had something she could have said but she held back I just know it.

I enjoyed the rest of the trip thinking about her and how she felt warm and smelled nice. I could hear her voice. She had a sweet southern accent.

These thoughts went well with the vibration of the window penetrating the side of my head as I rested it there. I listened to the steady humming of the buses tires as we rolled up Interstate 95 North this time.

It was funny recognizing all the things up ahead. I felt like a man of the world. I travel now.

I could see the signs for Massachusetts and the Pike I began looking for the lights that surround the city. It was still about an hour away....

Instantly the feeling of being safe at home has hit me. I am entering Boston on the pike. There it stands like an old friend. Just the way I remember it. There's a limo waiting in the pick up area. *A gorgeous classy looking woman exits, some guy sees her and says "Hey nice car how'd ya get that?" "I worked for it" she said "I bet you did"* he replied and went on his way. Oh yeah.. Its Boston.. I am home again

"Hey Bri" a voice said. "Hey John what's up brother"? "Good to see ya" he said "How's Dad?" I asked.

"He's ok, He's pretty worried about you kid" He replied. "Yeah, Elaine told me" I said. "

"I told Dad I would pick you up. So we could chat a little." He noted.

My concerns grow from this statement. I am the bad guy right now. I had a CHINS warrant and everyone here views Marie as poison.

The fact that anyone, but Dad having input regarding my well being is a joke to me. Elaine should have been happy to see I was gone. She can't stand me. So her input is pure bullshit. It's an act for Dad, I hope John sees this. She's new to him, and her act can go on for months if you live with her. John only sees her when Dads around.

She is his *other half.* "A worried parent." Oh please, her Leeann is the baby now all is good with me gone.

John has street smarts and a different relationship with me. John could get better information from me than Dad could. I could see the wheels turning and specific questions were being processed in Johns mind. I am a bit cautious. He doesn't know Elaine, like I do. I try not to answer directly and hope he can't read into the plans that are formulating in my head. I have hopes to bring Marie and the baby back to Mass. John has a hint of anger and dissatisfaction by the time we get to the house. I am up to something, he just isn't exactly sure of what. He quietly observes the "Reunion" as I say my hellos and get settled in. It's about 10pm and emotions are high, the feel of tired is mixed in. It's not a very happy moment.

Dad has been upset for some time now. Elaine feeds off of this she has been waiting for a chance to show her hate for me.

For right now it's *masked as concern for Dad*. John and Dad are just talking about the ride. They have both done time and have a language they share of their own. I sit in the living room trying to catch bits of the conversation.

Elaine walks in from time to time running her fucking mouth, with a lot of negativity. Dad has some questions for me; He wanted the details of when I left, and how Marie and I got to Georgia.

It's a Friday night. Dad said "You're going back to School Monday." Elaine added "Reform school" *If you even think of that whore, or think about going anywhere!"* Oh? Have I made a mistake coming back? I've only been here an hour.

Oh boy, how did Elaine just come out with "reform school?" *John was in reform school*. He *is* here right now. *Have they discussed this*? Elaine wouldn't even know what reform school is without Dad and John mentioning it. John and I are two different people.

I don't know what he did to have to go there. Its kid jail, Can Elaine be the judge and sentence me? I am not a fucking criminal. I am a father, and I have to do my job. I know her kids are *plastic*, phony users, looking for any ways they can latch on to people that have money.

That's a crime! Speaking of crime, Leeann chased Jimmy once while shouting and threw a butcher knife just missing him. It was fluffed off as a *cute little cartoon* incident. If a cop witnessed it, she would have been shot at with real bullets. Who needs reform school? Maybe, I should throw a butcher knife at Elaine. We could all laugh and reenact the whole thing and laugh some more.

Fuck this! I am headed out. I guess I am going to have to learn to speak with a Southern accent I am going down yonder to fetch me a life. *I'm loozin the bawstin axent and now imonna tawk diffrint.*

I know a few people that can loan me the money for the bus back. Maybe that blonde girl will be on another bus, we can meet and start a new life somewhere else with a clean slate. *"Between a rock and a hard place"* that saying is so stupid, but here I am.

After a quick visit to some relatives and some friends, I have more than enough money. I should be in New York before they even know I am gone. I will get *"the Chicago"* hot dog, *"mustard and kraut"* To eat while I wait for the transfer bus at Port Authority...... Off I go

I am not afraid to be here now. I was, when I was with Marie. I guess the familiarity has made me feel confident. *"How long before the Atlanta bus heads out?"* I asked the clerk in the window "About 2hrs and 40 minutes" he stated "what? Why so long? I asked. "If you're in a hurry take the city bus over to Newark, Which should take a half an hour then, a bus, and goes to Savanna from there within minutes" He added.

I am more confident, so why not? I saw the bus, and boarded. The bus headed down a few blocks and took a few turns and Oh shit! This is the heart of *graffiti* and *bad asses* and car frames in the street without parts, *"Stop here please"* I asked. The bus driver let me off in the middle of it. I ran back so fast, I passed the place. I'll just stay here at Port Authority mall.

The ride to Atlanta will be a straight shot. "Ahhh", Finally I was on the bus.

I looked out and remembered all of the "South of the Border" signs; they should be coming up, watching the changes from north to south, I feel *myself change* from my father's son to my sons Father. Cherry blossoms, black eyed peas, grits, fried chicken and Georgia Pulp. Not to mention, the heat lightning at night, it's kind of cool. Gil, Marie's father is on the road. Gil Marie's brother is back in Mass, doing drugs with my brother and *her fathers pick of the prize* Pete.

30
In too deep

The city bus from downtown
Macon, takes me to a few blocks from the
Trailer Park. It looks like its home now. I
am taking a day off. Before, I get back to
cutting lawns. It's too hot and I am too tired.
I have given in, and I should plan on being
here, that's all there is to it. I told Marie, My
family is upset at me because of my age. I
never told her what they *think* of her. She
isn't that stupid, I think she knows.

The boss at Days Inn had to fire me
for three *no call, no shows*. "I had a family
emergency" *Bullshit*! He wasn't buying it.
He did like me and talked straight. I spoke
with him about leaving home. He responded
by saying *"I wish somebody would have
punched me in face when I left" Sometimes
you have to learn on your own."* I think a
punch in my face would have sent me
further away.

I will have to add a few more lawns to the list. I check the Macon Telegraph classifieds. Not too many people wanted to give me a chance. McDonalds, forget it, I lasted one day, At least at Hardee`s, I lasted four days. A job in a furniture store.. They caught me *cat napping* within a week. Kmart wouldn't give me an interview. So, I head out to the truck stop and washed a few trucks, I continue cutting lawns as well, It's not regular, but its instant cash.

Some good looking, smooth talking kid named Tommy has been hanging around with Marie. She says "I think *he's funny that's all*. And he wanted a cigarette." Well he's not working his ass off to *support you and your child*. Tell him to buy his own cigarettes. If I weren't so tired, I would be funny too. I expressed my concerns. I guess the kid has a sister in the park. I have seen her she's a redhead with a great body. Maybe, I can catch Marie fucking the guy, and I can fuck his sister? That should be a good trade. I don't have enough to worry about? I need this asshole working on getting his dick wet. It's not a tough job, just ask. I wish she had panties on that first night,

Why was she up anyway? She wanted to get laid that's why. I can be so stupid

She has to play games. Why? If it weren't for the baby, Would, I still be so hung up on her? She has me by the balls. *Why can't she have integrity?* And be grateful for what she has.

I waited for signs, the only way I'm going to know, Is, if she tells me, or I catch her. However, I have a gut feeling and have had that feeling all along. She is a whore! When, I can prove it without any doubt. I will be done with her completely. I approach every person with a certain amount of integrity and assume I am getting the same thing in return. In my eyes, So far Dad is the only person I know, that has this genuine quality.

I watch her father play his games. I know there was *never* a job here for me. And to think of my conversation with him, before I arrived "*You better not hurt my little girl*" Months later "*I had my doubts*" Fuck him too.

Why is it a tragedy if his woman sleeps with other guys? But it's perfectly fine if mine does. He probably introduced Tommy *guns* to her. Well, let me just catch her and I can go on with my life.

Her father informed me today, that he has a plan for us in the near future, He said "Brian, I want to take you and Marie to Alabama so you can get legally Married" What? Oh Shit! *She isn't wife material.*

Her father thinks he can decide who *fathers her child*? Now he thinks he can pick *My wife*? Does he think he's God? If I call Dad now, I won't get the time of day.

I know what I want, it's very simple. *I want to settle down and start life as a family.* I had no Idea; Marie would be less than what I hope for in my significant other. *I expected to be in love and have the love returned. Two people happy to feel so much for each other.* But she is the one I am with. I hope there is something genuine in her.

Amy! She lives in Lynn now, Ill stay with her again. I will get a job, and see if Marie can behave in *my turf.* All I wanted was a family, now I have a mess of a life. *What's new*?

I made the call the next day. Amy told me Dad is very hurt. I told her about Elaine. She said she'll talk to Dad for me. She added that "he's not too happy" with Elaine right now, He thinks she's *screwing her Boss.* I said "oh she is" I knew that a few years ago" She laughed.

I called back the next day. She told me I have to find my own way back. But Dad will be happy to see me. I can stay with her, get a job and try to do what I think is best. *No reform school.* That's all I wanted. I have to tell Marie's father (*"Gil, I applied for a lot of jobs when I was in Lynn, My brother called and said I got an offer. If you don't mind, can I tag along on your next Boston trip?"*) "Sure, I saw one posted for this week, Ill put in for It." he replied.

31
A long road to travel

One to one, Gil is everybody's pal.
We headed out like old friends at five a.m.
*"You know some of them queers think their
actually woman*? Gil mentioned "What?" I
responded "Yeah, they really think their
actually fucking woman, I mean, like they
have woman parts and things, imagine
that?" He said *"I really don't know what to
say to that"* I replied. He went on about that
for awhile,

I am somewhat alarmed by his
words. We are going to be together alone for
24hrs. Come to think of it, *instead of
worrying about Terri sleeping other guys,
why doesn't he take her on his runs?*

My mind is racing, finally I ask,
"Why don't you take Terri on runs?" He
replied "Oh I was, until she lost the baby,
she jumped out of the truck and had a
miscarriage. She told me she can't go with
me anymore, because it reminds her too
much about it." I was very surprised.

What the fuck would the kid *look like*? Well, he isn't her father *anymore*. The kid probably looked like *Roy* or maybe *Tommy* ha ha, Shit! I forgot about him! Grrr Things happen for a reason. All I want is the truth. If Marie screws another guy, were done, it will hurt. I will be happy either way, just as long as I know the truth!

Gil is married and fucking his wife's daughter, yet he's upset if his wife's daughter cheats on him. What a nut job! And I am supposed to marry his daughter, who knows what she's doing? He *knows* she's doing, probably *more* than I *think* she's doing.

Where's Uncle Ed when you need him? Who needs him? This fucking group that's who!

We took a dinner break at TSA in Virginia. We showered up and got back on the road. We called home to the little women. They said everything's just fine here guys. *I am sure it is*.

After, a very long and tiring road trip, I couldn't wait to step away from the weirdness and return to what I know. It seems every minute with those people is like being in a place that is unlike the normal world I was living in.

Gil dropped me off near Fanuel Hall. I went to Haymarket, and got the City bus to Lynn. I sat down in Dunkin Donuts for a real coffee. That's a nice treat. I noticed some familiar faces, not too much has changed. By the time I got to Amy's house. I was cold and tired. Being down south has made my blood is very thin. I need another hot shower or some sleep.

Everyone here is happy to see me. John showed up later in the day. "Hey just in time, Cheryl and I are getting Married, and you are invited to the wedding." It's a week away. John stated. *It looks like I am accepted as a man with a plan.*

Great, it seems like I made my point here. If Marie can be *trusted*, I will have a pretty *good thing* for a *change*. I am working on it. I will *do my part* she should too. I'll take care of her and the baby. She swears he's mine. She has to think something of me.

What do I have to offer? Other than me, Marie can't have any other motives, from where I stand. So maybe, I am reading too much into her.

It is a better reunion this time around, Dad came by, he was curious about how I expected to support a family, Where I plan on working, and all the other frightening aspects,

These are the things that I should *not* be thinking about at this time in life. *It didn't work*, I am just as frightened anywhere in life now. With a little family support, I should be fine. I think that's not too much to ask. I am really happy right at this moment. Laughing, joking and getting time with my family. It is like I never left, I just got a little older.

I have to limit calls to Marie, I usually call collect. And for fear of surprises, I let her know when I'll call next... I am predictable and offer too much trust. I have to stop that!

One minute, I am like a detective, sorting out all the nasty details in my head. The next minute I am aiding the culprit.

32
Focused on a Dream

I spent the next day filling out applications. I think a call to these prospective employers in a day or so should do the trick.

To my surprise, Kmart in Saugus called. I was hired the very next day. *Hardware, lighting, rugs and furniture* these are the departments I will work in. I am a department associate. *Ah thank you, for ah shopping, ah can I help you?*

I enjoyed customer assistance you could learn things from people and you are able to goof around and just talk to customers, I spent a lot of time on that. Where else can you get paid to stand around and bullshit with people? Hardware and lighting were very busy for me with small parts inventory pricing etc. I wore nice slacks and a shirt and tie. No lawnmower here unless your buying baby. *What type of an area are you looking to mow? Do you want power assist? I mean these are things you should be concerned about.* In fact, that's not my department. However, Customer satisfaction is what I am all about, walk with me.

The lawn and garden guy was not so happy with my pitch, However I settled in quickly, and it feels great.

Amy likes having me at her house; she never really had the chance to know me. We play cards at night and just hang out. Later I usually run out to a payphone to communicate with Marie. This routine goes on for a couple of months. My concerns are growing for Marie

She has been hinting that Gil and Terri feel like the trailer is becoming a bit small and Marie spends a lot of time "hiding" in her room with the baby. Terri is pregnant again. I comfort Marie and send a few bucks each week. She is usually fine by the end of the call. I inquire about Tommy from time to time she says. "He has a car now so he is usually not here that often." Like an idiot this comforts me. Until around 11pm. As I try to go to sleep while visions of her in his back seat consume my thoughts. I feel like running down the street to give a surprise call. I breathe deep and slow and eventually nod off.

Every day at work, I have personal interactions with my Coworkers, on break and through out the day. Nothing too deep, just friendly hellos and how is life etc. It seems, before you know it. You have become friends. You have established a *relationship of friendship* which can sometimes lead to a *life long partnership*. At what point does this take place? I talk with everybody.

No matter how much I look, the young ladies here know I am *not* available. They all know I have a child and I am working towards bringing him and his Mother here.
Sometimes I wish I had no *conscience*. With the female population looking, as if they are competing for a top modeling job. My eyes are everywhere. And, they all think I am funny. That's always a plus. A few girls have given me phone numbers. I just shut it out of my head. I keep the numbers but I never call

My routine remains unchanged. I work; I go home to Amy, Dad stops in and visits. I call Marie and go to sleep. On weekends, I see Grammy Booba, and Then I go across town to Grampy McGee. Monday the cycle repeats itself.

(It is moving into the 3rd month. I
called Marie and Terri answered, she told
me Marie is getting some cigarettes. She left
a little while ago. I thought to myself, *OH
it's a ten minute round trip*. What's a while?
I asked, Terri said "they left about an hour
ago, but Marie knows your calling, so she
should be in any minute." I responded "Who
is she with!" "Tommy" she replied. "*What
the fuck!* I shouted Terri said "don't worry;
She *always* leaves the baby with me." I am
furious again. My heart is racing
Well she is obviously fucking him now.
Idiot! Grrr! I am so stupid. And the pictures
that go through my mind are just
disgusting.)

About an hour went by; I called
back, I was fully armed with my own
scenario. Marie answered, sounding like she
always does. She began *Singing the "I am in
the way" Song to me*. She moves into
"*Hon*", I'm being talked to like a child.
Guilty! Is what this tells me. Marie informed
me that Tommy has a girlfriend so *don't
worry*. I am sure he does, *her name isn't
Marie by chance is it?* I never thought to
ask. Marie told me… that Terri and Gil are
bitching, Terri is pregnant again and the
trailer is feeling smaller for everyone. Terri
is convinced that she is Gil's *wife, now* she
also wants to be a *Mother*. I guess when *she
cant sleep around she becomes emotional*.

Gil redirects her most of the time. *His penis is counting on her happiness.* I wonder what it took for him to bang her the first time. Twinkies? A Barbie? Maybe just a good spanking. To add to the disgusting images of this twisted relationship. Terri and Gil *talk baby talk* to each other. I know this *dates back* for the couple. Figuring they have been together for *years*.

The pressure is mounting over the past three months. If, Tommy asked Marie To "take off her shorts" just *once*. To me, there's a fifty percent chance she may have. He is as alive as any other 18yr old. What else could she offer? I *know* he asked more often than that. I can't remember her saying *no* to me. I am not the best looking guy in the world. This young *lady* doesn't know what love is. What could possibly stop her? Nothing! Plain and simple what stops me from thinking on these lines?
Her persuasion, I guess her Daddy has passed this gift down.

Terri must be angry that Marie is having so much *fun*. That *has to be* the reason she is *in the way* now. Girls and Guys are no different; we all have the *same needs*. The only difference I see is girls have *more* opportunities, this enables them to say *no* more often, Marie is almost a year older than I am, and she has had *many* partners. I have only had one. I have had two *offers* in the three months since I have been back.

I knew Marie "hung out" with Tommy so, I figured, I would "hang out" with a girl named Tanya, We went to her house, and she wanted to watch TV in the dark. She snuggled up to me and started moving in for the kiss, I got up and said "I have to go" She was offended and said. "What are you a fuckin fag?" We are *not friends anymore*. Tommy still hangs around with Marie. I am really hung up on this bitch. I can't stand it. I should be care free.

One hour into the phone call, it was decided. I would try to transfer to Kmart in Georgia. I didn't have enough saved to move her and the baby here. Rent is double what it is in Georgia. The only problem I had there was getting a job. Kmart wouldn't interview me *down there*. I went over 1000 miles away to get hired and return to work? No worst than *tennis shoes* I guess.

The next day, I went to Human resources. This is not a problem. By the end of the day, I learned I will be transferred to Warner Robbins, the next town over from Macon. It will happen in a week. Marie is happy with the news.

A few phone calls later, Marie told me *her father has a run to Boston*, so he can ride me back.

I will meet him in Chelsea at the produce center. That saves me a hundred bucks.

The rumors about my leaving have spread through work and to my surprise I was given a little party. One young lady that I had befriended. Actually began crying and told me how much she will miss me. *What am I going for*? I wish I could open my eyes grrr.

I said my goodbyes at work. At home, I waited until the very last minute. I actually called Amy from Dunkin Donuts. I asked her to look after my baseball stuff. I have a glove with Carl Yastresemski`s autograph, signed baseballs, trophies. Etc. I almost lost it all when I left last time. She told me *I better tell Dad*. I said "yeah after I get to Georgia." Because.. he will flip out.

That alone should be a sign to me. But, I can't *see* anything. I met up with Gil and he *acted very happy* to see me. We begin our return trip. Gil seems real happy. We laugh almost the next 24 hrs. We were making jokes about people we see. People we saw, People in General. We were also laughing at ourselves. The ride comforts my feel of returning. I can't wait to see the baby and Marie, Even though most of my thoughts are wrapped in a terrible situation, I miss her too.

We stopped in Savanna, Gil picked up a case of Beer. He placed them right in the cab of the truck. He cracked one open and slid one my way. I figure we have about 3hrs left of the ride. If I drink a beer every twenty minutes, Ill be really smashed by the time we arrive, Ah *fuck it*. He is going to have to pull over a lot. About half way through my second beer, *Gil begins laughing his ass off*. I said "What's funny?" He stopped laughing for a second and said "This road is bumpy, Every time we hit a bump, I think of all those signs on the side of the truck." "What signs?" I ask. He turned to me and said "You didn't see all those Explosives signs?" Nervously, I stated "ah no, what do we have that's explosive?" "Dynamite! But it's secured with foam and stuff. We have a load of TNT and these bumps; give me images of that coyote cartoon fella." He replied.

His laughter becomes contagious, by the next bump in the road. *I have a feeling that he wouldn't be laughing if we were really in danger*. I did have a great buzz going by the time we get to Macon. It was all hugs and kisses and more laughs with Marie then we settled in. I haven't even thought about Tommy. Marie seems very happy to see me. She certainly does have an issue with Terri.

She pulled me aside and began talking about Terri secretly, whispering just a bunch of gossip crap. Terri has expressed to Gil that she would like a bigger place, and she wants her younger brothers and sisters taken from Mass and brought here, so she could be the "Mother." We do have to move.

I started at Kmart the next day. Right from the start I had difficulty with an overweight arrogant department manager. "D-bag" She does not like me. This woman is giving me orders that cannot possibly be done by one person. She is waiting for the right moment. And then just four days into the job she *captured the moment.*

Another Manager requested that I cover patio for an hour. Fifteen minutes later "D-bag" told me to clean an area in the stock room where items were moved. I told her I would. As soon as I could be free of the Patio. She simply gave a cold hard look

One half hour later she called me into the office and said "Your Fired"! For non-compliance I tried to explain that the Store Manager requested for me to cover, she stopped me in the middle of my sentence and said "No, I am a Manager, and I gave you an order and you refused, good day!

I laughed at her and said I think you have some food on the side of your face and I then I left

Oh great, *let me see if that lawn mower still works*. I have the use of Gil's car for now. So I headed on back to the trailer park.

As I arrived…. I looked over and thought *Oh isn't that cute*, Marie and Tommy are just sitting on the porch having a smoke. As I try to control my speeding heart. I wonder is this a *before or after* smoke. "Hey guys what's up?" I said loudly. "Nothing" Marie said.

Tommy looked my way and said *"Well I'm out of here, hey dude, what are you worried about? Their all whores anyway"*. He got in his car and peeled out. Marie just looked and said "I told you there's nothing going on if you want, Ill tell him not to ever come around again" Oh really? I wonder what *did I just miss*? It was ok for him to hang around for three months until now and they are all whores? I think they just broke up.

I told Marie what had just happened at work, *she knows Ill work and we will be fine*.

She informed me that Gil wants us to take over the rent or find another trailer. Terri found a house to rent on Ponce Deleon circle.

The new landlord… The one that they will have is a few years older than me. He is supposed to be a really great guy his name is Jay. Terri seems to like him; she had nice things to say. Since they are moving and we are here… I figure we should keep this trailer.

The next Saturday, Gil went to a used furniture store, and completely furnished the house. I went over with Terri and Marie to clean up the place. Jay happened to stop in; he seemed like a nice guy. He asked, If I knew anyone that could paint and do small repairs. I told him I could, and I also let him know that I was looking for work, but I have no transportation. He said, He can pick me up and bring me to job sites no problem.

About a week later, Gil came back to Georgia with all of his kids, except Marie's brother Gil. He has a girlfriend, and doesn't feel like leaving her. Gil Sr went to Lynn with his tractor trailer and swiped all of their belongings and his kids. He planned it with his son Gil Jr. They did it while the mother was at work and unaware.

They all moved in and it seemed fine. Terri had her baby, and she was doing the Mother thing,

About two months later, One night around 3am, We got a call from Gil, He was furious, He told Marie, *he came home from a run, and got into bed. When he threw his arm over Terri, he felt another body and figured it was one of the kids. He turned on the light and discovered it was a dude. He punched Terri in the face and threw her out.* He told Terri the baby stays with him and his other kids. If she wants to see the baby she has to go through him.

Now he needs Marie to watch all the kids. So we moved into the house.

Gil worked a lot and talked with Terri often but details were unclear to me. Marie claims she doesn't know what's going on with them either. We developed a routine for the next few months. Gil came in one day, and said he was giving Terri a trial visit, If it works they are moving to Ohio for a brand new start. Gils Company originates near Akron. We agreed to join them. I have two sisters living in Cleveland. I am very happy about that.

33
Dangerous ingredients

The trial visit went well, a week later, we were loaded up and ready to go to Akron. Gil took the truck along with Terri and her baby. Marie and I drove the station wagon with the other kids. We were loaded up and headed north through Georgia, Tennessee, Kentucky, then up through Ohio. It was a rough 14hrs. The car was *overloaded* with kids and some of our things. It was almost noontime when we arrived.

Already.... It sure feels better than the south to me. But it still feels weird. Immediately we cleaned up the house and began moving things in. By the end of the day, you would think that we were there all along. We took the next day to look around and get to know the area. It feels good being in a city; it's a lot like Lynn as compared to Macon. I took a few days to adjust and I began looking for work. The job to have around here is at Goodyear. I tried; I ended up working at the *zip inn* a small breakfast place. They also had the BBQ express food service. I had no part in that. It was the owners *pride and joy*.

I told them that I cooked at the Days Inn. Once they saw my skills, they knew it wasn't possible. I began training on days to work the overnights. It was slow enough that I could get by without much difficulty. Marie has announced she is pregnant again. OH boy! Should I be very happy or should I worry? I counted back and forth and decided we will see If I am the Dad. I should know better when he's born. In the meantime, I remained positive and very hopeful. I thought people were just *happy* to get that sort of news. No problem, this *should* be a celebration, whatever. Everyone in the house is adjusting.

I called my father and let him know about the move. He was happy to know I am ok. He added that Grammy Boober was headed out to visit my sisters. She would like to stop in and see me. That's the best news I have had in some time. Marie seems happy about it too. On the surface everything looks great. I sleep during the first part of the day, Play with my son in the yard before dinner, and then I watch TV until work. Over the next few Months serious changes take place. Something is cooking. Marie informed me that Gil Jr called.

Marie's *brother* Gil and his girlfriend Sue are going to move in with the family. Her *father* Gil is starting to work less and he is collecting welfare benefits and getting assistance at the Salvation Army and local charities. Marie applied for Welfare; the welfare system informed her that she is too *young* to collect and should be on her father's case. *Unless* she is married. I guess proof was *NOT* needed in Ohio, because she was approved and her welfare ID has *my last name*.

I can't remember any wedding but, *the Mrs*. obtained many other services as well. Gil Sr. took me to various churches and told me to *go inside and tell them I have a pregnant wife and a baby at home, and I need food and cash assistance*. I *refused*. He began to *resent* me. He always has beer and cigarettes. I think we all have plenty at the house, I also work, I would go hungry, before I could do anything like that. He has also grown a beard and that's *way out of his character for him*.

During the time that we've been living here, Gil and Terri developed a friendship with another couple *Bob and Helen Crowley*. Having the kids in school, allowed them to meet people.

There was also a single mother named Lee that *they spoke of.* Terri didn't like Lee too much. But the Crowley's were, "as she would say" *O kee do kee*. The information I usually get, is delayed and not complete. Due to my work hours and sleep schedule, I am not around for the so called excitement.

(Until one day when I got fired for being *sluggish*. The owner would often come in at 630am, one half hour before the end of my shift. He saw that I was not all bright eyed, and ready for the day, so he let me go. If he came in around 2am, He would see I ran circles around the grill with the drunken rush. *He must drink at home*.) As I catch bits and pieces. I look to Marie to fill me in.

34
Simmering with animosity

Gil Sr. and Gil Jr. began to spend a lot of time together; Gil Jr. is working at a car wash. In a matter of days he found his drug connections in the area. *At home in Lynn he had my brother Jimmy and his friend Pete,* Here; he has found a guy known as *Rainer*.

Gil Jr. was not very happy to know…. that *Gil Sr. and I were allegedly "close."*
He has become jealous seeing his father talk to me like a "son" I am becoming the *common enemy*. In my view the only reason I am here is to be with Marie and my children. She is ready to have the second child any day now.

Her father and brother often drink
together. Gil Jr is the type of person *that
gains courage* as he becomes intoxicated.
His *balls get bigger* when he drinks. I can
hear the conversations from the other room,
and at some point, Gil Jr usually says "*I am
going to fuck with Brian*" Then he picks
fights with me. I want no part in it. So, I
usually just tell him, "I don't want to fight
Gil, so please, just go fuck with someone
else." (It's probably like Jimmy said I seem
like a *Pussy*) He usually seems to feel better
as he walks away with somewhat of a
bounce.

I am surprised his father doesn't try
to make some kind of peace. I mean he
wants me to *do the right thing* with his
daughter. I could get drunk and pound the
piss out of this moron But, I can't see what
it will gain and he was my friend, I have no
desire to fight anyone. I see myself as a Dad,
and I want my kids to be happy and feel
safe. I have had enough fights with the 6ft 4
inch monster.

It didn't matter; this became a regular
thing Gil Jr has something to prove.
One day, after the second baby was born,
Gil Jr wanted to *fuck with me*. I happen to be
holding the sleeping baby. He started
running his mouth. I was shocked, the room
was quiet and dark I waved him off.

He decided to spit right in my face. His father just sat back and watched. I took the baby upstairs. I tried to avoid the two of them.

Marie felt caught in the middle. To me *blood* is *thicker* than water. She can leave me one day, her *family is forever.* So I remain cautious. The whole group is nuts. If we were in a different place, *maybe I would smash this mother fucker with a beer bottle across his face. Or take a baseball bat to his fucking head. He can only push me so hard.* I am trying to be a father and do the best I can I am not even eighteen yet. I already have a few years into this. They should be honored *anyone* would step up and be a man, (Under *normal* circumstances, *Fucking morons.*) When Gil Jr. is at the car wash or hanging out with his drug buddies, Gil Sr. spends some time with me in an *almost* human way. I work a few days, here and there at local restaurants. I am inexperienced and it shows. I try to learn, so I can stay in one place. As I spend time with Gil Sr. I notice he seems weirder than he usually does. He looks tired and pissed most of the time. At the same time he is slightly unemotional yet focused or occupied. I have a picture in my mind that his brain must feel swollen in his head or something. I talked with Marie about it she says he has a lot on his mind.

35
Hunting a human

Marie told me that, *Terri* is up to *her* old tricks, she met a guy through the Crowley's, and she *may* be fucking him. Gil and Terri argue a lot and she storms off for a day or two. Nobody knows where she goes. The Crowley's know *of the* guy. However, they aren't sure where he lives. Finally, *Gil decided to throw Terri out again*. He is tired of her shit. Lee has been trying to help Gil, *and maybe start a relationship of her own with him*. She is a nice enough woman and she is more his age. Gil seems to be drinking much more and he doesn't laugh any more. I mentioned to him maybe he should forget Terri and focus on Lee. His response was "Lee *ain't nothing but a piece of ass, I don't give a fuck about her*"

For about a month Gil and Lee seem to be settling in together. Gil would sometimes put on his humorous charm and then instantly appear as an enraged man with a cold hard stare and an emotionless facial expression. He decided one day, that he would like to go and talk to Terri, He wanted me to join him. I was fine with it figuring I could have a better scope of the situation. *I thought he knew where she was.* We started out just driving around aimlessly. Gil decided to stop at a biker bar and ask a few questions. The bar was near the block that the Crowley's lived on. This bar had motorcycle parts hanging on the walls. Some of the parts had signs with a description, some examples are "Jerry 1972" or "Bull 1978" I couldn't even sport a five o'clock shadow so I stood right out. I was nervous… I figured, if I could hear my heartbeat. I think they can too. Gil *small talked* with the waitress. We headed out. We did a bit more driving around. But we didn't see any sign of her.

This searching became routine for the next few days. Gil Sr would take Gil Jr around as well. One day Gil Sr. came downstairs, He was clean shaven and dressed in his best attire. I said "Hey looking good, what do you have a job interview?"

He said "No, *I want to find Terri, and I want her to remember me like I was*" I figured maybe he thought she likes him more with a clean appearance. Now, he could have a better chance at winning her back, Whatever, It didn't really matter to me. We headed out. He drove to different areas this time. He told me his son Gil Jr. has some friends that got information that Terri was in this particular area. He stopped a couple of times and talked with people. He was in and out a lot, so I waited in the car. He had purchased a case of Beer for this search. He had plenty at home and a couple before we left. Surprisingly he seemed entirely sober. I had a couple for the ride.

Gil Sr. came out of a building and said to me "I have to wait until my son gets home. But Terri agreed to meet me at the Crowley's tonight. *I'm going to put an end to this once and for all*." That statement was alarming to me.

I thought about things this man had said and done in the past. (If he ever said, he was going to *kick down a door or something, He would*. And what was he putting to and *end*? She's been *gone that ends it right there*. He shaved, so she could *remember* him that way. Holy fuck! He's going to *kill* her.

I was so nervous I actually farted.. it was such a terrible smelling one, that Gil, began dry heaving and he pulled over to *vomit*. I tried to laugh it off; He stated "What the fuck died in you? That would gag a fucking maggot!" but this *is no laughing matter*. He has to wait a few hours now, so we headed back to the house. I sat in the dining room with Lee and Marie. Gil Sr. went to buy more beer.

I told Marie and Lee what I thought. Lee said nervously *"no, no, he, he wouldn't do tha*t" Marie began to think in my terms but she changed her tone and said "I don't think he would *actually kill her*" her tone was steady. I replied "I hope not, but it sure seems like it. I mean, what else could all that possibly mean?"

We all quietly watched the rest of the day unfold; everyone seems to have an eye on the situation. The girls made dinner as usual. After we ate, Gil Jr. arrived. The two "Gil`s" went outside and talked for about ten minutes.

They came back in Gil Sr. said "Marie, you and Brian are coming to the Crowley's with us. Lee, you stay and watch the babies. Marie and I headed out to the car. Gil Sr. said " Brian, Terri *will listen to you, so go to the house she's at, and tell her to meet me at the Crowley's, So we can talk.

"Ok" I replied. He continued drinking non stop, yet he still seems very sober.

We parked in front of the Crowley's house. Gil Sr. Opened a wood framed screen door, and knocked on the inside door. The Crowley's answered and they invited Gil Sr Marie and Gil Jr. in. I said "I'll go and meet *Terri*; I walked part of the way up the street.

Terri was walking quickly toward me, she seemed quite angry. I stopped her and said "Terri, Listen just *"yes him to death" and get the fuck out of there*, she interfered and said "NO! Fuck this; I don't have to take his shit anymore! I said *"Terri he's really fucked up right now, just tell him what he wants, and get out, he can and will hurt you, go away and never see him again!"* She replied Fuck Him! And she entered the house.

Gil Sr was sitting at the kitchen table with his back to the living room we could see part of his left leg. Terri sat facing him we could see her entirely. The Crowley's and Marie and I were on the couch facing the kitchen. Gil Jr stood at the doorway. Gil and Terri began talking quietly.

They talked for about ten minutes, Gil Jr paced around the doorway. All of a sudden, Terri got up and shouted *"Fuck you! I don't have to take your shit!"* She stormed out of the kitchen and passed us heading for the door,

Gil Sr ran towards her reaching into his pants at the back, he pulled out a small gun, he held it up and aimed it in Terri's direction, The Crowley's, Marie and I, ran out towards a back door.

As we ran we could here pop pop, pop, pop The Crowley's headed off towards the left. Marie and I headed to the right out towards the street, as we came towards the street. I could still hear popping. I saw the wood framed door close, I couldn't separate that sound, from the sound of the gun. I heard Gil shout *"where's Brian"* I pulled Marie down into a bush, and covered her mouth with my hand. We listened; I could hear footsteps on the stairs and porch

I heard the Guys get into the car and start it. Then I saw Gil's car leaving. He circled the block once, *probably looking for us.* We got up and headed to back the house, to be with the babies. A police car raced by us very quickly, without lights the officer looked right at us and continued on.

We got to an open lot. Just as we did, Gil Sr pulled up to us in his car. We stopped and stood frozen He said *"come here"* I asked *"where's the gun?"* he said *"Gil Jr has it, he's going to get rid of it for me."* He then said, *I'm taking my baby to Boston, I'm going to leave her with my Aunt, and then I will turn myself in.* He proceeded on. If he had the gun we had no place to run at that point. I was so relieved.

I wasn't worried about Gil Jr; I knew he was a *pussy* when I met him. His father was motivated to commit murder. Gil Jr just wanted to have his father's approval. Alone he is nothing. As soon... as we arrived at the house.. we checked the babies, they were fine. Marie began asking her brother, for more details. *He was very excited.* He said " *She thought she was leaving, but, I stood right in her fucking way, Dad shot her five times, and I gave her one in the fucking head, What happened to you guys? We were looking for you"* Marie said "we just ran with the Crowley's" I asked "where's the gun?" Gil Jr said *"I buried it out back near the fence"*

Gil Jr appeared to be very happy, He said *"When we got here, Dad told Lee to get her shit, and get the fuck out NOW!"* laughing he also said *"she looked scared and ran out. It was so funny"*

Just then we heard a knock at the door. It was the Police. They asked if Gil was here. Gil Jr said "I'm Gil" but I think your looking for my father. The police investigator sarcastically said "Yes is he here?" Gil Jr replied "No I don't know where he is.

The Police said they have a warrant and they want to check the premises. We let them in. Some went upstairs some were outside and one asked me if Gil was in the basement. I said "No he's headed to Boston with his baby." He said "Are you telling the truth?" I said "Yes" he said "then I am going to use you as a shield if your telling the truth you have nothing to worry about" he began checking with his gun drawn as I was held close to him as a shield. After a complete check of the house he concluded that Gil was not present.

36
Sick twisted mother

The Police remained in and around the house for about 45 minutes. They went back and forth to the cars; they were also making several radio communications. At some point, the original Police Investigator came into the house; He sat us all together and informed us, *Terri has died as a result of her injuries. He added that each bullet independently struck vital organs. She had no chance of survival.* Gil Jr and Marie acted shocked by the outcome. I just sat and realized I was right several hours earlier, and now I had a strong sense of guilt, Knowing, I had many chances to call Police, or tell Terri not to go. I had no Idea he had a gun, However, I had an Idea, he had a plan. And I knew Gil Jr was a part of it. The Police left…. noting that if we *hear or know* anything we need to call ASAP.

Gil Jr watched through the window. As the tail lights moved further away from the house...

He turned to Marie, and reached out with both hands. They held hands, and began jumping up and down. While Gil shouted *"We did it! We fucking killed the bitch. Yeah, we fucking killed her."* They both started laughing. I couldn't believe my eyes! First, For Gil to be happy, he's just a drug crazed idiot. But, Marie is the mother of my children. What have I just brought into the world? What the fuck is wrong with these people? And why did I hear, "Where's Brian?" *during the shooting*? And not where's Marie? *I am a sitting duck.*

I went to the fridge, preparing to drink myself into a stupor, allowing myself to sleep. After my second beer, the *missing gun* became a question in my mind. I believe Gil Sr was going to Massachusetts to turn himself in. My thoughts are on Jr. I wanted to stay sharp. I made coffee instead.

The dance between these two *freaked me right out*. I can see and hear them. I wanted to call Dad. But, I also want them to feel, I am *with them right now* because unfortunately, I am. I put my focus on Marie, and I ask if she's ok, I try to comfort her *as if she is in an awful hurt right now*. I have no idea what she is in, but if her and Gil Jr spend one minute *anywhere without me present* I'm off and running. That's my plan for now.

We all stayed in the living room waiting. I wonder if they are as afraid of the *unknown* as I am.

The light of day started in and snow began to fall. Gil Jr said "You know that snow is for Terri, I just looked and thought *what fucking planet are you on? You just danced over her death, now you're all fucking squishy and sentimental? You sick fuck!*

Marie just agreed with him. I wanted to see the three of these monsters go straight to fucking prison. That's where they all belong. How could she even look at her babies? First chance I get, I am on the phone, fuck this group.

The night has become day. I am exhausted and I have just a sick feel occasionally burping up the taste of beer and coffee. And a terrible taste from too many cigarettes. Marie is asleep on the couch; Gil has nodded off on the love seat. I feel it's a good Idea to at least shower quickly. I hurried through and found them to be deeper in a sleep. I feel better knowing *they haven't talked without my presence.*

I am fresh and ready for the day. And hungry, as I look, for what I can stomach right now. I heard a knock at the door. It was the Police.

The plain clothes officer is not the same as the *one from hours earlier*. He informed us, that we *are not under arrest*, but we have to go with him *for questioning*. He has a Murder, and we were present at the time. *At this moment, we could be charged with anything.* Marie became very nervous and announced

"I have to stay here, I am pregnant, and have two children in the house, Nobody else can watch them." She is pregnant? Again? Or is this bullshit? Because, she feels guilty and she thinks she'll go to jail?

"Are one of you the father of her children?" He asked "I am" I said, The Officer said "She can stay here, If we need her later, you can watch them, for now, your coming with us." He turned to her and said *"Don't plan on going anywhere."* She just looked at him without saying a word. Gil Jr lit a cigarette and said "I just woke up and need to go to the bathroom." The Officer said "You can go to the bathroom downtown, let's go"

37
Interrogation

He told us we were not being charged with anything yet but, he informed us of our rights.

　　　　Gil and I sat in the back of an unmarked Police car. We got to the Police station and we were sent to different conference rooms. I sat quietly…. Waiting to talk… because of the conversations between Gil and Marie and myself. And the Idea that Gil Sr *said "Where's Brian?"* I want to wait until Gil Sr Is caught, before I spill my guts. Some of the conversation from last night was on the *perspective each of us had, from our own viewpoints.* Gil Jr acts like *I know too much And* I should be quiet. In other words, *I am still a sitting duck.* Gil Jr has made me feel it with more *conviction.*

The Police Detective began to ask me many questions. Specifically, Where Gil Sr went I told him, *I think he went to Massachusetts*. He was determined that I knew exactly where. I really didn't know. He could have been in five different towns. He could have gone to Georgia for all I knew. For many hours, the detectives would ask a question or two and then leave for an hour or so. I was at *my breaking point*. I had to just spill my guts and get the fuck out of there. I told the detective, I was ready to talk. Just as I did,

He said "Great, Oh by the way, *Gil Sr turned himself in with Mass state Police*." I breathed very slow and deeply, a sigh of relief. I told the detectives the entire story, including Gil Jr and the gun. The detective stated that they checked everywhere around the property and found nothing. They can't include him without a weapon. He then noted that *Gil Jr told them I was the one that hunted her down and convinced her to go there knowing what was going to happen.*

38
Blood is thicker

We were free to go. *They didn't offer us a ride back*, without money; it looks like we had a long walk. On the way back Gil began accusing me of being a *rat*. He mentioned things that I said to the detective. *He was right, I said it*. I defended myself by adding that the detective told me parts of it, and *that you're the one that told him*. I knew the detective basically stuck a *knife in my fucking back*. I can't believe a Law Enforcement Professional just asked me to *help catch a murderer*. I gave him *two of them*.

He told *one of them* what I said and sent me off with him. He could very well have just caused another murder. I was there and I knew his role I told the police

This piece of shit was in the doorway, and said that he fired a shot to her head. I know he was physically part of this crime, I saw him! The weapon has not been recovered. I am completely fucked. I need to get away from here. This Marie situation is over.

We got back to the house, Marie wanted *all the details. And* she told me, "Your father called a few times he saw it on the news." I said "I better call him. I went to the phone. Gil Jr and Marie began talking. Gil Jr looked my way several times. He tried to talk to her and *listen to me.* My father said "Are you ok? I said "Yes" He continued "Don't say a word to anyone, *but John and I are on the way.* We will be there as soon as we can it's about a 12 hour ride. If you can talk, *tell me what happened*" I gave him a *rough draft* that Terri cheated on Gil Jr so he shot her. I knew *they were listening,* I left out many details. Gil Jr asked for some details regarding the *phone call.* I fluffed it up for him. I have no idea what Gil Jr and Marie talked about so, I tried to pay extra attention to everything. I went on through the day as if "we" were waiting for what happens next.

The day went on… we were all very tired so we sat around closing our eyes but not sleeping. Every now and then somebody would bring up a new comment about the *events before us*. We would talk about it, and get quiet again. This repeated itself for hours. We didn't really eat; we had various little things, here and there for most of the day. Around midnight there was a knock on the door. It was my father. He looked at me in front of Marie and Gil and said "let's go". I just got up and got out. I never said a word, no hugs, no tears I never looked back

When we got out to the car John said *"Hey Bri, You can stay with Cheryl and I"* Dad said "I called the DA, they said *you can come home*, when this goes to trial, they will use you as *a rebuttal witness*. I asked what that was, he gave me the details. We headed to Cleveland so we could sleep at my sister Linda's house. We will go back to Lynn in the morning after the commute. I started telling them all about the past year.

We got to Linda's at around 2am. We all had a few beers and talked. I was able to sleep. I already *feel better* but food might make me feel 100 percent.

I woke up to the smell of bacon and the sound of it sizzling in the pan. Linda is cooking us a nice breakfast. Already feeling the sense of my family, I smile. *"It's going to be fine."* I said to myself. Then butterflies zip through my mid section, *and I think of the kids, is Marie actually pregnant again?* I never asked. If I bring it up to my father, he is just going to flip out. *As usual, something will happen to set the course straight.*

My mind is taken over, by the events that have occurred since I met *that* family. The clinic, Sunset grill, trailer park, Red dirt, I remember talking to the store clerk at *Kwickie*, In Macon, She told me and old saying *"if you've been to Macon, you will go again, and if your born in Macon, you will die in Macon.* I hope, I see my son again, even, if it's just to tell him that. She told me that story after my second trip back. She seemed to believe it herself.

The traffic rush is over, so we headed back to Massachusetts, John did all of the driving it's his new car and Dads driving really sucks. He prefers to *talk and have beers*.

When he does it while driving, it creates a very *uncomfortable* situation. The first few hours of the ride the conversation was *focused on the Murder*.

That basically brought up all sorts of details of my traveling experiences. My father *was not proud of me*. But he was happy to see that I am ok, and headed home, He has been around, and knows that I am not the child, *I was when I left*. Hopefully, I can take what I've learned, and use it in the future.

Dad is in agreement that Elaine is an asshole. However, she remains his other half. We talked about everything I have missed

John is very excited; He is working for the Department of Mental Health. Cheryl has a great job with an insurance company. They have a baby girl a new car and they are looking forward to the future.

Cheryl is a sweet, caring and quiet person. Whenever, a humorous situation arises She laughs like "it *was silly but not too funny."* . She seems to like it when I'm around. It's great, that I can live with them for awhile. They live in Swampscott, The next town over from Lynn. It's a nice area with extremely low crime.

I can *deprogram* in a great environment. I will look for work in Lynn, Swampscott, Salem or Saugus. I am going to try to obtain a drivers license.

With three years of driving under my belt, it's a good idea. John and Dad are helping make me feel like everything's going to be ok.

We stopped in upstate NY for some food. Without anymore stops until Lynn. We made it by 9:30pm Dad wanted to stop at "The Franco" for a beer. He is a member; you have to be a Veteran. A "beer" is usually two or more Pitchers of draft. We stayed and played some pool and had a few beers. We dropped Dad at his house and headed to Johns.

They had an extra room, a complete bedroom all to myself. Wow, *who could ask for more*? John said "Hey you live with me now, don't worry about work too much. You'll get a job when you get one." Right now relax. We watched some TV and headed to bed. Tomorrow, we can get around and say hi to everyone. Jimmy is married now, to a young lady named Lynne.

She seems to like, the *bad boys* Jimmy, Pete and a few others. I am sure *they* want the scoop. John has had *some shit from Jimmy* lately, so he has a firm grip on *those issues*. John has been filling me in with more of what I have been missing here. I guess, When Gil Jr was around *Jimmy, Pete and Gil,* couldn't be separated.

They all have other friends, but, the three of them are the main click. *They like drugs*, whatever is the latest. They get high and paint the towns. Jimmy has lost his license so many times. And he has been determined to be a *menace to society* in a vehicle.

I have been in a car with him. *I was terrified*! I vowed to walk a million miles before I ever thought of doing that again.

Now, that I am removed from the craziness, with the chance to feel *at home, and safe*.

I headed off to bed no phone calls, no investigators, and no crazy people. John has a few personal days. He is taking them to help me run around, and to get to be my brother a bit more.

The next day we got up and had coffee and breakfast. We went to see Nana Perry, she is in her 90s and she's the best! She is a little out of touch. She wondered why I haven't been up in a while. Then we went to Grampy McGee, He is unchanged what you see is what you get. It feels good to see him. Then we headed to Grammy Boober, She gave her input to my previous situation.

She said she felt a cold hard feeling from Gil Sr. and the place itself felt dark and gloomy. She doesn't like Marie, but I have kids with her, so she will except her as part of the family, if that happens.

Jimmy is our final stop for the day; we will see Aunt Marion tomorrow. As we pull up to Jimmy's house. Jimmy and Pete are outside; Jimmy is working on Pete's car. I walked up and said hello. Lynne said "Hi Guys want some coffee?" "Sure" We respond. She went inside. Jimmy and Pete just stood looking at me like they were about *to settle a score.* "So what's up?" I asked. Jimmy said *sarcastically*, *"Why don't you tell me?"* Then he looked to Pete, they chuckled, as if they could see some bullshit coming on. "Tell you what Jimmy?" I asked firmly. He shouted *"You know exactly what! You fucking rat!* You ratted on Gil you didn't have to say shit! You fuckin moron!

John stepped over to Jimmy and said "What the fuck are you doing? This is your brother, and YES he *should have ratted on that fucking murderer!*"

Jimmy shouted "You gotta fight that pussy's battles? Huh, tough guy?" They began swinging, John held Jimmy down, until he could calm. It took three tries to get Jimmy to stop.

John and I got into the car and left. John is pissed about what just happened and it seems to have stirred up some thoughts John had about Jimmy from years past. I just sat in the car agreeing with John. What happened sucked and now it gives me a lot to think about for my own personal assessment.

My own brother Jimmy is *angry at me*, for doing the right thing. I cant except the idea that any human can take the life of another human. *Who in the world has the right, to think they can just end a human life?* We all have the right to life all of us in this world have an equal chance to live our life in its natural course. *What if it's their own? Or someone they love? Then it's wrong?*

Some maggot fired a bullet into someone's head. **With the intention of a complete *end* to that persons *existence*!** What makes what he did, ok? And *having to answer* for it is not ok? Fuck Jimmy! He's a dangerous piece of shit too.

News travels fast. If I stay away from Marie, Will I have to connect Jimmy to these people the rest of my life anyway? What Jimmy needs right now, is a good beaten. Oh boy, I thought when I left Ohio I was putting all the danger behind me.

However now I know Ohio and all the danger is with me. I have to steer clear of these guys. It never ends does it? This is my lifetime I just want happiness. What the fuck?

John and I headed over to Dads house. We intended on having some beers with him anyway. Now we can tell him about our visit with Jimmy. It will be nice if he knows what his *own son thinks of his brother.* Dad was sitting in his recliner having a beer while watching TV. We went in, and told him our story. He was pissed. He started yelling about the times that he told Jimmy, *Pete is nothing but trouble*! And how many times he asked Jimmy "Where are your friends going to be when you need them?" Your friends are assholes! "He went on and on" Dad knows Jimmy is small potatoes. *I know his friends aren't.*

When Gil Jr hung around with me, he was a *skinny little kid.* Now he is a much bigger boy with biker *wanna be Mentality.* That family has serious head issues; His mind is fucked up even more from drugs. The goal these guys are trying to reach is to become hard core bikers. This whole biker image is starting, so far, they all have long hair and leather vests, and they have a few tattoos. If you look close, you will realize Jimmy's are *cute little cartoon characters.*

A *real biker* would say hey "Here's "comic strip" when Jimmy shows up.

They bought engineer boots, they wear some Harley stuff, and none of them even own a bike. I heard Pete is getting one. I guess that should make them all official bikers.

I don't want to be a pawn in the game they want to play. We are in Lynn there are a lot *of real bikers*, Lynn, Lynn, the city of sin. The bikers love the saying; they wear printed *references* on shirts and hats etc.

My father told me, that saying actually started in the days when the Navy would come to town for shore leave. Lynn had bars on every corner, with prostitutes every where. The sailors would come into by train. In time, the MPs where waiting at the train station. So they left by cab, bus etc "Lynn, Lynn, the City of Sin, you never *go out* the way you *came in.* I like that image.. its, more real to me.

The Lynn I know, *I love.* I can't think of a better place to have all those adventures, it's got the beach. It would be an excellent place for a huge hotel From Lynn you can go anywhere.

You have the Boston skyline looking back *at you*, as if it were thinking *what's over there to explore?*

Over the next few weeks, I was able to get a job, as a *maintenance helper* at Mount Pleasant Hospital. It's really a good job for me. I paint, I do outside work, the guys I work with are good guys,
I work 7am to 330pm Monday thru Friday. It really helps keep my mind off Jimmy and Gil Jr
I am thinking a lot about the trial. It will be coming up and I have to go back to testify. I don't talk to Marie as much as I should. She said she *really is pregnant*. I will have to address this after the trial. She told me her father has a *complete blank* in his mind about what happened. And *I should just tell the truth*.
Jimmy and Pete have talked with Gil Jr and they want me to lie. I thought living in fear and watching my own ass was *behind me*. Now my brother James has me right in the middle. As if, I were in a spider web and crawled only so far. If I were.. a biker, or a badass. I would probably *do something* very nasty to *eliminate* the problems. My thoughts on God, and my idea of my Mother possibly knowing, *what I think and feel* are all too strong. For me to *act* on these thoughts, the thoughts alone give me a strong sense of guilt.

My favorite thing about the new job is the back fire escape. I climb to the top and watch the Boston sky line and the ocean I can see so far out to the Ocean. It feels free and it really helps keep my imaginations of a potentially brighter future a real possibility. Some days I think of my second child *I have strong feelings that he needs me.* So far the only evidence that the boys are mine is my hope and his blue eyes

Sometimes, I wish, I had no *fucking conscience.* I could become selfish and give up on everyone. I know the children never asked to be born… I brought them into the world and I have to do the right thing. I also have to worry about *who knows who* now. In Lynn *anyone* can have ties with these assholes. They have girlfriends that *were* generally *nice girls.* They just happen to like the *bad boy* image. These girls work in *respectable positions*, Banks, insurance companies, The RMV, if my name comes up, word gets around and now the web has widened. I knew Pete had a girlfriend at my bank, so I got an account somewhere else. But, I left forty dollars there, so Jimmy doesn't learn my business. It makes him feel powerful to have *the goods* on someone. No matter how petty. That way you wonder *what else he might know. Ooohhhh my fuckin hero.*

This is really childish shit. We are
supposed to be grown up now. And this
childish shit has become a life or death
matter. That is some very serious adult shit.
 John is becoming very close to me. I am his
brother and he has a brother's love for me.
He also stands up for what's right. If he
thought for one minute, I was an asshole
about something he would *call me on it*
immediately. From his viewpoint, I am in a
world of shit *that I didn't create*. I should
have *no problems* now. But it seems to be
the story of my life. How the hell do these
things find me? Life changed forever when
Mom died. It's like *she* was the sunshine
that *could burn* away *dark clouds*. I have
images in my mind that show an *evil King
deciding the fate these three children now
that their mother has died. He simply says
"SEND THEM TO THE LIONS!" John
escaped the lions den. He has become his
own King. Jimmy, he probably bumped his
head on the way to the den and thinks he is a
lion. I just keep running from the lions.*
At the Hospital, I am able to work alone and
at my pace. I prefer to be here than anyplace
else right now. It really is pleasant. I spend a
lot of time working outside overlooking
Boston and watching planes take off,
Feeling the presence of the Ocean. It really
feels great. I feel like I am overlooking the
world in all directions.

My mind has the freedom to sort out
all the things going on in my own world.

39
A little freedom

I usually take the bus to work; *I never spend any money on myself.* I've decided to buy my own ten speed bicycle. I saw it in the window at the bike shop in East Lynn. It is brand new, with the labels still on. It's metallic blue, I feel kind of guilty but I deserve it. On Saturday, I'm going to see if the one I like is still there. If it is, I will run down to the bank and get the cash and drive to the beach, to Nahant, all over the North shore. It feels strange not thinking about anyone *but me.* John doesn't even want any money. I eat and sleep there. I am able to bank almost all my pay.

Saturday, I woke up and got ready; I headed down to the bike shop on Essex St. in Lynn. *Yes! It was there and they are open.*

I *ran* down Union Street as fast as I could. I got to Saint Josephs church and *out of nowhere,* a car drove up on the sidewalk in front of me and one behind. These guys jumped out. One of them displayed a badge. I realized they were *under cover Police.*

One asked "What *are you running from*?" I said "I'm not running from, *anything* I'm running *to the bank,* to get money, so I can buy a bike I just saw."

My heart was in my throat. I gave them my information; they waited and finally sent me on my way. *That was weird.* What's the connection here? After thinking *you should only run while wearing a track suit* and it should not be so fast. I wondered why my life would *pause at Saint Joseph's church.*

The only connection to the name *Saint Josephs* is the Cemetery My mother is in. Maybe she was saying *I'm watching you I just wanted to look at you for a minute.* Ok Mom, hi back, Love ya, I have to get that bike talk to ya later…. The new bike….

OH yeah this is the best, the smile on my face is so big, *my face hurts again.* I rode the beaches, the woods; I even went to the sign that says *Entering Boston.*
With a feeling of pure ecstasy from the freedom the ride and the smell of salty ocean air entering my nostrils, after the smells of nature from the woods. This was a real treat. I am reaping the benefits of my hard work. My body is becoming so tired and sore but it feels so good. I will have to do this again tomorrow. (Where my thoughts)

I began doing it so much. I probably put more miles on that bike than the miles
 I put on Maries fathers car. I have had an occasional encounter with Jimmy and his *forestry pals*. They are only concerned with what I am going to *say at the trial*. Rumors are beginning to fly maybe to *heighten my fears*. One was that Gil Sr and Gil Jr will make *me the accessory* so Gil Sr can *hear my screams* from his cell as I *get raped* in mine.

The trial is coming up in a few days. Marie seems to be on the same page as I am. She can't stand Gil Jrs girlfriend. This has given me a little comfort to trust what she says. *We do have three kids together. "We" are her new family*. It seems awhile after the trial. We may *be together*. I keep in mind that her blood relatives probably have more meaning in her heart. *Intuition* is my friend, when I heard *"Where's Brian?"* I held her down in the bushes with my hand covering her mouth. She didn't even try to struggle, I didn't have to think. Like when a baby takes its first breath to give it life. *That intuition saved my own*. I really think she was *"with me"* and I think she was happy to be *hiding by my side* that very moment. Regardless of what occurred after.

John and Dad have been spending more time with me. They know I have a lot of things to worry about. *Flying in a plane to meet the Police detectives and meeting up with that family and then testifying eye to eye with a Murder.*

On the night before my flight, Dad and John took me the surf. It's a strip joint in Revere. I haven't seen *any skin* in months, so it should be a treat. Then before my eyes, was *Suki,* She was 6ft tall and built to *perfect proportion* with her height, She is larger than life and has *cat like* eyes, long auburn hair, her nude body has picture perfect detail, And what moves, My father got her to spend some *time* in front of me. I was in fantasy land. She smiled with a lure of *seduction*. This is more than enough to take my mind off my worries. I would love to return just to *see her*, often. I slept well with her images in my head. I had tomorrow on my mind but Suki clearly was good medicine. I had a slight beer buzz too. John and Dad had more than slight, for their buzz. I think they are worried for me. They know I am fine. The taste of fear is in my mouth and they know it.

The next day when the plane took off; it felt like I was heading uphill and all of a sudden the plane picked up incredible speed my heart began pounding like crazy. We leveled off and steadied out next it was like a drive in a Cadillac. The stewardess noticed that I was nervous she gave me plastic wings and a deck of cards. It was distracting but I still felt nervous. The world below looked like a toy model. The plane had to go to Toronto Canada before Cleveland for some reason. So the plane took a turn over Lake Erie. I looked out the window and there was nothing but water, no land in sight. The flight from Toronto to Cleveland and then a quick flight to Akron municipal Airport felt like two minutes. I got off the plane and *two plain clothes detectives were waiting*. They knew exactly who I was. I never saw them before. We went directly to the court house.

40
A wink of confidence

The Detectives brought me to the outside of the courtroom. Gil Jr, his girlfriend and Marie, with all the other brothers and sisters waited on benches. Marie was very pregnant! *I was very nervous*; Gil Jr just looked at me with a cold hard stare. He whispered a lot to his girlfriend. The court officer called out to me and said "*Brian come this way, they are ready for you*" Marie kissed me and said" My father wants you to *tell the truth*, its ok, I love you" I needed to hear that! Now, I believe she's with me on this and it's ok. I sat next to the Judge, I raised my right hand, and took the oath "I do" This court is now in session. It was quiet and I had the chance to look around the entire courtroom. I focused in on Gil Sr   He just watched as if he were a student about to be lectured in an educational facility. Questions were presented to me I answered clearly and slowly as the prosecutor presented his case. Most of my answers were *yes and no*. At times I was requested to give details in my own words. I *could hear sounds from the Jury in response to my testimony.*

The defense attorney fired some questions my way, His line of questions made matters worst for his client. I completed my testimony and with all of the details given. I could feel the Jury would probably *hang him* for this crime. Silence settled over the courtroom. I had *nothing further* to add. I looked him right in the eye. Gil Sr *winked at me*. I wondered if he was saying *good job* or your fucking dead. All I did was confirm what this man had done. I know the Crowley's were also present and the testimony they gave was what they had seen. If my testimony differs from theirs then things wouldn't be accurate. I exited the court, before I could say anything to Marie; the Detectives took me directly to the airport and off to Boston. *That quick.* I was greeted by my Father and John they wanted all the details. I told them about the wink. They said he was trying to *scare me* I shouldn't worry that's all he could do.

The next day the Prosecutor called he informed me that the trial had come to a close, the end result was *"Guilty of Murder in the First Degree!"* Gil jr was not affected I know he is just as Guilty. Marie also called. She had new concerns for her family.

She said the State Department of Social Services is making decisions, regarding her younger brothers and sisters.

She hopes to leave Ohio and come to Massachusetts to be with me. About three weeks later. She called frantic, She said *"the state of Ohio is going to take the kids"* so she had to come to Lynn Now! I had enough money saved up, so I rented an apartment, furnished it and asked my sister Linda to bring her back.

Once she arrived, it was an easy transition. I already had an apartment with everything we needed, and a lot of food. She told me stories about her brother and his girlfriend and she said *"her brother wanted me sent to jail."*

41
Trying to find that happiness

With Marie pregnant and a lot of new responsibilities; I had to get second job. I was lucky; Wendy's down the hill from work hired me.

I worked 7am-330pm at the Hospital and 4pm - close at Wendy's. I had no trouble with scheduling Wendy's took up Saturday afternoon as well. I had more than enough money to take care of us. She had the baby, I was present this time and it was a girl with *those pretty blue eyes*. (I feel good now; Marie seems to be happy with me. I have the family I wanted. We went to the park on weekends, and hearing my son *ask me about my work and waiting up to see me when I get home was an awesome feeling.)* Marie became very cozy. She made friends with neighbors. I wasn't too happy about that; I worked all the time, some of those friends are guys

What could I do? She does write to her father and she keeps contact with her other siblings including Gil Jr He told her that he's *coming to Massachusetts very soon. I really had hoped I would never see that loser again*

Around the time the baby became two months old. Marie told me she had to get an *abortion.* I said "What? Why? If your pregnant, why all of a sudden an abortion? I reminded her of the first time she told me she was pregnant. I stated firmly….

("You freaked *out on me,* when I was *thought to have suggested* it before.") She said" I know, *but we can't afford another baby*" In my mind, I was thinking of the dark skinned Puerto Rican guy that lives upstairs. *She can't justify the tan.* She's a baby factory. I said, "I'll take you there, but I want no part of it. *It is against my wishes*" She was fine with that. It was done a few days later.

She requested *Burger king* an hour after. *How the fuck could she eat*? Now, *she's a murderer too. It runs in the family.* I wonder if her Father grabbed a burger when he was done.

We got back to the routine of everyday life. And a few days later, While I was working at the hospital. Out of the blue, That horrible feeling I first had in 9th grade. Hit me again I can't escape, *I am going to die someday*!!!

It lasted for a few minutes. I thought about it for a while, the questions of *why??* It was so *overpowering*. Luckily Sonny, walked by he is a counselor for the patients, I stopped him and explained this *phenomenon*. He smiled and said *"you had and anxiety attack, Try to remember what you were thinking just before it happened and that's most likely the cause. Then you can address that problem and you should be fine. If you have more trouble or want to talk you can always come to me."* He was excellent; I think he just gave me the cure for that mess. I am so very grateful to him.

A few days before Thanksgiving, Gil Jr has arrived. He stopped by the apartment to *visit his sister and her kids.* He just looked at me, *like I was a virus or something*. Without saying a word, I could tell he has bad intentions. The gun was never recovered.

I have to keep my tired eyes open. I am *living* on pure *adrenaline*. After he left, I told Marie, I don't want him around. And I made my case, she said she understood.

On Thanksgiving Day, I was walking past Dunkin Donuts; Jimmy pulled over and said "*Hey what's up?*" I said "Nothing Jim why?" He said "*You and Gil should try to work it out, this is no way to live, and He's your kids fuckin uncle for crying out loud.*" I said "Big deal, I'm their father and that's what they need in their lives. Not some puke that shoots a chick after she's dead." So he can make a claim to being a real *bad boy*. Jimmy said " *I asked for him to meet us at your place in an hour so lets go over and wait*" I replied " Whatever Jimmy, Its pointless, and you should mind your own fucking business."

He responded "*Don't act like a tough guy with me, 'Ill break your fuckin face! Now let's go!*"

42
Happy Thanksgiving

We got to the apartment; I could see Marie peeking through the blinds.
I wondered what the fuck is this? All of a sudden like a blur *The door burst open*, Gil Jr came off the porch, *All I could see was the bottom of his boot, coming straight for my face*. I ducked and maintained focus on him.

I realized right away, I was just set up, Gil was waiting and Jimmy came looking for me. Marie was in on it. I'm lucky; *I wasn't hit in my sleep*. We exchanged a few punches; he got me in a headlock. I couldn't get away. We were on the sidewalk, I saw a parked car, my face would miss the bumper, if I went down, taking him into the bumper, we struggled for many minutes, finally with *everything* I had.

I took us down.... his face and head hit the bumper with great force; he almost passed out from the blow.

I said "*we wouldn't have this problem, if your father didn't kill your half fuckin sister.* He didn't have to do it in front of me. So fuck off and don't ever fuck with me again. I won't be so fuckin nice next time." John pulled up and said "What's going on?"

Gil was standing away from me catching his breath. I was catching mine. Jimmy said "*They had something they had to do, so they did it*"

I looked to John and said " Jimmy just set me up, Gil was here, well Jimmy hunted me down, knowing he was going to jump me by surprise" I looked at Marie in the window, She *was laughing very hard, and pointing at me, while doing some type of dance.* John said "C'mon Bri your going back to live with me" Jimmy sarcastically said "Happy Thanksgiving." John replied "What *the fucks he got to be happy about?*" as he pointed to me. John and I got in his car. We headed back to his house.

As I sat there on the couch I could feel muscle aches everywhere. My head was pounding. John asked, if I was ok I said "I guess so." We talked about how much Jimmy and Gil are juvenile type delinquents. *Insignificant pieces of shit.* John would like to hurt those mother fuckers now.

Good, I thought Gil can start paying her fuckin rent. Let them have a nice little sick twisted life, *in that shit hole apartment.* Maybe his girlfriend can come in and mess with Marie some more. I spent the next day on Johns couch. I couldn't move. I hope Gil feels the same. I thought about the incident. It's best that I am out of it anyway, hopefully that ended it. Monday I will head back to work, I should try to save for a car.

Monday…. while I was working Marie called she said she wanted to talk. I told her"*she said enough.*" She told me "they tricked her; Jimmy wanted her to be on their side of *things.* So he told her, *I have been sleeping with all kinds of girls.* When she heard that she was pissed. Jimmy told her Gil was going to kick my ass for cheating on her." *So she says.* I replied "What *girls? And when do I have time for that? I work 80 hrs a week to support you and the kids. Other than that, I am home with you.*" She said "I *know and I am sorry. I told Gil he can't come here any more. Please come home lets talk.*" "I will call in at Wendy's and come to you." I replied.

43
Unexpected Surprises

Marie knows all she has to do is open her legs and I am hooked I'm getting used to knowing that. We *hooked up* and she did her *Hon thing.* I told her that I will come by at various times over the next few days… to be sure Gil doesn't come around. Then, if it seems right, I will come back for good. She agreed.

I asked her if she was doing drugs, she denied that. I figured if what she said happened was true; it was too simple of an excuse. I figured she does drugs. I mean she *laughed and danced as I was beaten pretty good*?

I didn't even go near the apartment for about a week. Finally, I stopped in and found he wasn't there. But, a very large decorated Christmas tree took up the entire living room. I said "Where did that come from?"

She chuckled and said "My friends *gave it to me*" I was thinking I'm sure they did *give it to her.* "What friends?" I asked, she mentioned some female neighbor's names. *Yeah whatever,* I asked her if she has been fucking anyone. She denied it with the usual "hon thing" So I left and told her I would be back the next day to move in she was very happy to hear that. I went to work at the hospital for the day. Then I went to Wendy's. A short time there…

The manager took me off the grill to mop the floor around the salad bar, I went and did it. A bus load of people came in and the Manager told me to get on the grill and hurry it up. I said "after I wash my hands." She said "you'll do what I tell you, when I tell you!" I said "I just touched a germ filled filthy mop and you want me to cook food without washing?" She responded "You're fired Get out of here now!"

I just turned around and headed out. I decided I will go to my apartment and tell Marie what happened. This was hours before I was expected. I walked in and saw my son watching TV. I could hear moaning from the bedroom, I ran in and saw the neighbors naked ass cheeks and Maries knees moving out to the sides as he pounded away.

I shouted "You fuckin' whore!" He jumped off, she jumped to the floor, pulling blankets over her. She started screaming "I don't know what happened, He tricked me into it. I swear"

He put his clothes on real quick. I just started beating on him; she ran past me and into the kitchen, I ran after her. She fell to the ground, and hid under the table. I realized how *pathetic* she looked, like a naked little piglet. I will admit she looked terrified. I turned and walked out, I could hear my son say *"I hate you mommy."* I smiled, He is a good boy. I should send her a *thank you* card. All I ever wanted was the truth, for four years I waited. Now, I have it, and that certainly ends it! I knew I should not marry this girl. I am freaked out. But after the abortion, I knew the truth. Dad always tells me "go with your gut feeling."

I should try, it's not easy. What if, I read someone wrong and they are telling the truth. It would be horrible. I know at times, people think I am lying when it's the truth.

I can't wait to tell John, I went straight to his house. He was on the phone, I waited. He sounded like he was comforting someone. He works mental health so; the family uses him as sort of a shrink. The news I have for him, I feel excited to tell.

At the same time, I am very nervous and shaken. I wish he would just hang up. Just then I heard him say "Alright, *Ill tell Brian, Yes, we will be there, Love you too*" And he hung up the phone. "*What's that all about*?" I asked, "Aunt Ruth Died," He said After a slight pause I said "What?" He told me that Aunt Marion called him and Dad,

I guess Stephanie called Aunt Marion, I didn't know what to say. I wished bad things to her for so long. I am surprised, but, I am not freaking out. I gave John the details of what just happened to me. He was pissed at me for caring and pissed at Marie for being a whore. He said yeah, yeah, yeah. He heard enough.

It's sad to say, but sometimes a funeral can seem more like a reunion, I walked in not really expecting any feelings. It was a respect thing. I saw Joey, he is now Joe, He's a big biker looking dude. He has changed *projecting a sense of genuine quality*. If I had never met him before, I would say "he's a great guy." Then Stephanie came over "*Hi Bri you ok honey" she asked through her tears*. Goosebumps rolled through my body, from my shoulders upward and down simultaneously. I felt the reality settle over me. Ann joined Stephanie *we became a cluster of tears*. I fell apart crying, was I sad for them?

Or was I freaked out over things I've thought. Or has *my life finally put me to tears*? I have no idea. I went to the casket, I said a prayer, and knew she was gone from here, If she meets her maker as the next step. I wish, I could find forgiveness to put in a *good* for her, I can't. I walked away in tears, I feel very *sorry for her* right now.

Gail is a grown up nice looking young lady. I can't believe my eyes. I gave her a huge hug, and told her how great she looks. Uncle Ed just sat there as the grieving widower, I didn't even look his way. I left with John; we went across the street with Joe to have a few beers. We wanted to catch up on everyone's lives. *Joe really has changed he is a great guy now.* We spent the remainder of the wake at the bar and relatives came in a few at a time. We had our reunion right there in Players Pub.

The family sure can drink. I had no idea some of these people drank so much I had no idea I would have cried so much. I think I felt compassion for the girls, Ruth was their Mother and it is a terrible tragedy I know too well.
I will attend services in the morning. And then I will get on with my life. I don't have to work two jobs now and my primary job is at my pace it's a good time to get my head and life together.

The next morning after the service, everyone gathered at Aunt Ruth's house. I couldn't imagine that smell penetrating my nose again but here it is. I feel like dry heaving. For everyone else, the mood went from happy to sad and back again. This is her family. I sat quietly taking it *all* in. "Brian, son, you look good" Uncle Ed spoke; I looked towards him and gave a slight smile of agreement. "When are you going to bring the *wife and kids over?*" He asked, at that very moment, *I could hear a small explosion in my head. As I felt my right eye plunge inward and back* "What?" I asked slowly, He said "I haven't met your family"

I figured of course you haven't and you never will why would you? I said "Yeah well soon" He has an incredible nerve, just thinking such a thing, let alone asking. Does he want to look at my kids as *fresh fish*?

The sight of Uncle Ed put me back in a place I *never* wanted to be. Like, if I have a bad experience in a carnival ride. They stopped the ride and let me off. *I choose to never go back on.* Here I sit, buckled in. I got up and gave Joe and the girls a hug then I walked out.

*(Jimmy was there. I stayed away
from him too. He acted like they were all his
closest relations. He sat back talking like he
is now a grown up big shot or something.)*
The only way, I can get this smell off me, is
to go to Johns, shower and change. John
came out after I did, and we headed off
together. We talked about all the changes
that have taken place over the years. The
two surprises, Gail being grown up, and Joe
turned out pretty cool. John and Joe have
things they like equally such as beer, darts,
and pool. They decided they can meet up
and hang out from time to time; John liked
the idea, and asked if I wanted to join in. I
told John, I might join them sometime.

(The thing is.. I like to have beers,
just not as much as them. I get drunk too
easy I'm 5'10 @ 160lbs. These guys are
235lbs and up they can take it better. They
suck down a beer every twenty minutes;
they also buy rounds, so you keep the same
pace. I like *social drinking*, not to the point
of being trashed, a *nice buzz* is good. These
guys are in a race to get drunk, a quick shot
with a chaser, not me, thanks.
This is when John says yeah, yeah, yeah,
whatever.) We went to John's we changed
and cleaned up. John said "Hey Dad wants
to meet at the club" *Seeing as we all have a
day off now.*

The Franco is two doors down from Maries, "I don't want to be there." I replied, John said "c'mon, you'll be with us" I said "Alright" Great, I thought, we can start drinking at noon time two doors away from where my ex and kids are. After, I caught her being plunged by some maggot.

I say *plunged* because I now see her as a *toile*t, a disgusting, vile, pig.
There she was, standing on the porch with her brother and some very tall *hard core biker* what the fucks up with that? I wondered as I went inside the club. John and Dad were having the usual fun playing pool and sucking down pitchers.

I was reviewing the images in my head of her knees moving to the sides. "Go get 'em lucky" Dad broke into my daydream "Oh I'm up? I asked. I overlooked the table "Nine down there two rails," As I point to the pocket. I made the shot just as I called it. "*You unconscious bastard*" Dad responded.

Hello, I just called it *how am I unconscious*? I thought, he always says that when I make a shot. That's the type of teasing that reminds me that I am his youngest and being with him and John really can spark me up. In a while, I felt much better the game of pool, them, and some beers.

Go get 'em you lucky unconscious bastard! At least he feels he can pick on me, For Dad this is good loving fun. If he picks on someone he really thinks an awful lot of that person.

It feels good to know how much he cares, but he can be annoying with his trash talk. I learned a trick shot once. *I spread out three balls and told Dad I will get them all in and I would hit three rails. I did the shot just as I explained.*

He laughed and said "You gotta be shittin me. Go get 'em Lucky, You unconscious bastard. Grrr I cannot get around that one I guess.

I had so many thoughts running through my mind that is was difficult falling asleep that night. I decided that I am free to be with any I choose. I was somewhat excited to see what being myself and thinking about my own "wants" was going to be like.

44
Free do as you choose

The next day at work I saw a *new girl* working in the café. She was around my age and she looked so nice that I could imagine her on a magazine cover her hair was long, with small curly waves, various shades of brown, she had tan skin and a body that could create sexual fantasies.   I had to say something;

I turned to my boss and said "Hey what's with the new chick?" He said "ah, ha, she's quiet nice, isn't she?" I said "well, kind of" He laughed, and told me "she is single, and You…. are one, of about a hundred people here, that want her" I agreed and said "well, Its nice to at least have her around, huh?" I figured he was right; I went on to doing my job and disregarded any hope of getting personal with her.

A couple of days later, I was sent to the outside of the café where they stored food carts. I had to patch holes in the wall. The kitchen staff has a habit of crashing carts into them. We put up rubber bumpers, but they still damaged the walls.

I had all my supplies and started working. Kitchen staff was working all around me. And crash! I heard the cart hit the wall. An unfamiliar voice said "Oh, *I am sorry Brian*" I turned to see the *fantasy girl* looking at me she had her hands covering here nose and mouth. As if to say, oops, I said "You know my name? I mean, its ok, "Hi" She replied "I'm Michelle, I heard your boss call out to you a couple of times" Oh, well nice to meet you" I said, She replied "Nice to meet you, Ill try to be more careful" I responded " No, it is job security keep up the good work" we laughed and we got back to work. I spent the rest of the day thinking about my moment with this lovely image of life's art. Now, she has also proven to be a normal human with a nice personality. I have a great pre occupation for the rest of the day.

The next day… my meal at the café was almost double in size, I looked at my meal and then at her she smiled and she said "anything else?" Wow, special treatment. This is very nice. She handed me her number and said "call me." I couldn't believe it.

Later that day we talked, I found out that she lives down the street not far from work.

We decided we would meet at her house and we could watch a movie or something. (If she lived ten miles away and I had to walk the entire distance, I would have. I mean, *a hundred guys at my work would too*. Then, there's the rest of the world of maybe thousands of guys that would want this very opportunity. I think she smashed that tray on purpose. (I figured she was a little vixen.) After I hung up, I showered and went to her house, her parents weren't home. She turned on cable and searched for a movie. We talked, just a bunch of small talk for a little bit. She said her parents work until 11:30pm so we had a few hours alone.

We stopped talking and moved close to each other, looking into each others eyes. Finally, I moved in slowly for a kiss. It was long and passionate. I started kissing her neck and back up to her lips. I became lost in her; my kissing was soft and slow, down her neck, we undressed without really missing a second of each other. We exchanged kisses to each others necks, I moved down her neck and all over her perfect breasts. I kissed her tan soft stomach, and decided to go south from there.

The smell of her skin was extremely arousing. It was more beautiful than anything, I had ever imagined. I was so aroused, I slowly moved up and into her. We starting slowly, we were *making love*. I responded to her sounds and we moved in perfect synchronicity, for so long our stomachs were soaked with sweat and sweat was dripping from my head. My kisses are passionate and we began moving faster, working together, like a well oiled machine, faster we moved, and finally we reached our climax. Out of breath we laid next to each other. I watch her wet stomach move up and down with every breath. I could see her heart beating right there.

I felt a high that I could ride on forever. She is the most beautiful thing I can even imagine. And right at this moment, I can't imagine anything else. My mind and body are in harmonious ecstasy. We spent the rest of the night in each others arms.

I woke up realizing it was a new day. I woke her up and she smiled what a lovely vision to see first light of day. I went right to work from there. She is scheduled to be there an hour later. I didn't want to talk about last night with anyone. I wanted to see her and see if she has the same feeling about this as I do.

She came in and she was difficult to read without words. I had to wait for a chance to speak with her. My Boss and I had to get lumber for a project this will take us off grounds for hours. I will have to wait and talk with her tonight. My boss thought I had a brighter disposition than usual I simply said "that's 'because life's good." As soon as I got home, I called her. She said "You didn't tell me you are married and have kids" I said "I am not married" She interfered and said "You used me! I don't want to talk to you again!" She hung up. I called back, her mother answered and said "She is moving out so please don't call here again" what the fuck? I know I talk too much at work, Everyone knows my business, but how did this happen? Was she asking about me? I think she really felt like I did. When I see her tomorrow, I can fix it. I got to work the next day. My boss told me, to see his boss. I went to her office, she told me I to bring a lot of my personal problems to work, It interferes, and they have to let me go. She gave me an extra week of pay, so I left feeling like I had a bonus. I should listen to Dad and keep my mouth shut.

It's a warm and Sunny day; there is no place I have to be. I also have money. I have a wonderful feeling because of the time had I with Michelle. I guess that makes me *one in a million.*

The other guys at work must be pissed. All they can do is look and wonder. Once, A while back I heard a guy talking shit about someone he slept with, he said "It was like *fucking a jar of mayonnaise*" Quizzically, I thought "what's it supposed to feel like?"

Now, I know what it's supposed to feel like…. I walked along wondering if I should look for a new job or just enjoy the day. Jimmy drove past me and stopped. And for some reason, I really didn't care. I am usually nerved up when I see him. "Brian what are you doing out of work?" He asked. I told him I was fired. He said 'Oh yeah, Hop in." I said "Nah, I am headed out to look for another job" He firmly said "Just get in the fuckin' car!" Pete was with him. I got in the back; He drove like an asshole over to his house. The car stank like weed.

45
A Death sentence?

We walked into Jimmy's living room, Pete pushed me down onto a chair, and said "sit down" I just looked at him I was a bit shocked. He pulled out a gun and pressed it to the side of my head. He began telling me the things he doesn't like about me, he went on for a solid five minutes. *I couldn't hear his words at one point just his voice.* All I could do was think, I sat frozen; I could feel my brother Jimmy watching, but I couldn't look his way. My heart was beating. It figures, I had such a wonderful time with Michelle and now I get to pay with my life? *Was she a departing gift?* Was this the plan for my life?

His speech was given in a manner as if he were a judge *sentencing me to death.* And when he gave his final words he pulled the trigger. I didn't hear a blast, I didn't feel pain, and I thought this is it? This is what I was worried about? It's not bad at all… I feel fine. A smile came over my face…I looked up and noticed Pete appeared to be frightened.

I can't tell what he saw in my face. But, he was afraid of it. So I grabbed a hold of the moment, and shouted, so loud my lungs vibrated in my chest *if you ever hold a fuckin' gun to my head again it better be fuckin' loaded!* They were both in surprised from that. I never even talk back. They knew they were only having fun with me. I really thought my life was over. There is a big difference. Jimmy is nothing to me now as far as I am concerned!

I will tell John and Dad, but does that make me a pussy or a rat? I wondered. If it were loaded, I'd be a *dead pussy rat*. Fuck them, this is my time and it should be as good as I can make it. I don't seem to have as much *life enjoyment* as these drug addicts. I called John and told him. He called Dad the end result was… Dad is going to go one on one with Pete. Jimmy told Dad he didn't know that was going to happen. And he wasn't sure if the gun was real. - Obvious bullshit -

46
Times are changing

Pete agreed to Meet Dad at a park. Dad got there a few minutes early just In case he was going to be *rat packed.* " *Attacked by a group*" Pete walked slowly up to him, some words were exchanged and Pete sprayed Mace into his eyes. Dad couldn't see, he ran to his car got out of there… he drove away blindly, *in case this was the chance to be beaten while he was unable to defend himself.*

Pete, Gil and that tall Biker guy spend a lot of time together now. The Biker guy is Jay, I learned through Jimmy. That night John heard a car pull up to the house. He looked out and saw Pete Gil and Jay. Gil shouted up to the window "Hey pussy, come on out, so I can take a pot shot to your fuckin' head." John decided *fuck these guys* He called the Police. They don't see so much action in Swampscott so a lot of them arrived, Gil and his friends took off in different directions.

They got away, but they left the car. The Police broke lights and things on the car so they could have it ticketed and towed. They suggested that I go to the court, so I could obtain a restraining order. After the Judge heard about the Ohio business and current events he approved the order. This will be effective for a year, and if violated. Gil will spend a mandatory two years in the house of Corrections.

I am sure he will violate the order. And *I will be at fault for his incarceration in their eyes*. I have determined now, that Marie and I are not together. I have no reason to have contact with these people. I got a Job in Swampscott at Bradlees. This was a whole new scene with working class people and finally a chance to try and enjoy a trouble free life. I decided to keep my business to myself.

A month later, I was called into court on Child Support. I pleaded "No *Contest*" The Judge told me. I can request paternity testing. I declined, I said "I know they are my kids" I started paying my support, and did not try to see the kids. I figure in time if things settle and can be somewhat healthy for everyone. I may be able to establish a relationship.

For now, I testified…. and *Marie and Gil have a father that's in Jail for life.* In an argument we once had she said *"You took my Father from me, so I am taking you away from your children!"* She will always feel that way. Blood is thicker.

It's very sad because, I know I would be a patient and understanding Dad. I would not want my *children to ever see the hurt I've seen.* I think these kids are losing the best thing they could have for their growth at this time in their lives. I will hurt too, but I will be alive. That's what counts most. In time my older son may remember me he is almost five. I lost my Mother around the same time. He has his mother and maybe this gives him a better chance. I will just work and wait….

Being at Bradlees is familiar because of my experience with Kmart. It's better for me because it's different in many other ways and I need change but I need an easy transition. So it works out well

I work in the receiving area. It's me and two others. The job is pretty routine. Once you learn it your on your own. I have gotten to this point and now without distractions, I find, I have so much time to really think.

Sometimes too much time I'm working daytime and John works nights. I am in a new place and I don't know anyone.

Alone and Lonely, All I can do is reflect on all the experiences I have had. You would think if I weren't humble, I should be getting there. I know I have always been humble. *I have always been right from the start.* All though, things change when you have something you *really love.* I always wanted a family, *not millions of dollars or fancy things.* I just wanted the simple things in life. All those things begin at home. I stayed through all I could with Marie; the big problem for me now is an entirely different hurt. I can't get my kids off my mind. I created them, and I think the love you have for your kids is more powerful than I could ever have imagined. *They never asked to be here.*

Even songs on the radio make me stop, and they actually bring me to tears. The only thing I can do is wait. It can be weeks, months or years. I can only hope it will be quick and that the kids have less hurt than me. If I had a house and money and daycare or whatever is needed. I wouldn't even try to fight to take the children from their Mother. I just don't think children should be away from their Mother, no matter how good or bad she is.

She is the Mother. I can't be where I'm not wanted. This is the most pain I think, that I have ever felt.

At times, I feel as If maybe one of my children are missing me at the exact same moment. I look out to the world and wonder if they are looking too. This is not like any love I could feel with *anyone but my own Children*. That's the reason, I told the Judge *No Contest*. I can feel it in my heart, think of it as a Fatherly instinct.

I have heard of Mothers instinct. I just think its *parents instinct*. In one of our fights Marie said, *they're not your fucking kids anyway*. I actually laughed, that didn't hurt. *I knew she was wrong*. Until something happens, I will just pay my support, and wait, until it's safe to see them. It's absolutely, too dangerous for me to be there with the games with guns, threats and deceit. If this were a game of Chess, I'd have been in check so many times. It's a stalemate.

I had to go; Checkmate in this game would mean the end. I have to choose *living or dying*. Plain and simple the children can be in my life, *if I stay alive*. If it takes eighty more years, I will try to be here for them. I often notice, That I stop and look at things, I as an 18year old wouldn't normally.

Like spending about ten minutes admiring rain droplets on the leaves of trees, the daylight reflected them, making them look like thousands of tiny lights.

I would love to point that out to my child. And then maybe, they could point to something for me. I try to stay busy and "have a life" that way I am not so lonely

I have been saving my money; I was able to get a license and a car. It's A 'shitbox', but it runs. Now, I can rely on myself. On Fridays, I have to drop my support payment at Marie's house. It's always a difficult task. Having a car, gives me a quick getaway. Marie and Jay are a couple now and he treats me like garbage anytime he sees me.

It's usually only about one minute a week, so it's not a big deal.

I travel around Lynn at times, but being in Swampscott is like being a world away. I go to Dunkin Donuts in Lynn after, I drop my payment, and I hang out with the regulars. Ritchie, Annie, Frank, Linda, Meatball and Carl and a few irregular, regulars. It can be entertaining; we usually sit and watch people come in and out all night. With every customer, *there's a different story.*

We bitch about politics and current events, we tell stories about our lives they love mine. I spend most of the time with Frank; he is the only one that doesn't mind having *beers on the weekend.* We go to the Charlie Horse on the Lynn way and play pool. That works out good for me. On Monday nights John, Dad, and I play pool. Fridays with Frank gives me practice. This keeps Dad on his toes. Ritchie and Annie are married. She used to work at Dunks, now she's a regular, Linda is Ritchie's sister, and Meatball is Ritchie and Linda's Brother. It's a family affair. Carl is a very quiet nice guy. He looks like he's smiling all the time. I wonder if he is. Meatball is a large man he has no neck and it's *hard to hear what he says.* I think his tongue is too big for his mouth. Frank calls him marble mouth when he's tired of hearing it. It's really kind of fun.

Many people that I knew from Lynn, when I was younger, come into Dunks. At times, if we see each other we stop and say hello catch up a little. Every night you can count on something happening. I know on Fridays. The people I worry about are at a drug house in the projects or another shitty neighborhood. You never see them around here.

We usually hang out from about 7pm -10pm unless, we have beers, then we leave around 8:30pm and we stay at the Charlie until closing, unless *one of us can hook up*. Then it's anyone's guess. Then my routine starts all over again...

I get to work about 730am. If I am earlier, I can have coffee and a smoke with the boss, its good that way because, you get extra break time. Any other way you're late. Kim works at the lunch counter, she's like the food service *bartender*. We talk a little; she has the gossip on everyone.

She's short, very pretty, with dark hair, she keeps it in a pony tail and she happens to have a great ass.

One morning she told me, I should ask her friend Lisa out. She told Lisa, if *she wasn't taken*, she would go out with me in a minute. That alone gave a great boost to my self-esteem. I wasn't really attracted to Lisa, *I asked anyway*. Even though I really enjoy hanging out and listening to Kim, she is a *real hoot*. I could enjoy going home to her at night. Lisa is tall with long blonde hair. We went to her house. I felt like, I should be *respectable*. I guess that was the wrong move! The next day, she told Kim that I didn't even try anything... that ended that. I thought ok No big deal. I've been there before. I feel like *trying something* with Kim every time I see her.

I finally put it out there. She said "I cant, I am going to get married, and I've been with the same guy since like 8th grade." I said "If you ever wanted a last hurrah, I'm willing to help out. That wasn't the smartest thing to say…. I've burnt my bridges here. If I try *to hook up* now, I am just a dog. I have to wait until someone wants to *hook up* with me. Nothing like running straight out of the gate, it's for the best though

It's working out well for me; I can focus on my job. Whenever, I get into clicks at work. I become too distracted, and do a lousy job. This whole *trying to meet girls* is hard to figure anyway. I get all dressed up, style my hair, shave and buy the latest cologne. I have had young woman flip me *the finger* for looking their way. Other times, I've gone out without a shower messed up hair and whiskers. And young ladies gave me little cute cards with their number on it. I met one young woman, in the Charlie Horse *that way* and she was *all over me* at the pool table she said "I can't believe I'm doing this but, lets go to my place." Funny, she was a *Michelle* too. Hmm

My routine is sweet and simple now; I go to work then home and sometimes, Ill go to Dunks and see what happens. I play pool on Mondays, with John and Dad.

On good weather days we play handball at the beach, then we hit the YMCA for some swimming. The Y and playing handball started because Dad wanted to lose weight. I like it, we drink less. Personally, I like a few beers around 7pm or later. Dad can start after his morning coffee; I was at his house one Sunday morning helping him fix his car, about 9am He said "Want a brew Bri?" I said "What? I am not even done with coffee," I tried to have beers one Sunday around 2pm I was asleep by 8pm. I think it was a waste of a day.

47
Legends Die

Since Marie is getting support, and
I have a restraining order, all that's pretty
good right now. Direct family issues aren't
good at all. Nana Perry, Grammy Boober
and Grammy Mc Gee have passed away all
within 2 weeks of each other. Nana was in
her 90s, God Bless her. My other
Grandmothers were in their 70s. It's a
tragedy to loose any one of them. Grammy
Boober was where everyone went for
Holidays. The family became so big; she
had to rent a hall. Aunts, Uncles, Cousins,
all sorts of people of marrying age and
having children it has become a very large
family. Now with her gone Aunt Marion
will take over the Holidays, She wants to
down size it and keep it at her house. I know
she will do an awesome Job. It won't be the
same without Grammy, Everyone went to
see her, and not because they have to *they
want to.* She was an institution, She never
sang or danced but you just knew *you were
loved for who you are, that was the
attraction.*

Grampy McGee is a tough guy, He is the center of attention when were at his house, *Grammy McGee was quiet and stayed alone most times*. He likes his scotch, now he will like more of it. His fighting days are over, now he just talks more when he drinks.

Jimmy's wife is divorcing him. He decided to act out at each funeral and argue loudly. When Grammy Boober passed Jimmy yelled out the car window at his soon to be ex.

You fuckin C word", *Dad screamed "Do you mind? I just buried my Mother!"* Jimmy quieted down, but he didn't seem to care about Dads feelings. It's all about Jimmy all the time *"I'm right and everybody's wrong"* that's his way of thinking. Dad loves giving chances. I think Jimmy has used all his chances with me. I am supposed to be the little Brother; I haven't felt that way in some time. Fuck him its no wonder *his wife's finally leaving.* I am surprised she stayed with him as long as she did.

The final straw with her was when his daughter accidentally broke the remote for the TV, He decided to use his *parenting skills* and got right in her face, *screaming like a wild man and broke her toy asking her how it feels.*

His wife tried to intervene he chased her outside and down the street *as the Police were driving by*. He was cuffed and stuffed right there. I wish I could have seen them take his ass down. Imagine the look on his face when he thought he was going to beat up a woman, and got thrown down by two big cops instead. *Ha ha ha that's too funny, and I'm supposed to be the idiot or pussy.*

Dad was right about Jimmy`s friends, one or two of them are fucking his soon to be ex wife. One guy said "Wow, *Jimmy must have a little dick cuz she's so tight when she pisses it whistles*" I pictured the teapot sounding off while she was on the toilet and the guy saying "hey you making tea?" *Ah NO! I'm going to the bathroom!* I didn't take any time getting to know her.

Lynn, Lynn, the City of Jim, Jimmy used his skills to hook up illegal cable; He learned trunking systems on Police frequencies. He rewired cable boxes so you could watch free pay per view movies. Police new him by name all over the city. He could bypass alarm systems. Any time a new security measure went into place Jimmy found a way around it. *He could be rich if he used his skills legit.* He just likes the drugs, that's payment enough for his efforts. Most of the time when he was caught *it was his friends turning him in.*

Many people know Jimmy is my brother, they like him, when Jimmy is on your side *he has a heart of Gold*. And they like me. Some of them tell me things he says about me and a lot of it is *horrible*. I am being made to be a real shit bag. So, I find that I am often defending myself. Just for the sake of *principle* and my own character.

All I can do is begin to feel *resentment* towards him. My father always says with anger "You don't *hate* anyone!" So I *resent* him.

Hey Kim's looking good as usual, *and she's staring right at me*. Maybe she wants that last hurrah. ("Brian, come here" She said, I went over. She continued "My friend Denise saw you the other day at Dunkin Donuts. We were in the car and she pointed you out and said *yeah I wouldn't mind knowing him*" I told her I knew you, I was going to come in so you guys could talk, but she got nervous and backed out. I told her I can talk to you today". She said "will you?" I said "of course." Here is her number) I said "What's she even look like? I mean she knows what I look like its only fair" She agreed and invited me to her house for a party Friday. Denise will be there. Kim told me she was small and cute and lots of guys try to hit on her.

Well that sounds good to me. My father says "If *you want to be happy Marry an ugly girl*" I say "if you want to be happy, Marry a girl that actually loves you" *If she does, the rest should follow*. I know When I love anything… I am in it one hundred percent. I think were all the same in that way. I went to Dunks after work; Ritchie, Annie and Meatball were there. I told them about the girl, Ritchie wanted to be funny and said "Oh yeah, I remember her, she was *hot baby* she was tall, with long legs, and I think I could see her muffin." Annie punched him and said "Oh leave him alone, Ritchie's the one who wanted that girl" we all laughed, Then Ritchie said "*Hey, don't go for the one you want go for the one that wants you and you'll be happy that's what I did*." Annie punched him again. Annie said "Don't worry Bri you'll find someone" Ritchie just sat back winking to suggest *see how I get her going*. Meatball said something and laughed instead of asking… I just laughed too.

All day Friday, Kim would tease me, and act like she was trying to be my girl. I enjoyed it she likes to have fun. On my way out of work She said "See you tonight" I said "Not if I see you first" I headed out, ate some food, showered up and got dressed up with my fancy cologne and feathered hair.

When I got to the house Kim ran over and said "Hey Bri, I want you to meet my friend Denise." The only words that can describe her is cute, she was short and way too cute. We got along great.

We started dating for a few weeks. One time she was with me while I dropped off my child support. I told her my story, and then out of the blue she said "Why don't we fight for your kids, we can live together you, me, your kids and my kids" My response was "I like the idea, but we've only known each other almost three weeks. Why don't we wait awhile on that?" She just smiled. I think she's very cute, I could certainly fall in love with her. I was feeling real good about her. I spent many nights with her.

One morning I woke up and got ready to head out as I approached my car I noticed all four tires are flat. It could be anyone at this point, her former husband, my brother and his friends who knows? My car stands out. It was in front of her house. All I know is that I had to call in for work. I stay at her house a lot, and called in late a lot. My boss is pissed, we have a truckload of shit that has to hit the floors,

I took two tires at a time. All the way to the junk yard and replaced them.

The tires had cuts in the sides and couldn't be repaired. On my second trip *James* saw me and offered a ride. I was tired and figured why not. We got to Denise's and all he had to do was see her.

Now he will find a way to weasel in on my business. Around 12 noon, I called work and told them I was all set to come in. They told me "*they were all set* pick up your check Friday your done." Oh well, it was fun, I told them to tell Kim I said "Ill miss her" the boss said "go fuck yourself."

48
I should be incarcerated

Every time you have a change in status, *you have to notify the court*, they modify your support order according to what you make. Its all arranged before a Judge, And logged as "appearances." Reporting a job loss is one appearance a few days after that Reporting new employment is another "appearance." The amount of "appearances" are always included in the "file" that is presented at the time you see the Judge

Change jobs once or twice and you're a real asshole in the eyes of the court. (It looks like you have appeared before the court multiple times over this child support case.) I got a job with Joe right away at a moving company. I appeared for the second time in two weeks and the Judge called my name he read the previous case history and loudly stated *"This man should be incarcerated!"* I almost shit my pants and thought to myself "he wants me in jail because *I pay my children support and don't want to fall behind*? I am here to tell them where I work so they can tell me how much I have to pay it's their fucking system. *This fuckin Judge should go to jail for scaring the shit out of me."*

Someone from the probate division stopped him and said something. He turned to me and said *"You should have one job and keep it, Stop wasting the courts time."* Funny, if he were having a heart attack or something, and I was the only one there that knew CPR

He would be humble to me. But for now, he could put me in jail, just because he says so. And if it's in error, try to get out. It is Heaven on earth and he's God. Didn't he start out as a lawyer? He has no idea what I've been through. He just looks on a piece of paper. I went by their rules, and I am a Piece of shit. *He's a piece of shit.* I would love to be in the ER while he is gasping for breath, and say *This Man should be incarcerated!*

Have another drink you fuck! Wait until Dad finds out about this. We have pool tonight. Well Judge, just tell me how much I have to pay, *your wasting Brian's fucking time!*

Dad was bullshit and he told me his stories about his run ins with Judges. We played pool, As usual John and I went out we had beers and drove around. We drove by Denise's and I saw Jimmy's car at the corner a few doors down. I knew it, he wasted no time.

I called her number and got no answer. I figured he would get up and out around 7am so I got there at 6am, He was gone. I went up and knocked at the door. She confessed, I guess he told her, John and I, have it in for him and he gave her some bullshit examples he produced some tears and next thing you know. Oops, its like she was lying there naked and he tripped and fell in, dick first. I told her, "I was glad we didn't fight for my kids and good luck with Jim. He'll make you so tight, when you piss, it will whistle.

Too bad, Dad met her and liked her. John did too, She was great, until that happened. Its ok.. while I was at the courthouse, a girl named Melissa gave me her number. I called and was going to meet up at her house. She's blonde and tall. I wonder if Ritchie saw her muffin? I think that I'm going to. At this point, I don't think any of these ladies care about being committed to someone. So why should I? One girl told me, " *Brian you only think about one thing*," she was wrong, but we ended it, because that's what she thought, that should be my theme *fuck em and forget em.*

For the next couple of months, I was all over Marblehead, Beverly, Everett, Lynn, Saugus Malden, Once *I brought a girl home late. I wanted to bring her at 11pm*, just like her Mother asked, but she wanted to stay longer.

Her brother pulled me out of my car as I dropped her off. He was drunk and he tried to kick my ass. I told Meatball about it. I think he said "*Let's Go, show me where he is*" We found the guy sitting in his car outside of his work. Meatball grabbed the door handle, ironically, it was rotted at the hinges, and so it fell off the car. Meatball said something, and the kid actually pissed himself. *Fuck with the bull ya get the horn* Like Dad says.

49
Fun for me

I started going to the strip joints.
One night I was in the surf talking with John
and we were talking about the ride from
Ohio, and we mentioned New York, The
Bartender was a sexy little Asian girl and
she over heard our conversation she said
"I'm from New York I heard you guys
talking, I'm Sara" "Hey Sara, I'm Brian,"
That's all I said. The rest of the night the
beers were on the house we usually don't sit
at the bar either. We are usually by the
stage, However, just seeing nude woman all
the time, *does sort of lose its flare*. I can't
believe I just said that. We exchanged
numbers and we will take it from there.

The next day at work, Frank drove
into the parking lot at the moving company,
"Hey feel like some beers tonight. He
shouted from his car. Four guys turned
around and said "You buying?" He didn't
know what to say. I laughed and said "Hey
stranger what's up? Sure I'll have some
beers, what do you think the Charlie?" He
said "yeah Ill meet you at dunks around
eight"

Joe looked at me and said "So is he getting us beers or what?" I said "it's fuckin lunch time, and you've already had your share" He laughed Then he said "Come to the Scotch mist after work, to get primed, we have a blast every Friday."

After work we headed over to the scotch, they were setting up for a live band. I heard them practice these guys are good. So I called Frank he decided to meet me there. We were there for the night, at some point Frank started talking to some chick he knew *Lisa, she was the sister of one of his friends* so they had a thing going on. I called Sara she wasn't working so she agreed to come see me.

She was there in about an hour. Now, I was comfortable and with friends and family. Joe and I are becoming close too. It's a blast. I am in my element with people I know and care about, with loud, live music and a hot Asian chick. I was like a rock star. It's a night, Ill hear about for years to come.

Its funny what being carefree, and confident can do for you, Every one I saw there, had good things to say "hey dude, what's up, *you're the goods* etc, I think Sara was the goods, but she's with me, *so were the goods*, Any time, I looked at her, she was smiling and looking right in my eyes, like I just saved her from the evil villain. Guys were hitting her like bumper cars and bouncing backwards and sideways away. I took Sara home so we could start a nice little relationship.

We had sex… The kind you read about, She was loud… so loud, John was outside the room "A hem, Ahemm, I could hear him. However, at this time, I am in a place that Ahems don't bother me. I'm almost there, And finally I yelled, "Almost! One second YEAH! Oh Yeah. Ahh what? Oh sorry, did I wake you up? We'll be quiet now. Gnite"

And then I was down for the count, with that really big smile I've been talking about. The next morning, I felt like a super star, She was there, naked, and on her stomach. I gently slid my hand all over her back side, feeling her curves, and kissing all over her back and bottom. She had to feel as good getting them, as I was giving them. Kisses that is.

I had no choice we had to start all over again and I held off for over an hour. She must have felt really good about it because we showered and went out for breakfast I couldn't even spend a dollar if I tried but she had plenty of "ones".

We decided to spend the day in Revere. Later that day we went to Kelly's she wouldn't let me spend any money there either.

We finished our Kelly's, she had roast beef, and I had a burger. We had ice cream and walked the beach. I notice a lot of guys around here; recognize her from the strip joint. They all want to say hello. *I am not going to let myself get too serious.* Some of these guys, l wouldn't even make eye contact with any other time. From big bad bikers, to really creepy looking dudes. Quite a few ladies looking her way too, I haven't spent anytime in Revere except at the strip joints. Eating and walking has made me tired, Coffee doesn't sound good right now so I decided on Tea. We went to Dunks. The Dunkin Donuts in my area has a bunch of cute chicks running around. Here, they are older *foreign woman*

The woman looked at me and loudly said "Malp you?" I looked at her twice and said "what did you just call me?" She leaned off to the side to make eye contact with the person behind me and said "Malp the next person?" I said "You just want to Malp everyone don't ya?" *Oh may I help you? I was able to make the translation*

She decided to continue waiting on me. I asked for a Tea with milk and two sugars, *I happen to be looking at the cookie selection* as she said "Cookie bags?" I said "yeah, ah, two chocolate chip, and an oatmeal raisin" She appeared to be angry, she held the cup in one hand, and two tea bags in the other and repeated Cookie bags!, I said Oh *two tea bags yah, Ill take the cookies too though.* I have to get used to another language? I am in another town now.

We enjoyed our treats at a near by park and relaxed the rest of the day. That night, I was able to see her in her own play ground. We went to the lounge. Everyone there knew her, and I had the opportunity to discover she *likes drugs*, *Coke* was her thing. I am not impressed by drugs so I slipped out an hour or so after we arrived. I was too tired and freaked out to go anywhere.

So, *half buzzed*, I went to Dunks in Lynn, Some regulars were there, and some late night regulars. I just hung out, with *regular coffee and regular conversation*. It's surprising how many women come in to *juice up on coffee* that late. They are dolled up like their going dancing. I think a caffeine buzz combined with drinking makes me talk way too much and think too much

When I stop and think about it I am not really a dog, I was just paying Marie back. When I am in a relationship I want to have a mindset free of worry. Now, I only care about the truth, trust and what branches out from that. Integrity, along those lines I guess drugs are a huge turn off for me too. *People smoke weed and that bothers me* but not as much as other drugs. It's like a switch. I turn off as soon as I know someone does drugs. *I am so hyper* at times, people ask me *if I am on drugs*, "Just life baby" Is my answer some don't believe me, and they are convinced I am on something, Sara never mentioned it but, thinking back, I was hyper and having a great time being me. She probably, thought I was "coked out." Oh well, I wont be falling in love with her.

We are all human, we like to know we are good looking, or were liked by other humans, whatever reasons it just makes you feel good. I get turned off now, so easy. Is it Maries fault? I go from one girl, to the next. When I am out with John, he says "*I see your fuck tumor is going off again*" I look at the woman, he asked me one night, If I knew how many guys were in the place? I said "I don't know two?" He replied "Brian there were seven guys and five girls. And all the people that work there. I am beginning to think I just won't find the right girl, and I am getting tired of all this sleeping around shit. It was great at first, but some people look better with *clothes on* and some of these ladies that act like, they have *some great prize* we are working towards. They should really be happy that the *interest* is there, because many times that *great prize* was a *huge let down.*

I never viewed myself as a "single" guy. I can be happy just being myself and being by myself. The thing I feel is… that I am supposed to be a family man. To be that way it takes two very special people. I cannot find that in the woman I have met. I know all about me and my sense of commitment and that makes me feel special. I think maybe I am too picky? I decided to ease off woman and hang around more with Frank.

Frank is a great guy but some people think he's gay. I try to keep a distance because; I don't want to be thought of as gay, *just because we hang out*. He is a little guy and has feminine qualities at times. He talks like a man and really bitches when he sees a guy *act like a girl* he says things like "Yeah, ok faggot, keep it in the fuckin closet," So he is hard to read. I think if he's going to be gay, it hasn't happened yet. He doesn't like woman that think they "their shit don't stink". He bitches about them too. He isn't afraid to let them have it…. Once, a chick cut in front of him in a line while we were waiting for tickets then she just smiled like she had the right or something. He loudly said "What the fuck, just because you have a pussy you think; you can do what you want? Get in the back of the fuckin line! What do you wipe, back to front, or front to back?" She said "*side to side*, faggot." I just laughed, If I said something like that, she would have said something much worst, I think. Then again, I don't think, I would ever talk like that. I did enjoy watching Frank talk to her like that. He mouthed off at one woman, and her boyfriend was behind him. Frank apologized that day. It was still a lot of fun, watching these hot shot asshole broads get taken down a notch. He seems more feminine when he's bitching.

He loves sweet nice girls; in fact he gets along great with all people that *are down to earth...* period. Frank has a coupon book. We usually go half on the two for one deal 50/50 on buy one get one free.. We go where ever the coupons send us. We could eat in Marblehead or On Newbury St in Boston, without the book we would end up at Wendy's. One New Years Eve, we went to "By George" in Boston; the wait staff was delivering *complimentary champagne to all the tables*. Frank asked the waiter about our bottle he told us they ran out. Three bottles were brought to other tables within the next ten minutes. Frank was pissed. He said "No Champagne huh, Order anything, and add a lobster to the meal *fuck em watch this*," He ordered Duck and filet Mignon; I had Filet Mignon and Lobster with all the extras. Frank was very pleasant, and added a touch of sophistication. We enjoyed the meal, had chocolate moose, and one final drink and we casually got up walked past the Madre D, Who thanked us and asked for us to return soon. Frank said *"Why thank you and happy New Year,"* We got to the exit, and ran *down the street so fast, Frank got stomach pains. I was laughing so hard, my sides hurt. "No fuckin champagne for me, but the bottles kept coming, fuck them. Thanks for the free food assholes" He was still angry for an hour after*. He is fun and means well.

Frank has money, however, all it takes is rubbing him the wrong way and well his meal is free. No matter where we eat, if something wasn't right with the service "A bitchy waiter or waitress" I prepare for the escape. He usually says "dine and dash?" The very second he feels the attitude. If his food wasn't cooked right he is *very understanding* just don't give him attitude. I like his way of thinking but I thought my stealing days were over. I was laughing, and telling Dad about *By George*, He said "you're lucky you didn't get caught, you could end up before a Judge who will say "Well I hope you enjoyed your meal," as he sends you to jail." I was like, "yeah, I know Dad, I know" "Top *of the hub* has the right idea, the wait staff only bites into their tip here. The only way out is *in the elevator*. We only ate here once. I could picture the news reporting live from a restaurant near you. (" It seems a local man has taken a *two for one deal* a step further, and has made it a *two for none* deal. Local merchants are *not cleaning up* and wondering why. And what motivates this *dashing diner*? And what can be done, to prevent the distaste in the mouths of these merchants? And help pass the gas brought on by this brazen act of eating on the run. Live at Pewter Pot *Almabetradenm Piktyuesdre*, news 12 Boston)

I have an idea; tell the *help* to leave the fuckin attitude at home. We all have problems. If I am trying to enjoy a meal that I am expected to *pay my hard earned money for* I don't need to be treated like a *second class citizen*. The *courts have that covered,*

In fact, Joe told me today, that I was hired to work on a contract, doing office moves at General Electric. The move is complete. I am no longer needed. Oh boy, I am not going back to court. Ill just get a job and continue to pay the amount already established. Around tax time, I discovered this was a big mistake. I got a *refund* of $2500.00 The DOR *intercepted it.* They reported that based on the amount of my pay increasing. I should have *gone before the Judge* to have my support increased. Therefore the *refund will go to Marie* as back support. I also have to go before a Judge now to have it modified upward now. I wonder what she will buy for my children. Cigarettes? Booze? Drugs? Ah, I know, a new leather Jacket and boots for her biker boyfriend. And then she will say thanks for the *Bonus.*

50
Outside paying in

The new job is in Salem at
Vincent's Potato Chips, I am the receiver,
it's a noisy dirty job but I like it a lot. The
building has a truck lift, it picks up a tractor
trailer truck and the raw potatoes roll out,
it's very loud, the potatoes hit a big bucket
called a hopper, Then, they are brought
across a conveyor belt, into a stone
separator, then they move to a peeler it is
more like long grinding wheels. They are
sent to a wash bucket, and then a slicer and
finally into the frying oil. I operate all the
belts, hoppers, peelers, slicers, and maintain
the flow.

It starts at 630am, production stops
at 4pm, the cleaning ends at 630 pm Heavy
duty cleaning is on Saturday morning 6am
to 130pm. That's how I had the extra pay.
Extra hours, No matter, *Marie and her biker
boyfriend*, I mean, "my children" are entitled
to the extra pay, not me, when I go to pay
the support I am met at the door and not
invited in. I can go to court and ask for more
rights. I need a lawyer that costs money and,
if I get those rights. I could be *killed*. I
should just work and *be happy that I am
able to help the poor girl.*

She is a *single Mother you know.*
The fact that her brother, and a biker live
with her, and contribute financially, do not
matter. The Murder and threats are different
issues they have nothing to do with my
obligations… so I just pay my money and
shut the fuck up. I wonder what the kids
look like and how are they? Well, maybe
someday Ill know. If not, Well then that's
just too fuckin bad I should just shut the
fuck up and pay, or go to fuckin jail. This
can go on for over 20 years. I am sure that
the children have some of my DNA, so they
have *the potential of going to College.* Her
DNA will lower the GPA… As students the
support will continue.

What if I do actually meet someone?
And we have kids, what happens then?
Maybe, I should just stay far away from
woman now, work hard, and try to put as
much money away as I can.

If you tell the truth in court, *anything
you say can and will be held against you!*
I was asked to list my savings. The support
worker said "You have that much! And your
children's Mother had to go on welfare. You
are going to have to pay that welfare back."

I thought "Oh, ok, maybe, I should just slit
my fucking wrist. It's better than giving
Miss Mayonnaise's *all my money.*

It's better than Jail. Send me to Uncle Ed that's an idea. I work 65 hrs a week.. and I am 19, in my third year of 40 plus hr weeks.. just because, I tried to do the right thing. I have the potential of being a real shit bag. Hmm If I have to go to jail, I should make it worth my while. I am a *second class citizen* now, and in the eyes of the law, Mayo girl is first class all the way. *She owns me now*, just because the *lid wasn't on her jar one night*."

I know the system is trying to do the right thing for *children*. But they should make sure all the facts are there. As a Father I should have different consideration. Especially under these circumstances, each case is unique *The support and interceptions are leaving me broke. I try to work more hours for more money. Marie is reaping all the benefits from it. I should work under the table. The DOR will have no record of what I make and I can get ahead. I haven't been able to save lately. Lucky, I live with my brother. I pay for food now and my car and cigarettes. I don't have money to go out and I'm too tired to go anyway.* I toy with all these thoughts for months. One day while dropping off my payment I notice Marie is wearing a Maternity top. Hmm, Is a tiny little biker dude in there? Ha, Ha, Ha, Good, it's not my problem. I thought "We" couldn't afford another child.

We couldn't afford a Spanish one.
Marie and Jay the biker can easily afford
one with the money I give them and welfare
and his drug sales. *He just bought a new
Harley ya know.*

I passed him in my $200. Shit box.
The sun reflected off all his chrome and I
was blinded for a second. I have to reflect,
and believe that someday it may all be ok. I
mean, I should think about people that love
me and don't want to hurt me, I have friends
and family, my health. It can always be
worst. I know that. I just don't think it's fair.
I have been fucked over since, I was five.

That's fifteen years of shit that
keeps piling up. What have I done to
deserve such a tough time and when is it
going to change? It has to get better
sometime.

Who knows what the future holds?
I have moments that I am knocked so far
down. And I am able to climb back. Family
and friends are such a treasure. Monday
nights are tougher now. I am always tired..
because I have so many hours at work. I get
up at five in the morning, I am not a
morning person and add beers to that.
Tuesdays at work I am usually grumpy.

I wonder if it shows. I get along great with everyone at work.

I guess my attitude about the hours and support has gotten to some of the people here. My Boss told me I seem grumpy sometimes. I told him Ill try to be happier. I tried for a couple of weeks.

We are moving into winter months, and when that happens, you add an extra truck load of potatoes each day and store them. Now, I am going crazy all day. I got yelled at and decided to yell back for a change. I blew up at a coworker. I figured I will be fired for that so I just walked out the door.

51
I have Potential

For about a year, John has been
telling me to work with him in the State.
I keep telling him, *I don't want to work
around crazy people*. He says they aren't
crazy they are "developmentally delayed."
They are like kids. And they need help
trying to do what we do all the time, and we
take it for granted.

I decided to go with him one day
just to see what it was like. The campus had
a Main hospital and houses. John worked in
a house. I visited the house and noticed the
clients were really great; they were regular
humans but they were somewhat slow in
some aspects of life. They all have
individual personalities and unique qualities.
I liked it, so I applied. It took two
interviews, And I got the job.

I was assigned to the second floor
unit. My clients have more needs. I was
assigned to work in a behavioral unit. I
began training.

We trained with limitations, like blind folds, wheel chairs, Non verbal communication. Etc It was intense and gives you an entirely new perspective of the needs of other people. And your own appreciation of the things you have.

I went over each client's profile, and I became familiar with everyone in my unit. Each person has an individual service plan. Specific to each individuals needs, I learned a lot and I had an ambition to do well. Not too long.. just a few months into the job. I became very good at what I did and I was promoted to an entry level supervisor position

I began training new staff and scheduling, giving input to "The team" Of care givers from social workers to nursing.

When I go to Dunks I tell Frank about all the things that happen like clients "going off" what we did to correct the situation. I didn't stop there; I began telling everyone I know. Like my sister Amy, she is one of those book smart people. I figured I am increasing my vocabulary and maybe she won't search for difficult terminology to use while we verbally interact, she loves talking in a way.. that can make you feel really stupid.

Grampy McGee thinks I am nuts, He said "You *don't want to work around crazy people all day eventually, it rubs off on ya,*

He is a bus driver and wants me to get my Bus Operators license, he is also close to retiring and He has a really cool belt buckle with a bus on it.

He said "get that license and I have something I want to give ya" I'm pretty sure it's that buckle. He's had it for years. He decided to call a friend at a training bus company, and I can train early mornings, this way I can keep my regular job, its second shift anyway. I can have something to fall back on

I wonder what my kids look like now. I wonder if my oldest still likes the "he - man" toys. I guess it doesn't matter, as long as I pay her that money that is really what counts in life, well in my life. Maybe Ill just get licensed, and work only as needed. I was thinking of doing weekends, and times off my regular job, but its not going to benefit me in anyway.

Bus companies will train you in hopes that you will drive school runs for them. Once you're licensed you can work anywhere.

It's the same as a class B truck driver license, So having the license will open up some doors. The licensing course is like *drivers Ed in a long yellow car*. It takes a few weeks. I took the course and I got my license. I starting taking trips like athletic runs, Science museum, casino trips, water country, Canobie Lake; *I never went to these places as a kid.* The first time I saw a circus I was 19yrs old.

I continued working with the State and that's going very well. I look at these "charter jobs" as *weekend getaways*. It's not too different from The State. You have to keep a bunch of people from going off.

On the bus I say "*Keep your heads and hands inside the bus*" very loud and clear. From that moment on.. it's a quiet ride. The quiet is important, those buses have a lot of mirrors for a reason, you need to see and hear everything. You're responsible for the safety of 60 plus people at the same time. At my regular job, I have to be very patient and work a process watching cues and working in steps. I use some of what I learned from both jobs in each of these positions. What it boils down to is setting firm limits and continuing to be a nice person. *Kindness goes a long way.*

To me, that's just common sense anyway. The funny thing about the bus runs, I am going places and doing things, I would never have the chance to do. When I know we are taking a bus run to a beach, I pack a bag. I'm not there to smoke cigarettes with old guys, while having coffee in the hot sun.

Your there, you might as well enjoy it. I *think of it as a reward for all my hard work.* I had a two week Bus Run that brought me to a country club every day. I took vacation time from the State and went to a pool every day. I had the best tan of my life, even better than when I lived in Georgia.

Once… I had an all *girl college booze cruise run.*

I am their age and being hit on by a few of them. They were trashed. I probably could have had some fun. But it's my job and my license so I just enjoyed the attention and the fun.

Having 60 drunken college girls just playing around for the night was wild enough. I saw more than enough. It just confirms that men and woman are no different. Were all pigs given the right circumstances.

52
At first sight

Another funny one to me was Disney on Ice. I drove *the characters* to and from the hotel. It was awesome, watching them skate flawlessly.

When they stepped off the bus they looked like cats walking across a freshly waxed floor woo ho woo. They were very nervous you can't blame them they have precious ankles but to see them look that way it was a *behind the scenes treat.*

The chance to meet famous people on the bus was always there. Famous football player's, celebrities, *it's the world walking right through your door.* The fall foliage and Christmas lights runs were other cool times. I would wash all the windows on the bus even if it was just cleaned. The reflections of the lights and colors were just as cool as the direct view.

I worked both jobs for about a year. The state job began taking up so much of my time. I couldn't handle both.

On my off time, I basically hung out with Frank. One night, we were in Denny's I was bitching about the women I had dated in the past. As we sat there I noticed a very pretty girl with her friend. *I said to Frank "why can't I meet a nice girl?" I pointed and said "look at her, she's been smiling the whole time, she seems very happy just to be hanging out. You can tell she is easy going, and has no motives. Girls like that wouldn't give me the time of day." Frank said "Ok go tell her you're in love, and you want to take her home" I said "I have to go talk to her. Be right back" I talked to her for a few minutes, at first you could see she was taken back for a second. But she gave me her number. I will call her tomorrow for certain.*

Frank just fluffed it off *"ok Brian is back he is looking for numbers"* I said "Hey Frank ya ever hear of love at first sight? He said *"Yeah every time I'm around you"* I said "No really" Yeah ok Bri whatever"

She had beautiful eyes, tight wavy curls, she smiled often, and when she does, her eyes smile.. This must happen a lot.

Because, the shape around her eyes had permanent little smiles.

The image of her face is the only thing on my mind. I can't wait to call her.

I called the next day, "Is Becky there?" I asked, "This is Becky" she answered. *I had a feeling she was too good to be true and there was just a chance that she may have given me the wrong number.* No, she gave me the right number and she was hoping I wasn't just trying to get her number, and then maybe never to call.

It seems to me we were both hoping to hear from each other equally. Right then, I felt strangely connected to her. We decided to get together and spend some time getting to know each other. We went to Salem for our first date *Salem Willows*. We had so much fun; we even got the 50 cent strip of pictures. We played video games walked the beach, ate fried dough and most importantly *we laughed so hard all night.* It was natural and carefree happiness…. just because we were together.

A day or two later, I woke up and saw a piece of paper on my windshield. I picked it up and it simply said "*Just passing by thought Id say hi*" A huge smile grew over my face.

I haven't stopped thinking about her, and she is thinking about me, when I'm not around and she isn't afraid to show it. *She wasn't just passing by, she never comes this way.* I have never felt this way, I feel like she is part of me. The best part.

We began spending every minute we could together. We both work second shift, *I would get out of work and drive as fast as I could, to be with her.* Then we would spend hours together the hurry was always over once we were together.

I met her in late October. By the first week of December, I told John, I wanted to ask her to marry me and give her a ring for Christmas. He told me I was crazy, and I should buy her something very nice to show what she means but, I should know her for a year, before I consider marriage.

I didn't agree. I bought her a stereo anyway, she was happy; she already knew what she meant to me. I knew I wanted to be with her all the time.

In March, I couldn't take it any more. I had to ask. When I did, she responded by saying *"It's about time"* We both *expected it to happen in December.* And we both patiently waited.

We knew it was the way it should be. We are made for each other.

I think we *fell in love at Denny's*. I do believe in love at first sight. We moved in together right away. I think her parents were not very happy about that. Hey they were young and in love once too. We had a very nice routine. We had our friends. We both agree on *keeping good people around you*. And avoid the shit bags. I told Becky everything that has ever happened in my life. As to the children, on our first date I had to *drop off a support payment*.

I told Becky, that *I believe at least one of the children are mine*, even though I was told *their not my fuckin kids anyway*.

Becky still loved me for who I am, with no surprises. We continued to grow together. We both had good jobs, Becky changed from fast food to an Auto dealership.

We had a cute little apartment we got two cats. We had the support of everyone we knew. My father thinks the world of her. *I think he likes her more than he likes me.* This is exactly where I have been waiting to be. *Becky is my dream, come true.* I have been waiting all my life for her.

Sometimes, I would look at her and say "What do you see in me?" I couldn't imagine how she saw "the me" I wanted the *love of my life* to see.

I figured she would have had to go to the ends of the earth and back to realize the depths of my soul, yet, she sees it. And I see hers, we are soul mates. She has never had any trauma or tragedy in her life. That explains the smiles.

Becky really *celebrates the Irish* in her. I thought she would love Grampy McGee, The first time she met him, He had asked me about the buses, So I told him I did get the license, and I'm looking into going full time. He said "Good, I have something I had on my bus, and I want you to have it, so you can keep it on your bus."

He held up a *sawed off baseball bat* with leather wrapped around it, and nails were sticking through the leather. Then he said " *If anyone gives you any shit or even looks like they want to play fuckin games, show them this they'll think twice about fucking with you"* I was shocked and said " Grampy, Ill go to jail, just for owning something like that" He said "suit yourself, Its always worked for me"

I wondered what Becky thought of old Gramps now? She was surprised... I think *she looked to the situation as a television moment*. A real life cartoon, Luckily Gramps can seem silly when he does things like this. She did like Gramps. I let her know he was a tough guy when he was younger. Aside of that, he was his usual playful happy Irishman self. *He is a lovable guy once you get to know him.*

I met her grandmother "Nan" she reminds me of Grammy Boober. Its too bad Becky didn't meet her. Becky and I *have the same respect for elders.* The respect she has for her parents is much like my respect for Dad. It seems Becky looks towards the world and life in the way I do. We really were *looking for each other.* Now that were together, we have a start to the future in the way we both wanted. I don't want any change in the way we feel. *We are two young people that are in love, the way it's supposed to be.* I wake up every day and look at her and I want to say thank you. She wakes up adjusts her eyes and looks at me as if *I am the morning Sun,* her smile adds to the beauty on her face.

It doesn't matter if its cold, raining, snowing or too hot.. to us, the *days seem like sunshine and it's around the mid seventies.* Every day I realize, if I had to wait twenty more years to meet her it would be worth the wait. No doubt, I talk about young love and happiness.. but to be with someone you feel such a connection… it goes to the depths of your soul.

Once you feel that connection you are no longer individual, you have another half I hear some folks say "hey where's your better half?" I feel my better half is right here with me… she is in all of my thoughts and feelings.

As I went through life talking advice from *that "little voice" in my mind*, I knew *I had my mind and it was my friend.* That little voice wants to consider Becky as much as it's considering me now. To feel the happiness for a day or two is a treat, to feel this happiness everyday is a blessing, And to know my other half feels the same is pure Heaven. *I am building my future; it's full of excitement and electricity.*

We like to see Nan on Sundays for a big dinner; Becky loves Nan so much she wants to *be like her* when she gets older.

Becky doesn't care about money or material things, she wants the wisdom that a *good life delivers* as you blossom through your family and the people that help you grow in life. To be established as Woman that faced "many years of life and can look back with a *positive and thankful* view." Nan is smart and loving and she looks forward to her family. She thinks I could use a few pounds, but she would *never* tell me that. She is worried though. Becky just tells her, "He has to slow down a little, and then, He will fill out. I think Becky has the beginnings of the wisdom she is hoping for. She just doesn't know it yet. She has the biggest heart.

We spend Sunday evenings with Dad and Elaine, *Becky is not so impressed with Elaine*. She knows I have reasons not to care for the woman. Becky is finding her own reasons *she tries to see the good*. She loves Dad; Becky looks forward to hanging out with him. Dad is very smart, and when Becky is around, He acts like he's *quite intellectual*, Then he asks "*You ever play Jeopardy Beckidy?*"

We laugh when he slips like that. Around her he does, and he tries to act like it never happened. *We usually order pizza and have a few beers.*

I continue to have Mondays with John and Dad. Becky has Thursdays with her Mom. Becky has two other sisters at home with her Mother and father. They are a close family, Becky is the oldest. We are growing together at a wonderful pace. The way we feel now is like *our lives have woven in with the past and the future*. Becky can see a picture or even hear a song that relates to a young boy and she instantly has an image of me. *It's like she's been with me all along.*

Becky is working on wedding plans with her Mother. I am trying to do good things for my clients. I am beginning to feel *some stress from work* and I don't want that to create any stress for Becky, if I have to change careers to keep the harmony in my life, I will. Keep good people in your life is one part, keep *good feelings* in life any way you can. I look to my elders, and I notice they only speak of the *good things in their lives*.

They talk about so many wonderful memories. You have to think that over so many years the wisdom and the happiness they talk with, is what *they use to keep high spirits*. Nan is a good example of this. My Grandparents were too

Whenever Nan wanted to tell us a story *she got prepared* it was a quick wipe to the table adjusting her glasses making sure she had our focus, then she would let it out. *Enlighten us with her memories. She proudly shares*; we are honored to be people she wanted to share with.

Separately, Becky and I have had these "moments" from our families all our lives; they always had a place in our hearts. We accepted the experience of our elders as a personal gift of love and affection. Quiet, one to one conversations from people that have seen so many things and they feel the importance of giving a lifetime of knowledge that connects the past to the present. Together, *we are in touch with this knowledge, so much we feed off of it.* We haven't even married yet. However, we have plans for our children.
We want them to be the best they can be. We will give them the best life we are capable of no matter what; we will always give them the gifts that have been given to us our knowledge and experience, with patience and understanding. We have so much ahead of us our minds are racing. *We have dreams.*

Dad he loves his Sundays, We called him one Sunday and told him I wasn't feeling too good. So we couldn't make it. I could hear all the excitement leave his voice.

He just wanted his moment. *It's his moment*, as well as ours but as you get older you have a *better appreciation for those moments*. Life gets so busy we sometimes seem like we just don't care or like we don't want to be bothered. Its human and it happens. *I stop and think of the water drops on the leaves. Then, I call someone, it could be Dad, It could be John. I could say "Hey Beck, Have you talked to your mother lately?" It reminds me of all the little things we forget to see.*

Becky has tuned me into wind chimes; And art, she is also an artist, that's her personal choice. And it's done in her personal moments. She includes so much detail, every line every shade, every brush of the hand in her art work is applied with depth of thought. She will not be satisfied with any drawing or picture *unless it speaks with all the things she was thinking as it was done*. She pays so much attention to detail, we stood over thousands of clovers one day, and she looked down and said "Oh," Then pulled up a four leaf clover, not once, not twice but on three different occasions.

We want the same things *a lifetime of little memories* that we can talk about when were older; we want them to be special and happy. We want to share with our children things that were shared with us. We want them to have the same great appreciation. There is too much negative in life we want to grow off this positive energy that happened the day we made contact. *All it took was one tiny spark.* We are fueled for a lifetime. I have the feeling she is bringing out more sensitivity than I already had.

53
I fight authority

I love my job… and my clients make me feel like *I am someone they can count on* to be there when they need a little something of a reliable asset. One day… I had a magazine, A client "Tim" pointed at the back and became excited.

(He is non verbal… he can be non compliant and assaultive. Usually, from the frustration of trying to communicate, he is really just a teddy bear with a big loving heart so big when things are good he wants hugs, sometimes a little too many, but that is something that can be corrected in time.)

The backside of the magazine had a picture of a dunk in donuts coffee. I asked Tim if he wanted dunk in donuts coffee. He sure did. I went on my lunch and got him a decaf. He sat down and drank it while giving me an occasional pat on the hand. *Letting me know it was a very nice treat*. I got an Idea.

I went around searching for pictures of anything relevant to him. I put all the pictures together; it had toothpaste, people he knew, cars, water, anything I could imagine. I posted it on the wall and called it *Tim's communication chart.* It worked, he met all of his objectives, He had zero assaults, he actually began sounding out parts of words, and He is *thirty years old* and has never made sounds unless frustrated.

The chart work very well. It enabled Tim to go out on a *one to one* trip to the coffee shop. Due to his previous assaults he was not a candidate for a community trip, *especially one to one.* He had been in many physical restraints some escalated to that point just over the fact that somebody didn't understand what he was trying to say. It could have been a belly ache.

His annual review came up and I was his direct care representative. The Director of the facility ran the meeting, she presented his "team" with his objectives and how they are met. And what plans should be placed to meet those objectives or what he needs to have new objectives. *The team* consisted of Doctors, Nursing staff, social workers psychologists and caregivers; a legal guardian was also present. About three minutes into the meeting…

I was asked to present my *doctorate or available educational degree or equivalent work experience.* The one that allowed me to make my own determination on the proper care required for this individuals needs - because I went ahead, and devised the communication chart (without the need for the *team* or the direction from the team).
Without any idea what consequences can result from such behavior? This could be disastrous.

I was taken off the unit, the chart was destroyed and his medication was to be increased. I was beside myself. I was told that I will be demoted, and I am lucky I wasn't charged with abuse for my actions. Later that day the Social worker Bill said "hey if we fix every one just like that… we won't have any jobs left."

I sat in the parking lot, Marc, the principle psychologist was near, and He was looking around his car.

I asked if he was ok, He said "I saw a cat go under the car; I wouldn't want to start the car and hurt the thing." He added "Why do you think they do that?" I paused and thought for a second.

I was going to say "Well *they are curious and as your vehicle cools down it makes ticking sounds drawing their attention and they seek out the noise and wait, it's the animals hunting instinct*"

I simply said "*I don't know maybe their fuckin retarded*" I knew, I was very upset about what occurred in the meeting. Marc was there, *he knew too*. I want Becky to be proud of my accomplishments and I don't want to put any stress in our home life. A few days later, I was on a new unit. A senior staff person gave me a credit card and told me "I had to go to Kmart and spend as much as I could, buy a stereo, furniture, clothes." I asked why, She told me the clients name and said "He has too much left in his account, If we don't spend it in the next few days He will get less with the new budget." *He is also deaf and has everything he needs* I said "He obviously doesn't need that much, so why should we waste money that can go elsewhere?" She became hostile and told me to just do what I was told.

As I walked though Kmart I decided that I wanted no part of it. I did what I was told I made a purchase; I bought the deaf client a walkman. When I returned I showed him how to use it. *He walked around smiling with his new headset.*

I was written up for "Violating his human rights and mocking his handicap" to make matters worst my response to the written warning was "WHAT?" I continued to work on the unit. I began getting stomach problems. I called in sick and started using personal time. I finally got to the hospital to be checked. The doctor told me. I had an *acute ulcer*. I didn't think it was cute at all.

I am about to marry the woman of my dreams. Its perfect and I can't let anything interfere. I would shovel shit if I have to. I am proud of my accomplishments but, I *realize I am not the type of person that can work here*. I resigned, just three weeks before the wedding. Then, I went to a local bus company to work *as needed* until after the wedding.

At that time… I can work a permanent schedule. John maintained his position at the facility. He told me *I rattled the wrong cages*. And no matter what I did… the ultimate goal was to force me to want to leave. He's seen it before. I miss the high points in the job, but I lost *the feeling at that meeting* and had time to accept the changes. My future in mental health was done. I've got big plans… my *future* is working… on "her" wedding plans.

When we were choosing the Church, Becky asked what I thought, I figure with her asking me maybe it didn't matter *where* to her as much as *why*. I suggested "My Church" Saint Mikes, It was where I was baptized, Received first Communion, Conformation and now Holy Matrimony. We went to talk with the Priest, *He didn't seem very interested. I was not very familiar to him. It has been sometime, since I was present in Mass.*

We called Becky's Church; The Priest was very happy and helpful. He suggested Marriage classes due to our ages. We are young. She was nineteen and I was twenty one. We told him we are ready. The classes were informative and reminded Becky and I about the commitments we are making. We really just sat with him and developed a friendship; I think he wanted to *know who we were as a couple*. We wanted it even more now

54
It's so electric

We are ready and everyone we know and love is going to be with us to *celebrate our union*. I couldn't feel any happier about what is going to take place. And then as I began walking up the steps to the Church I had to stop….

And I realized, I had been here before, and *my life was "paused" for a few minutes. In a very dramatic way at the time, I wondered what connection I had, to Saint Joseph's church. I figured it was My Mother stopping me for a look.*

With the biggest smile on my face I continued on, to *begin the Life* I have been searching for. September 27th 1986 In front of the people we care about our family and friends We made our vows and for the very *first time in my life* I knew with all the confidence in the world, I was about to make a *promise I can keep* " I Do"

Then I kissed my Bride.

Together the electricity that surrounds us is felt by everyone. I have been to weddings they were all very nice. Ours was filled with so much excitement it was a true celebration of two hearts.

Even relatives that were on the rocks had a rebirth of affection. I guess Elaine invited Uncle Ed, *I wouldn't have, I hardly noticed.* Frank was my best man. He got every ones attention, When he did… he unfolded a piece of paper that was a big as a bed sheet and he said

" *I wrote a little something for Becky and Brian, and we would wish them all the love, but you know they have that, I just want to say may their troubles be little ones, and may their little ones be no trouble at all"*

Then we drank the toast and everyone applauded. We danced and went through the entire ceremony without a care in the world, At the very last minute even more electricity was felt, Becky's mother and Uncle Ed both " *Pulled a kibby"* As John calls it, *they both had seizures.* I think it was from the toast for Becky's Mom. We waited to find out if Becky's mother was ok, we were told she will be fine; *she started a medication and was not supposed to have a drop of alcohol*, not even the toast.

She should be fine. I knew that, but Becky was very upset. After the air cleared we headed to our hotel in Danvers. We took route one through Peabody, Our car had all the signs *just married: Becky and Brian written all over it.*

At the Peabody line the State Police had a sobriety check point set up. We stopped Becky was still visibly shaken. The Trooper asked if I had anything to drink tonight. *I thought to myself is this fuckin moron real? I said "Of course I did! I just entered into the religious sacrament of Holy Matrimony with the person I want to share my entire life with! Who doesn't toast to that?!"* Luckily another Trooper might have thought *"Is this fuckin moron for real?"*

He pulled the other trooper aside and allowed us to go and congratulated us and sent us on our way. Becky was so *upset about her mother*; she looked terribly sad and worried. We had a night cap, and we held each other until we fell asleep. Becky seemed better in the Morning. Our plan was to go to the hospital to see her Mother before we headed out on our honey moon. Aunt Marion gave us the use of her cabin in Maine for the week.

We wanted to explore country roads in the peak of the foliage, and maybe take a small plane tour over New Hampshire and Maine. We also love North Conway and the Kangamangis Hwy. Becky was pleased to see her Mother was laughing about the incident. Becky's father thought his wife was trying a new dance, he wasn't afraid to give us the repeat performance.

With our spirits brightened, we headed out to begin the first days as Mr. and Mrs. It must have been a time for *Becky's and Brian's* we had a Nissan and we noticed a ford mustang with the same exact writings, somewhere in New Hampshire, We hope they are *as happy* as we are.

Our first year together was *sheer bliss and totally uneventful*, we had a normal life and it feels like this is what it's all about. Words cannot express that much happiness

55
The woman with gloves

The next year, I was called into court. The courts informed me that Marie has uprooted and left no forwarding address. Any payments I have made will go into an *unwed Mothers fund*. For now, the ongoing payments can stop

I still haven't seen the children. It's rumored that *they went to Georgia or Tennessee and months later she is said to have gone to California.* This is fine with us. The potential of unnecessary Crisis is lowered dramatically. We started to wonder if Becky could conceive. It didn't seem likely.

I have hopes that we will have children together. I can picture what *our child will look like.* A couple of months later we got the good news, we are going to have a baby born out of love! *Without lies, deceit or manipulations* the trust *we have* for each other is what we are growing from.

We began preparing for the baby; our rent was going to double for an additional room. Becky was worried. I told her I would *work five jobs if I have to*. Her trust in me made her feel better. I am still driving buses. At times the driving time gets cut down. And that creates a serious loss in pay. I asked the head Mechanic if he needed someone to fuel the buses between my run times. He was happy to sign me on. It was full time and the pay wasn't really too bad. He asked me one day if I ever did and oil change so *I lied and said of course.* He wanted to make me His PM Mechanic, Preventive Maintenance on the fleet. I started the next day at a higher pay rate. The training Mechanic figured out that I was lost within minutes. He agreed to teach me. And that he did.

It was time for Becky to have the baby; we went to the hospital because her water broke. She wasn't feeling contractions. After she was hooked up to the monitor
I could see the baby's heartbeat was slowing with each small contraction. I asked the nurse if that was normal she looked and told me to *relax Becky is not going to have the baby tonight*. The Nurse will give her a sleeping pill and she should give *me a valium for crying out loud ... as she put it.*

I continued to watch the monitor Becky began feeling the contractions. And sure enough as the line that indicated the contractions raised, the line that indicated the babies heartbeat sank. *I wasn't asking that bitch again.*

I found an older nurse with rubber gloves running down the hall, I stopped her and asked her to look. She appeared *concerned and told me she was going to get the Doctor to double check.* He came in he looked at the monitor and became really concerned, he took a breath and said *"Sir you can wait in the waiting room we are going to prep your wife she will need a C section we'll call you when ready"* I was relieved.

At that time *smoking was allowed in the waiting areas*, I had a smoke and I could hear a baby crying and I remember thinking I wish that kid would be quiet, so I can hear if they call me.

That kid was my little Tiger, Becky was taken in for an emergency C section and it was done because the cord was wrapped around the baby's neck. I was extremely grateful to the woman with the gloves.

I could have shouted out a piece of my mind to *Nurse fuckin know it all.* I was too grateful for my little tiger. He was six weeks early. We were still concerned about the nurse with the sleeping pills and her competence level. *So we are on guard.* The Doctor we chose checked the baby out and said his lungs were under developed and he would need medication. We did have some trust in him. The next day we were told the baby is losing some weight he was 5lbs 4oz he is now 4lbs and 11oz. He will have to stay until 5lbs. That could be a few weeks…..

56
Our Family Strength

Later that afternoon, we were told that the baby will need a *spinal tap* because they saw him move in a way that looked like a *seizure*. I was there; to me it was a *piss shiver*. What fuckin seizure?

They gave him this horrendous procedure, and later told us he is fine it could have been gas.

The next day, a nurse approached us, and told us the *baby has stabilized*, he basically went *into cardiac arrest, from serious blood loss when they did the operation.*

What fuckin operation? I guess our faithful Doctor has a partner and he put our baby on her case load. Even though the baby was premature and had an apparent seizure.

She decided to go ahead and circumcise him. He was going to be in the hospital for a few weeks anyway. They could have waited, I think.

We decided to use Becky's, doctor from her childhood. " Harry" He came in and backed off all the tests and drugs and eventually, he helped the baby adjust to this new life and come home. It was around five weeks.

During that time we moved to a larger apartment.. We wanted to go through a realty company figuring *we wouldn't get screwed*. We met the agent at the apartment we chose and we saw the landlord all was fine. After we got outside I remembered we have cats, I asked him to check and see *if cats are ok*.

Ross was his name; Ross went inside for about two minutes. (The hallway) He came out and said oh yeah *cats are just fine*; we gave him his finder's fee and moved in. The landlord came up to see us a day or so later and saw the cat. He flipped out and said *no fuckin cats in this house*. We had to bring both cats back to the old apartment we asked the neighbor to look after them for a few days. A week later we found out kids were doing *satanic rituals behind the house and hanged our cats. Thanks Ross you piece of shit.*

57
Unexpected road trips

We got adjusted to the new apartment. The lead Mechanic at work has been teaching me everything. From oil changes to engine repair, brakes, front end work, and it's all on buses. The parts used on buses are much bigger and heavier than on cars. So I shouldn't have any trouble if I *choose to fix cars someday*, if the bus thing doesn't work out.

Becky still works part time. She likes to volunteer for things, she is a giving person. She saves box tops and can tops and all sorts of things, for the kidney foundation and cancer society, and various organizations that help people in need. She wants to cut her hair for cancer patients. I tell her she's always helping other people and never asks for anything, I ask what she wants and she says she's already got it.

We are in a good place *bills are paid* we work and have our down time and on good days we load the baby onto the back of one of the bicycles. And we ride around the city and up near the beach. Becky likes riding as much as I do. The baby usually falls asleep a few minutes into it. I guess he likes it. The smell of the ocean air feels good.
It's nice to cruise at a steady speed and enjoy the early evening air. I need days where I can relax with Becky because stress can just drop onto my lap from other areas of my life without any effort on my part.

I haven't had any concerns as far as Marie goes. However, I was told by one of Jimmy's friends that he *used my name in New Hampshire and received a speeding ticket.* I figured I should call New Hampshire State Police to find out.

I called and he did. (Or I did) I spoke with the Trooper that pulled him over. Jimmy was doing over *100 miles an hour in a 55 zone.* The Trooper said he can't drop the citation unless, I go to Berlin NH. To show him it was someone else. I took the day off and went, John came along *in case I ended up in jail. Who knows?* We took the three hour ride.

When the Trooper saw me he said "*It wasn't you, who was it?*" I replied "I don't know." He said "well then *I can't drop it, because you obviously know, who it was. I want his name.*"

This Trooper *forced me to come here for nothing* so he gets nothing, Fuck Him! My intentions were good…. his weren't

I realize now he lied to me. He wasn't going to drop the ticket. He was going to add charges. *Nice abuse of power Asshole!*

I told him someone in the local bar informed me of the infraction. So I don't know who. He said "well then you will have to *return to see the Judge*, I am not dropping it." Great, I thought it's already cost me a days pay, and my gas and time. I get to do it all again. *Jimmy sucks*;

I went to New Hampshire again about 2 weeks later. The Judge read the charge. I said "Not Guilty," I added that *I wasn't even here*. He asked the Trooper if it was me, The Trooper said "No" The Judge dismissed it, but gave *me an attitude when I asked for documentation as evidence… in case I am pulled over or a warrant appears.*

I guess, I was an asshole second class citizen for *not even being there*. It must be my face. I suck in the *eyes of Justice*. I felt like Its heaven on earth and The Gods don't like my face.

I confronted Jimmy; He responded by punching me in the face and ran away like a kid that just pulled a fire alarm. The funny thing was it didn't hurt. I was worried about that for years. Well maybe he didn't get a full swing. Dad is pissed at Jimmy, but Jimmy flips out when he tries to talk to him. They both end up shouting and Jimmy takes off *he is right and everybody else is wrong usually*.

I mean, who am I? To be upset, it's *not like he did me wrong*, it was the Trooper that should be pissed I guess. All I lost was two days pay and the cost of meals and 12 hrs in my car, to correct something he did. I suck for being pissed. *Oh well, Ill get over it*. No big deal. Hey that's what big brothers are for.

58
Always ready for adventure

Now, that... that's behind me, I can
try to live the normal life I am entitled to.
I really am in a great place and my life is
wonderful.

*Every now and then Jimmy rears his
ugly head. But*, I waited so long to have *this
life.* My wife is *all that,* she is everything to
me. I have my baby boy. My smile never
fades. I change his poopie diapers, I burp
him. I say Da, da, da, da, da, da, da, da, da,
and da, all the time, he will say it soon and
you know it. I sing songs to him, I play on
the floor, we nap together, I get a beer and
he gets milk and we watch TV what more
can a guy want? Nothing, Becky has made
me King of the world. You know the saying,
I feel like a million bucks. Well, yeah, why
wouldn't I? At this point, I decided, I want
to be the best I can be. I went and got my
G.E.D. *high school equivalency.* I did live in
a trailer park and the projects so to a *normal
middle class person* this is like getting a
diploma from *community college, it means I
tried later on, but I tried.* "Slow, children"
grow up to be "slow, men at work"

Becky and I spend a lot of time with Cheryl and John, They came to the house *for the celebration*, we had dinner, cake and pictures. I was proud; to know all I had to do was try. I have new dreams; Even though some Cops are shitbags. I always *wanted to be a cop*. I can't take the test without the diploma. I can't get the job without a great score. I have to stop smoking; I have to focus on *the goodness* in my life, and try to see the good in the world. If, I expect to have any more dreams come true. With Becky and the baby in my life, I have so many dreams that feel *ok to dream about* and realize *they can come true*. This is my life, and I have a strong hold on it.

Cheryl and John together, are like us… they have no motives just a simple happy life. We have the family cookouts, we go to pioneer village, and Forest River Park, and they have a daughter and another baby on the way now. We baby sit for them they baby sit for us. It's all good.

John always asks why I want to be a Cop. I tell him *I have seen how things look and to know that's different than how they are*. I think I can have an approach to find the *real truth* and make a lot of changes. Hopefully, it can make a difference for my children. He just shakes his head and laughs. We have different views here.

I like what I do for work. I just want a career in Law Enforcement. Maybe I can establish some fairness in the system based on what is real.

I saw Gail on my way home from work and offered her a ride home. We chatted a little. She told me her Dad (Uncle Ed) Met another woman, she's a nice lady and he is so happy. I'm remember thinking *He is? Good for him, who gives a fuck.*

I said "Well we all deserve a little happiness" She asked me to come in and say hi, I figured… I should eyeball the little woman… the *odor was present*, Not as bad, the place looks less cluttered. There they stood, Uncle Ed and a short blonde woman. He smiled and was very surprised to see me, He introduced his little woman. He talked about how happy they are. I smiled and told him *I know all about that happiness*. I told him I had to get going and I left. I tried not to think too much about it.

As I drove away…. I thought about *"good things come to those who wait"* and my belief in God and how you should try *to find forgiveness*. I will never find forgiveness, not for him. I draw the line there.

I have to search for my childhood, and no matter how hard I look. I am not going to find it. One thing I will not do, is *wish bad things* on someone. I already know bad things will happen in life. I start to wonder if Uncle has had these dreams, and does he feel like I do about his own life. *He was severely injured once from that saw.* Does he follow this hope that there is a God? And is his *life moving in directions based on his thoughts and feelings of that God?* If so, why have our paths just crossed? And now his life has brought him to a better place, Just like mine has.

I am not happy or sad I just wonder. I also fear if his feelings about these things are anything like mine. Will I become a Monster and beat children when I am older? I sure hope not.

We are not alike… we are nothing alike. It is strange that we *met again at this time.* I stopped thinking about these things and returned to my current happy life and I gave my son a much bigger hug when I got home.

The very next day I got a call from Dad; he asked if I heard about Uncle Ed. I said "I saw him yesterday." He said "*Well Uncle Ed had a massive seizure and died this morning."*

Dad was unaware of what has happened in my life with Uncle Ed, so he sounded somewhat saddened and he knew I fell apart at Aunt Ruth's funeral so he asked *if I was going to be ok,* and he tried to speak with comfort in his tone. I am actually in shock.

I think I just witnessed a *wrath of some sort*. And to think the scariest thing is, I *may have been the last thing he was thinking* of when it happened.

I have been to a few funerals; Anyone's loss is a terrible part of life. You can't prepare for these things; you go in with a guarded feeling. I had no idea what I would feel or how I was going to react when I saw his body.

As I stepped in the doorway to the Funeral Home, I was taken by what I saw. Uncle Ed's *kids were laughing and talking like they were celebrating somebody's birthday*. Ann turned towards me and stopped laughing she must have remembered my reaction to Aunt Ruth. She held me and said some comforting words. I told her "I was ok" I went to the Casket to say a prayer.

His body looked no different than I remember as I saw him lying down on his couch.

His hands were not behind his head and in his pants this time that was the only difference. The people in the room remained quiet and as I turned to leave *I was obviously not crying or even affected* so they slowly began chatting with a bit of laughter and eventually returning to the celebration that I had redirected.

The return to the house at Camden St was just a continuation of the celebration. I waited to see if anyone was going to shed a tear for this man. I am mistaken the *little woman* was upset. The kids half heartedly rubbed her back and said "Well he is in a better place now" *and all those kind things.* A better place? He looked more comfortable on his couch. I saw more, than I wanted to see. I left quietly; I was really taken by the actions of his children. That is their father. There should be some sense of sadness in their hearts.

I went to my happy life and got back on track. I noticed an advertisement for a Mechanic with a much higher pay rate. I told my boss, I should apply. He challenged me and told me there is no way, I will get that job *if I did, and he would give me his one week paycheck. I am really going to try now.*

I went to Meineke on RT one, the owner works on cars, with his guys. The work here is different than regular mechanical stuff. "Under car" repairs, In addition to what I already knew this type of work requires strong knowledge of cutting torches and welders. And a real *talent for removing rusted engine studs for the exhaust system*. I told the guy, I am a hard worker, and I learn fast. He won't be disappointed. He hired me, I went back to my Boss and gave notice, I asked him to pay up, and He laughed and asked if I really believed he would give up his pay. I really didn't but, I had to ask. I started a week later. It was not hard the owner was a real professional, He was *not the nicest person to know*, but he was a Genius, when it came to his business. He taught me everything. In time, I could remove a bolt from an engine that was no thicker than a toothpick in the center. I could weld with my eyes closed. All the guys here had equal experience. And expert custom pipe bending, we began doing brakes too. There were five of us. *One could pick up where someone else left off, without having to think.* Without, any turn over in help. We all became friends. At this time, this is the number one Meineke in the country, from what the Owner says. We sure were busy. Becky is going to have another baby. We are saving for a house. *We almost have the down payment.*

I also just got a very large package in the mail.

It's a paternity suit for child support. Marie now lives in New Hampshire;

The State of New Hampshire wants me to pay her $240.00 weekly and $19,886 in arrears.

I told Dad he suggested talking to Elaine's cousin she works for the court and can help me with a lawyer.

This time I would like to establish Paternity.

I haven't seen the children in 9yrs.

I haven't heard anything from them in 5yrs.

59
Penance?

If all the circumstances were ok,
Even if Marie only cheated and that was it

I would have no concerns. *I believe
if my child needs anything I should be
responsible to provide in their upbringing.*
However, my children and I should also
have had *every opportunity to have our own
relationship.* I did some checking on my
own and more than the Murder and the lies
and the fist fights and moves around the
country. And the idea, that Marie made all
the choices regarding our destination. I
found out Marie is going to Marry an
engineer from New Hampshire electric and
my kids already call him Dad. Their
financial situation is more than adequate

They are doing very well. *The
paternity suit is dated on Marie's birthday.*
Wow what a gift. She took off, not me. I am
not as angry about the support. It's the
arrearage. I did what I was told to do.

Becky and I went to see Elaine's cousin. I refer to her as Aunt Bea. She is a middle age Italian woman. *With Becky and me standing there you would think she was Becky's Aunt. They have visual similarities.*

Aunt Bea introduced us to Jack Malone *my new lawyer*; He looks like the guy on mad magazine. She says he is the best. We discussed the cost of the tests and his fee and a meeting time. It was a few days later. I saw Aunt Bea and she went on and on about him. And then she said "Jack asked how *we are related* and she told him through *Marriage*"... and left it at that.

I am paying this man to do *the right thing for my wife and my family*. I hope he has the right thing in mind. I met him alone; he wanted details of the past, so I told him.

He asked me how *Becky feels about the whole thing*. (This is a red flag..)

(Instead of saying *she and I are one and we are pissed*. She knew this could be an issue and she was with me when I paid support payments and wasn't sure of Paternity.)

I said "She's very upset." He set up the Testing and took his fee $2500.00 from "us".

The test results came in and I *am 99.99 percent the father of these Children.* Now we have to go to court and the Judge has to make it legal. In court the Judge approved *the entire amounts.* I panicked! I wanted to *contest the arrears.* That's what I told this man when I handed him his fee!

My lawyer patted my hand and said "Just think of it as Penance" I was SHOCKED what fuckin Penance are you talking about?

He left looking at me as if, *I were the lowest life form in the world.* I went to work, worried all day how Becky was going to feel. I got home and saw she looked upset. I asked what was wrong.

She asked me to sit down. She told me **My Lawyer** called her for a meeting and he told her *not to tell me because he is my Lawyer and can get in trouble for talking with her about my case.*

When he saw her He said "**I am going to help you because Bea is your Aunt**" My specialty is *Divorce law and Brian has to pay this woman a lot of money for a long time. And this will create an awful marriage for you. I am going to help you get out of it.*

Think about it and come see me when you're ready. He thought he was doing Becky's aunt a favor. He figured….. His friends niece has married a real shit bag. Now, I am fuming. I called and wrote the Board of bar overseer's office. And I made the initial complaint.

It became *he said, she said* over the next few months. Basically they determined that *I was angry at my lawyer for not getting me a better deal*. They dropped our accusations.

I decided to go a different route and began writing the DOR and New Hampshire welfare division. The knowledge I had, was that Marie is engaged to an engineer at New Hampshire Electric and she lives on 14acres. *She never needed the Welfare or any additional assistance*. I know she is only tapping another resource.

I will not be able to have any kind of a relationship with the kids. Her fiancé is giving all of them the support they need in everyway. *She has a brand new car two of the kids have brand new cars.*They have cell phones and a very comfortable life. Based on the Law, Child support is required when the financial resources for the children are inadequate. *They are more than adequate.*

The arrears included have me paying $291.00 weekly. I only brought home $535.00 weekly. Now, I only bring home $244.00 a week. I cannot support my family on that. To no avail... I was disregarded and continued to pay everything

After several phone calls, Marie agreed to allow me to meet the kids. We would meet in Newbury, Mass. Just at the New Hampshire border. It was Marie, the kids and myself. We met at Friendly's restaurant. She pulled up in her brand new car. I was surprised my oldest son was bigger than me. *The two younger ones had my eyes*, the middle child looks like Marie, my daughter looks exactly like me with long hair.

My middle son said *"Wow you don't look like what I pictured, I thought you had tattoos and a beard and stuff. Instead you look like a camp councilor*. Marie bragged about my oldest saying he's a straight A college student and the youngest was doing really; well, she will be going to college too.

Then she pointed to my middle son and said *" Him, he's nothing but trouble"* *He steals, lies and smokes cigarettes and when ever I see him, he has a guilty look on his face"*.

I stopped her and said "Maybe he just thinks you're going to blame him for something and that's why he has the look" She said "NO Guilty! That's what he is! She did all of this in front of the children. My son looked horrified. If she was half a person and, if it was true. I figure she would have boosted all the kids, just to show me what I miss out on. We talked a little more; *her negative bullshit was really getting to me*. My oldest son said "Hey at home they usually put a cherry on my ice cream" She said well *your in Massachusetts now don't expect much*. Nasty Bitch!

They got up *leaving me the dinner bill* and she turned and said "*Oh thanks for the car, you pay for it.* I went to a payphone to call Becky and tell her I am ok, She was very worried, Becky knows about the Murder and everything.

I figure I am going to pay this for a long time and I should try to develop a *relationship with my children*. I called and spoke with my daughter. We were doing great.

I heard someone pick up an extension I have *nothing to hide so I continued on*. I told her songs I used to listen to and wonder about them. She asked my all time favorite movie.

I said the "Wizard of Oz", Just then she said "I have to go" she sounded nervous.

Ten minutes later she called back crying and said *"Mom listened to the call and told me I have to move out, and if I think you're so wonderful, I should live with you"* I said "Excellent, I am going to buy a house. Becky and I would love to have you live with us, we already talked about it. She hung up….. *Becky always wanted a daughter.*

Marie called back and said *"Your not allowed to call my kids ever again, and the only visits you will be allowed to have are Monitored!"* Then she hung up.

I guess taking my daughter…. could fuck up *her car payment.*

Becky and I have just had our second child another son. His birth went much easier than our first. He spent two days in the Hospital. Now we are finding the house we want. We figured it would be our home for years to come and it was going to be expensive we decided to get a two family. The rental income will help.

We got a house on Deer Park. Of all places this is where I met Marie. *She lived at the other end.*

With all the bills we have to pay, I really need to work a lot, all my efforts with courts and DOR have failed. I have this arrearage so I can't get tax refunds. They are always intercepted. And then Becky has to appeal to get her portion. I won $1000.00 on a scratch ticket and the lottery had to *forward the payment to New Hampshire*. I got a check that said $0.00 Marie got $1000.00. And with interest and penalties, my original debt, that I have been paying, *went from $19886.00 to $22775.00*

I am doing side jobs, working at Meineke six days, and I shovel snow. And I have no Insurance. The court has ordered that I provide insurance to the children. Welfare should not foot the bill. I have to find a new job that has insurance I can afford. My present employer wants $175.00 weekly for me to have a family plan. That lets me bring home about $70.00 a week. Becky had a boss that *wanted more than what Becky was being paid for*, to put it kindly.

She quit and became a waitress at the Ballard in Saugus. She also started making cakes for their functions. *We are struggling*.

I was able to find a job at a hospital doing repairs, on their delivery truck and maintenance, sometimes backing up the Security team. The pay was the same, *but the benefits were excellent.* I started getting nausea often and a stitch in my side. I brushed it off as stress. *Dad hasn't been feeling good either.* He can't hold down food and he is nauseous. He is scheduled for a colonoscopy.

After the test, it was discovered *that Dad has a blockage.* They will have to do surgery. They went in and found it was a very large tumor but he also had small tumors everywhere. On his liver, small intestine they were all over. Its no surprise, he was on the test sight for the Atom bomb during the Korean War. Cancer was eating him away...

His doctor told us that my father is so sick he will only *survive a few months* they rerouted his intestine to make him more comfortable.

When he woke up from surgery He smiled and said *" I feel like a million bucks"* He was in great spirits... but we knew he is the type of person that wants the truth and he always said he is not afraid of dying.

We asked the doctor to tell him the truth and when he did Dads voice became very soft and broken and he appeared very meek. *I wish we waited now.*

Dad knows his fate. I feel so sorry for him. *He is a good man and deserved to have his golden years,* he fucked up when he was young, but he is not that guy anymore

He is getting sicker by the day. It shows even in his voice. He used to talk loud and clear with a unique manly sound. Now his voice has a squeak and is so soft you have to say "what" a lot. I try to be myself when I am at his house and sometimes he perks up and forgets he is sick for a few minutes. To me that's the best medicine.

Elaine has a way of bringing him back down. One day I had him acting like nothing was wrong we were laughing and just living. Elaine came in and said "John what's going on? You were awful a minute ago and now you're all perked up and laughing" He said angrily *"Thanks, I was feeling fine, for a fucking minute!"* And to make matters worst. John's wife Cheryl has been sick.

She thought she had TMJ well the Doctor did. She actually *has a tumor*. And she is not doing well with the medication. Cheryl has progressive cancer and has only a couple of weeks to live. Becky just told me she is pregnant. I am worried about everything, and I am stressed. I am in no position to help anybody. *My side and my Nausea are worrying me.* I will not see the doctor. For fear that I could be very sick. I notice, when I am at rest, it doesn't feel as bad. So maybe, I am just over worked. I begin to pace myself.

Dad is getting pretty bad now he has good days and bad days. Aunt Marion's daughter is getting married. Becky and I went to the wedding. I sat with Dad and Becky and Elaine and her oldest kids.

Dad went outside for a smoke and Elaine and her kids came close to me at the wedding and said "Your brother John has problems right now and Jimmy is useless *You are going to have to take care of your fathers funeral*"

I was furious! I said "Really, ok, I will get a second Mortgage if I have to, but do you think, I am supposed to take care of that?"

My father is married to this woman and her kids are his step children they own their own business and always go to him for advice but I am supposed to take care of it. Those losers deserve to rot in hell. Happy fucking wedding, I just went outside smiled at Dad and told him I love him.

The night after the wedding... Cheryl passed away. John is doing serious drinking and he leaves his kids with Cheryl's Mother. I guess Cheryl had some major insurance and John will collect some serious cash and not work.

I am feeling so nauseous, all the time, I can eat, and I just have a stitch in my side and an upset belly. I got checked in the ER, they figure it could be a urinary tract problem. I saw a specialist and he gave me sulfur medication. I took my first dose on the night before Thanksgiving.

60
What Now?

The next morning, I got a call from Elaine; she said *"if you want to see your father alive again you need to get here now."* Wow she could have put it another way. I went over… Dad seems barley conscious and his breathing is labored. Aunt Marion Elaine and I stayed with Dad. *He slowly regressed throughout the day.* Around 6pm he passed away.

I went home and told Becky I felt very nauseous and had a cup of hot Tea. Seconds later I vomited. Whatever was in my stomach making me nauseous was also protecting me from pain. The feeling of someone ripping my stomach out from the inside was so intense, I told Becky I had to go to the Hospital.

I can't even remember the drive there but I pulled in backwards to *make it easier and faster to leave.*

I walked into the ER taking *off all my clothes*, it was November yet, I was *sweating profusely*. The nurse asked why I wanted to be seen. I told her about the pain. She asked *where I ate*. I told her it was not food poisoning. I have been sick awhile.

She told me to calm down. And again asked what I ate. I shouted for them to give *me something for pain or get a fucking gun, I can't take the pain*. She laughed, I said I am serious. I told her about the rock on my head years earlier, and that was like a pin prick compared to this. They did some tests and in awhile the nurse came in and said "Oh my god your *white cell count is skyrocketing*" we are going to give you something for pain. But just to take the edge off, so we don't mask the symptoms. I pointed to my stomach and *said all of this hurts there's your symptoms now please give me something for pain.*

The on call surgeon was the same Doctor that treated my father and he knew who I was. He said "Brian I am worried that you could be as sick as your Dad was". Oh boy. I was heavily sedated and had cat scans and blood work and a lot of tests. *I was in and out.* At one point, I began thinking of Becky and my children at home. She has a new baby on the way.

I wasn't able to father my other children. Is it my time? I got up to my knees and said" *Please don't take me now, I promise, I will not take another day for me, Just keep me here for my children"* The next day the Doctor came in and concluded that I have a *severe infection in my prostate* and I will recover with intensive antibiotics and pain medication. He would still like to do a colonoscopy later just because of my father.

Jimmy came to visit. I think he just wanted to get the scoop. The nursing staff asked, *if I wanted to go to my father's funeral in a wheel chair.* I figured I was there when he passed. I said goodbye. What would every one else say, if I was there in a wheel chair. It's not right to be visible at his funeral like that. I know he will understand. I declined.

Becky and the boys came up to see, me they looked so worried. My sister Amy came up and my nephews. I was released after a week. The Doctor told me, it will take a few weeks to feel stronger. My mid section felt like a large bruise. With every step I took.

I was off work for about another week. The Doctor has me scheduled for a colonoscopy for a few days before Christmas.

I told him, I wanted a later one than that. He informed me that it's extremely important. I told him if I find out I have Cancer a few days before Christmas it's not going to be the best thing for my family, just wait a few days after, and let us have Christmas.

I had to sign a release *refusing treatment*, but the test was going to happen on New Years Eve. John got the insurance money and nobody has seen him in weeks

On New Years Eve they took the test. During the test *he found some polyps* aside of that it was all good. Jimmy came to pick me up. He walked me outside and turned to me excitedly he asked *"So do you have cancer or what?"* I said "No, they just took some stuff out and they will test it, but everything appears fine"

Sadly…. he replied "Oh, really?"

I couldn't believe my ears. *He wanted me to be so sick I could die*! Fuck him he is no *longer my brother*. He just killed me off. I have given him too many chances, and now he has proven that he *really wanted me dead. Fuck him*!

I found out the reason he was in New Hampshire when he got the ticket was because he is involved with Marie's sister. Fuck them all! *I am killing myself to have a life and these fuckers want me dead.* I will get better, and I will fix my life. Better than it ever was.

61
I asked for more time

Becky and I like our Sunday drives and we always go along country roads. The problem here is *sometimes, she cries*, when she looks at the seemingly simple life the people seem to live. In the country they have a lot of land with peace and quiet and a just simple way of life with cute little houses set back *in their own little world*. We would love to live in the country. I tell her all the time we can work hard and buy a house in the country someday.

We *face big problems and we work hard to beat those challenges*. She believes we will someday have all the things we want she just gets sad when she sees the trouble that we face. And now it's even tougher. I just missed all that time from work. We are about to have our third child. I can't take on more work just yet. I am still recovering and exertion causes me to dry heave.

As I began to feel better, I wanted to make up for lost time.

I purchased a junkyard truck and began collecting parts to *make it a plow truck*. I figured this would be *instant cash*. Becky had the baby. He is born on time and very healthy that was my worry.

I work at the Hospital doing forty hours maintenance and thirty hours as security. I have the plow working now and I do some driveways. Our money has become steady enough to *catch up on the bills*. I went to the court and asked for a modification to bring the amount down, *but it was declined*. I work about one hundred hours a week. I work any shift that was available, sometimes not even leaving work. Becky would often call me crying, and telling me *she felt like a single parent*. I really couldn't change anything. I hope Becky isn't thinking about Marie and the money as much as I do. I send information that proves she doesn't even need any support and shouldn't get the amount I send. People bitch when cigarettes, tolls and taxes go up. Those things equal maybe $20.00 a week. My bills just went up almost $300.00 a week and instantly increased my responsibilities. The Courts and DOR Coming at you full force. When a person seeks out a complaint for support they are *the payee*. The questions page is so informative; it gives hundreds of questions and answers.

If you are the *provider* your listed as the (defendant)

I saw the word *Defendant*. It begins as a *lawsuit* for Paternity there are two questions and two answers. *How much do I pay and where do I send the money.*

The questions like *I had a lot of overtime, when the order was established my actual pay is much less what can I do.*

That question isn't there nor the answer.

The law states that, because I was a child of fifteen. My father could get a CHINS warrant. *Child in need of services* I was not *legally responsible* to decide anything. Yet, I am *legally responsible* to pay all this money. I really notified so many agencies. I was trying to prove that this was not helping one family as much as it is hurting another family. The truth is I paid support in the amount required. Until the payee made a decision to allow the initial order to expire

When that order was established, I didn't even complain. For one thing, I knew the support was needed. Imagine if taxes and tolls went up $15600.00 a year.

And you had to pay it. I have to find a way to make over $45000.00 a year just to make this seem fair to my wife and children at home in the eyes of the law.

Then to pay money to *a Lawyer who has his own personal agenda.* I feel like I gave a guy some money and said I heard you're the best at what you do. Here's $2500.00
(*Please take this money and do you're very best to ruin the lives of a wonderful woman and her children. Take any chance that her children have at a normal life and future and rip the hell out of it. Take off your fucking belt put this family over a coffee table and beat them for years until they break. Just because you, found it in your heart to play God with these precious genuine hard working God fearing individuals… If you think you're going to help your friend by sending this man up the river, Check with your friend actually say…* should I fuck them over?)

I know Aunt Bea actually thought of me as a son. She lost her son years before and he would be my age. I don't think she wanted him to save Becky from a terrible man like me.

My wife and kids, what penance should they pay?

The DOR should represent both sides get ALL the facts then make the determinations. It is FAMILY court isn't it? Penance was something I paid, *when I looked out at night and wondered if my children were ok, and if they think of me as much as I thing of them.*

Jimmy came to my house talking shit about the support and I asked him to leave. He began screaming like a raving maniac so loud that the neighbor called the police. They came in and arrested him they suggested I get a restraining order. He is doing *too many drugs to give a shit about the value of another life.* Becky worries that he will come in when I am at work. I went to court and Jimmy had to be there too. He contested the order, and showed the Judge his attitude and the Judge approved it. Wow the system just treated me like a human. I am very grateful. At least I can protect my family from Marie's... *future brother in in-law?*

Without any options, *I complain, I do work hard. I should feel lucky to be able.* Some people I know just don't try and they have nothing. I want a good life and I will work my *tail off to get it.* Becky sees so much in me, and it's very sad that her life has to suck so bad now, just *because she loves me.*

The lawyer really helped her out huh? It can get worst and of course I am sure it will.

When babies get check-ups they check for lead poisoning. If a lead level is around 30 it is certainly lead poisoning. If its 10, that's the bottom line of an *elevated lead level*. Our baby has a level of 10. That figure is reported to the state. The State requires checking the home for the cause. The state sends you *the information* and you have a certain amount of time to obtain the licensed professional to do the inspection at a fee of around $450.00 if any amount of lead is found. It must be removed. *Our baby is going to be fine*. The doctor said to feed him spinach and the level will drop. Thankfully, he will not be affected by the amount. It is the number that requires reporting is all. We feel better knowing that. My nephews had lead poisoning and it is horrible. They were eating paint peelings.

I paid the inspector to check the house. It's the law. I know I have no peeled paint. The inspector came, got his $450.00 He said "*look you do have lead in the paint, but it's all intact and I cannot find out how your baby has a level. Do you have fishing weights? Or scratch tickets from the lottery? The stuff you scratch off is lead.*"

I said "No"; He told me the water is fine in Lynn, "does your baby drink water from another area often?" The only difference with my youngest is he drinks a lot of apple juice. My other two drank milk. He told me that even though the lead problem isn't from the house. It has to be reported to the State and a licensed person has to remove it. You cannot live here until it's been re-inspected and certified. For another $450.00 the actual abatement is going to cost $40,000.00 and we have to live away from the house for about one month.

After we did all the research and the process began and we were able to *refinance the house to pay. Our Mortgage went up $500.00 a month;* the quality of life for us was already pretty bad. Now our kids have no family unit to speak of. We both work all the time. I told the lab tech at work she said "You should have brought him here, and she would have said the level was 9. She checked the apple juice; it had trace amounts of lead. The water must have lead that they use. He still drinks it, but he eats green leafy vegetables and his level is way down. I am going to have to ask the court for a modification again.

62
Piss on you

The judge read my request out loud. *I requested that the arrears be dismissed and that the current weekly amount be reduced.*

Marie stood up and shouted. "No, I want the amount increased. My car is getting old, and I need reliable transportation to take my kids to various appointments" The Judge asked me why I made this request. I told him the actual amount was based on overtime and the arrears were established based on that amount from the time Marie applied for welfare.

Welfare had her complete the paternity papers. The Judge told me he *knows how the system works*. And he asked what is different. I told him about my regular pay and the issue we just had with lead removal. I added that Marie lives with her Fiancé and they have a comfortable financial situation. Marie brought Jimmy along as a witness.

Marie told the Judge *her witness will testify that I have a plowing business* and my wife has a cake decorating business. The Judge asked me if that was true. I said "I plow a couple of driveways for gas money and my wife makes cakes at her work. As an extension of her actual job"

I am the one requesting help here and have real difficulty trying to provide for my family. The Judge asked Marie if she had evidence of my plow business she didn't. He then told me, *her fiancé can be as generous as he wants to*. That isn't part of this case. And Marie's children are *my first children and they are my first priority*. I already admitted the fact that I have additional income.

So my request for a modification is denied and her counter claim for an increase is continued to enable her time to prove the amount of my additional income, and if she can prove the income he will grant the increase she requests.

Heaven on Earth, And that was the lord speaking, I was able to alter my schedule to work 75-90 hrs a week at the Hospital and now I have 25hrs a week at Meineke again. To try to save my home and family

*It was nice to see Jimmy too. He is
so helpful. He looked very happy at the
outcome. They started laughing in the
courtroom,* the Judge just looked at them
and looked away. I informed the Judge
about the restraining order but it didn't seem
to matter.

I thought it showed a great
disrespect for the court. I enjoyed Jimmy
entertaining me with threatening looks. I
guess I could have avoided all this if I just
got the extra jobs and didn't try to seek
justice with the legal system. I have *some
balls being upset about this whole support
thing.*

Working at Meineke proved to be
too tough. I have to try and keep clean,
when I leave Meineke I go to the Hospital.
At the Hospital; I wear a white shirt and a tie
half the time. It was at a point where. I
didn't know what day it was or what time. I
only knew, when I woke up, Becky had an
outfit waiting. I knew my destination by the
clothes that were laid out. I decided to give
up trying with Meineke.

My boss at the Hospital is very
happy with my performance. I am the team
leader. I work with outside agencies, Police,
Fire, and Med, flight etc. I attend Quarterly
Hospital Safety Committee Meetings.

I basically oversee the Security Department. I continue to perform Maintenance as needed. I haven't seen or heard from John in over a year. Someone came in and told me they thought he was with my sister Amy and they saw him in a bar in Lynn Called the Golden Circle.

I went to Amy's house and asked her about him. She said he came by and asked if he could use her address for mail. And he wanted to know about Dad. That got us to start talking about his funeral. I wasn't there. She said a lot of people showed up and there were lots of tears. He touched a lot of lives. I asked what she thought about Uncle Ed's I told her his own Daughters didn't seem to care. She said "Maybe he molested his daughters" I said "No he liked to beat me, Jimmy and John, but he didn't have a sex thing for his girls"

She said "Why not he molested me, but don't tell anyone, Please"
I had no reason to think she made it up. She never talks about very personal issues. I am beside myself. So *dropping my draws for the beating was a sexual game* for those fuckin monsters.

I had to get to the Circle to see if John is around I want to see him. I went and stayed for several beers.

He never showed up, It was a chance anyway. I couldn't get Uncle Ed out of my mind. The grave yard is just around the corner. I remember him saying *Ill piss on your fuckin grave* to someone once. I had enough beers to fill that order and then some. My life was perfect until he *cast a curse over my life and future with his sick twisted fuckin games.*

At five years old that piece of shit beat the innocence completely out of me. So far I haven't been able to shake it completely. I thought to myself. *I can actually piss on his Grave.* I think I am supposed to. It closure, Even though I got my closure when I left his house.

He wanted me to bring by the wife and kids? What the fuck? I have to piss so badly.

I have never been in the Cemetery at night. In fact, I usually visit Moms grave on bright Sunny days. *I want to think of her in the brightest way.* Ed is buried past hers and down a little. I am driving as fast as I can. I am dancing in my seat. If I get up I will start pissing. (*My thoughts race back to the hate, I first witnessed during that first beating. He was worried about piss huh*? I think if I did this first, then I should have gotten the beating.

So I owe him one He wasn't worried about piss, he was breaking me in and I was injured so bad just for him and his *precious wife got to gander at my fuckin bean bag.*

I turned into the Cemetery on two wheels. I could hear my tires screech. As I past Moms grave I was doing about 60 miles an hour I skidded to a stop. Two rows in and there he is. *And like a tornado, a series of events took place at seemingly the exact same moment. Uncle Ed forced my body onto the coffee table, (I could hear a loud Crack! And a scream that could break the sound barrier, it was my own. All the while, Uncle Ed shouted with rage (Crack, scream and "YOU) thundered throughout me simultaneously, you want to piss the bed in my fucking house" he continued, Huh, you want to piss the bed? You'll never piss the bed again you son of a bitch!" My body tried to lunge forward as my hands covered my backside. I was shaking violently "Move you're fucking hands or Ill break your fucking fingers, Crack again and crack again Crack. My ass, my thigh, my testicles and my hand. Suddenly, it stopped; his physical and verbal abuse had halted. I cried uncontrollably bouncing with pain as my pants and underwear sat around my ankles. "Pull up your draws and go kneel in the corner" he said calmly. I moved as quickly as I could, anything to be taken away from that very moment.*

Bouncing with pain as my pants and underwear sat around my ankles.
I had to piss so bad drops were hitting my leg. I held it so tight. I shouted "*You cocksucker, you want to hurt me, hurt me now, mother fucker, I'm going to piss down on YOU And all over your fucking face you piece of shit*" Here I am, I can do it. *But you know something mother fucker, I wont! I'm not going to do it, you suck! Enjoy eternity!*"
I could feel more drips hitting my leg.

I got in the car and raced out of the Cemetery and pulled in behind the snack shack at Browns pond. I must have pissed for fifteen minutes. As I stood there pissing I said "*Sorry Mom you knew I wasn't going to do it, But I had to let him know I could.*" Feeling relieved in many ways. I headed home to my family.

63
Ready to succeed

The experience that I am getting working with local authorities is giving me the incentive, *to try to get that cop job I have always wanted.* I've taken the exams, and so far I have only scored 92 and lower. I hear you need a 95 or better. Those jobs start at $45000.00. I took the Corrections exam and I am waiting for my score. It's not a cop job, but it can lead up to something more. Either way, it is experience and a professional career. As a cop you are Law Enforcement. At work I have similar duties with limitations. Hospital Security....We are not Guards with badges and a notepad. We are dressed in a suit jacket and slacks with a shirt and tie. We approach any situation with a hands off, "talk him down," attitude. Just about every time it works. *We are your friend and we stick by you.* I like the approach.

I want to be Professional and in Law Enforcement, Security can get ugly though…. you are not Law Enforcement you become a "rat"

You never know what you're going to run into. We are always up to date and ready for anything. One minute you can have an irate person or someone seeking a trip to Bridgewater for treatment (Drugs) or an overdosed person on crack, oxy or alcohol poisoning. It isn't just patients. Employees can create Security issues. It was alleged that an employee in the Security Department stole a patient's cash $1500.00. The Security Department was responsible to protect the Patient's money the employee was *well liked by everyone*. He was a very funny guy, I liked him.

My Boss has been put on "Front Street" by administration. If we can't do our job then we aren't needed. In doing my job I have to find the truth and report those findings to administration. In the professional world that's *responsible*. In the human world you're a fuckin rat.

Things change when you're a rat. We are not investigators. In fact we are really a visual deterrent.

However, because we have access to so many things and off hours *anything that comes up is directed at Security*. Namely "me" and we have to defend accusations all the time. In doing so we have to seek out the truth and correct the problem that created the accusations. Sometimes that can create surprising consequences

So many people work hard to make their place in the world. ER Nurses are no exception. The hierarchy is much like that in the animal world. Someone wants to be the Head ER Nurse. *They went to school and they save lives*. They are important people. At the end of the day, if everyone did their best in a situation it really doesn't matter who is the leader and who is the middle person.

When a crisis arises "act on it," and do your best that's all. You are still a human. One day a patient went into cardiac arrest. The ER staff acted right away. They went right to the Code Cart that's normal procedure there is a Code Cart at every station. An *important Medication was missing*. The patient could have died. Administration decided the head nurse will check *the contents and secure the cart on their unit*. Then they will secure it with a numbered plastic lock, One *that's easily broken by hand in case of an emergency.*

And for added protection they will have Security sign a separate document that shows that they checked the lock on the code cart to ensure it isn't broken, and then all Medications should be available when needed. The Head nurse saw a security officer in the trauma room and she asked him what he was doing he said " *Just checking the Code Cart*" She flipped out and came storming at me shouting "Since when does a five dollar an hour Security Guard check Code carts?!" I told her we check the locks and we have been for months. Now the head nurse is furious, we seem to be checking their work. *How did we get so much Power!?* I tried to explain, she wanted to hear nothing from me. I am probably a six dollar an hour Security Guard. Police have limited rights in the Hospital so they have to get approvals from Five Dollar an hour Security Guards too. Especially regarding patient access or information, The head Nurses husband is a cop she's real pissed at us already. Word gets around. The Rumor is… that we think we can do anything we want. And we are rats.

One day my boss asked me if I had sex in the back rooms behind the lab during an overnight shift. Housekeeping found a spent rubber in a barrel.

The only males in the building that could access the area were *me and the housekeeper* that found it. Excluding so called *professional staff* ... The housekeeper reported it so it wasn't him. *It had to be me.* I am Happily Married, but that's not good enough. *Happy people fuck.* I don't use rubbers; well *maybe you did last night.* Otherwise maybe she wouldn't put out.

Or maybe the *male lab technician had a guest.* After checking around, I found that to be the truth. *He was fired it's a serious public health issue.* Oh boy, I really am a rat and now the lab knows this too. The kitchen staff and the housekeepers are related to each other by departments and actual family and friends. They like the Security Guard that allegedly stole the money. I allegedly placed the focus on him. So they smell a rat

At times nurses from the inpatient unit and the Er have to access the Pharmacy. When that happens two keys are needed. They are held by the Nursing Department and Security. My boss called me in and asked me to find out *who entered the Pharmacy* over the weekend there are no log entries. I asked why.

He told me that some things were messed up on a counter and the computer was advanced. I didn't understand what that meant. But I figured I would check. The head *female Pharmacist was dating a male nurse*. I will start by talking with them. *The head Pharmacist made the report*. They work Monday through Friday they are day shift people. She had all the access she wanted. I came in early to ask her for the details to what she found. She told *me she usually advances the computer* from Friday orders On Monday Morning. That was already done. And someone left medication "crumbs" on the pill table where the drugs are counted. She was hostile and actually somewhat accusative towards me.

I thought, I should find the Male Nurse that she dates and hear his side of things.
I found him actually going to see her. I asked if he knew of the Nurses going into the pharmacy at all over the weekend. He asked why? I told him.

He looked puzzled. He informed me that he *saw his girlfriend advance the computer on Friday*, so she wouldn't have to in the Morning and she said "*she would clean the pill mess Monday too.*"

They were in a hurry to leave Friday they were going Horseback riding. I reported my findings and for some reason *both employees found jobs elsewhere*. She must have fallen and bumped her head, I guess. But the end result is *I am a rat again.* Everyone that talks with me now is *very careful of what they say*. And they are not comfortable.

The head cook was beginning to talk shit about me. My boss is beginning to think I *steal food from the café at night*. There is food all over the building I could not ever be hungry enough to steal food. And I never even knew him

He is a friend to the *Security Guard that allegedly stole the money* so he is intentionally fucking me over and a lot of people want me out now. I decided I have had enough with him. I got home found his Instant messenger name and acted like *I was a young girl that wanted to hook up* and we texted for hours that week. While I was home and he was supposed to be working. *Fuck with the bull you get the horn.*

I saved the conversations printed them and gave it to my boss. He was fired!

Now, *I did fuck someone over*, and it's clear. No one feels good about me now that works here. My days are numbered, but just in time. My corrections score came in its 97

I am trying to stop smoking and I have to do push ups and sit ups and run. I started out slow… in two weeks time, I began getting into it. I passed the interview. *So I decided to leave notice and I trained my replacemen*t. I have to pass the mental test and the physical agilities. I am confident that this will happen.

The interview was not what I expected. I had three interviewers. A regular guy kind of like your *average Joe,* In the middle was a brute of a man with a *very angry tough* look. And then an older woman that seemed like your *typical Grandma.*

One of them would ask a question and as you began to answer *another would ask a different question a*nd they acted out the visual role you expected them to have. You wanted to yell at the guy in the middle and you wanted to be sweet with the old lady and you felt like confiding in your average Joe.

I passed, so holding my temper with the tough guy was a good thing. *Oh it was close.* I was told not to quit my job just yet. I had to go on different days to do different things. I took the mental test it was determined, that I have a touch of OCD, in this field it's a good thing. I knew the hard part would be the physical stuff. I know my days are numbered at my regular job now.…

I have applied for other jobs too. Campus Police jobs are sometimes open, I apply to them, when I see the openings. It can lead to a City cop job.

All you need is to be academy trained, and then you can go anywhere. August 2001 I went to Medfield Training Academy to take the final tests. The push ups sit ups and running. I had one minute to complete 20 push ups I did 37, I had one minute to do 35 sit ups, I did 46, I had 13.5 minutes to do the mile and a half run. I did it in 12 minutes. I was very proud and happy. In fact, I have completed all the requirements to go into the academy. *We were told congratulations we are the first group to pass everything on the first try.* You are allowed two tries.…

I drove home and told Becky she was very proud of me. I will continue doing my job mostly the Maintenance stuff.

I have trained my replacement he is a good guy and he is fresh, I paved a way for him to ease in without too many problems.

64
Black Widow

I sat down feeling muscle aches and relief that I passed the physical stuff. Becky and I were sitting in the air conditioning in our living room and the phone rang. The message machine picked up. I could hear a young girl's voice. I figured it was Becky's niece. *I was still glowing from the Corrections thing.*

Becky decided to replay the message. "With panic in her voice" she called me in the kitchen.

I listened to the message a young girl and she said *"Brian your son is dead call us right away"*

What the fuck?? I called back and said "What the fuck is going on?! The girl told me she is Marie's youngest daughter and Marie asked her to call me. I asked what happened

She said… "*Ma threw him out because he's 18*, she let him stay in the trailer on the property, She went out in the morning and heard loud music coming from the trailer, she went in and found *him lying there in a suit and tie*, He took all kinds of pills, and left a note saying *goodbye*"

I am in disbelief all I know is I want to go there and be with my other children.

My oldest son at home is thirteen now and I asked if he wanted to come with me. *He could at least meet his brother and sister.* I wasn't afraid of any trouble based on the circumstances… I also feel an incredible sense of guilt…When we got there Marie ran to me and held me tightly we both began crying. *It is all reality to me now.* My other children were there. Jimmy and Gil were too. Everyone seems freaked out. And they seem *almost human* right now. I asked Marie what happened she told me *he was depressed and didn't want to live.* "Oh" I noted. I knew what happened, her daughter already told me the truth. *You drove him to it you fuckin monster. All because you thought the support would be lowered. The amount stays the same for one, two or three children. You aborted one baby now you gave another baby a life so fuckin bad he didn't want to live it.*

We stayed for a few hours. I could see a little of her nastiness beginning to shine through. I decided to get going. I will return for the funeral.

I am riding on adrenaline. I asked my son if he was ok. He was fine. We talked about her new fiancé *he seems like a great guy*.

I wasn't going to bring my son back there. I asked my father in law if he could go with me. He is an awesome guy. *He wanted to be there for me*. We went; and it was the *most horrible thing I could imagine*. But I couldn't imagine…

Seeing my son in a casket and seeing my other children helpless, I try to comfort them, *but I am an outsider*. When ever I approach them, Gil or Marie approach and redirect the children. This ensures that I remain an outsider…

Thank God my father in law is there. Marie took the time to say to him "Thank you for coming, Brian needed that, I know *he doesn't have anybody*" and then she smiled " My father in law just looked at her, His face expressed some surprise. I felt sick, nervous, anxious, angry, and sad, I was shaky and I just wanted to get away from there. At the end of the service, my father in law and I got in my truck and drove off.

.

The first thing he said to me, was
"That woman is the black widow"

He is very religious, and *never has a
bad thing to say about anyone.* He is the
nicest person anyone would want to know.

I got miles away and my truck
stalled. The alternator is junk and the battery
died. I had to ask for help. I flagged a couple
down and they offered a jump. It was
enough to get us to a station.

I thanked them and then I fell apart. I
burst out crying, shaking and I apologized. I
told them I just left a funeral and I am upset.
They understood and told me *they drove by
it a ways back.*

We got to the house I was so happy
to see Becky and my boys. I have so many
things going through my head. I begged for
life so I could be here for my children.

I have witnessed a lot of people
dying; I have even taken bodies to the
Morgue. I have *never felt like I do now. I
feel doomed;* I feel heat throughout my
body. I shake uncontrollably from my mid
section up. My face feels like it's on fire.

65
I can go to her

My employer told me *to take all the time I need*. I wake up everyday feeling the same. Somehow, during the day *something takes the shaking and the heat away*. Today it's a call to my daughter.

I want to work *past the past and be a father to them*. My oldest is 21 and my daughter is turning 18, they can have some relationship with me… without the *involvement of the mother*.

The support still goes to the Mother until my daughter finishes college. It's been 4 days since my son passed.

I just got a phone call from Amy she just told me my sister Linda had a terrible car crash and died on the scene. It happened in Ohio.

I can't make the trip. *I just sit here in disbelief.* Amy isn't upset with me she understands.

Jimmy asked how I could be affected by my son's death. Seeing as where I *haven't been in his life since he was three years old.* He is my son and has been all his life and I am affected.

I wake up in the morning and I have coffee and a shower and then I sit almost all day and I stare into space. My youngest son has a tiny pool in the yard. He plays in it. I just watch him and *say yes to all of his questions.*

One morning he was playing and he would say *"Dad watch me do this"* Dad *watch me do that, Dad, My response was yup, Yup and Yup. Finally he looked at me and He said "Dad, I replied "Yup", and he grabbed my shirt and demanded my attention and he said "I am right here!" I looked and smiled and said "Yes you are"*

My three year old son just woke me up, suddenly I feel awake. *I still feel a sense of doom*, yet I can focus a little on the world around me. He brought me back into life.

It was amazing… He turned me around and I was able to come back to reality

I returned to work, my boss asked me to see the Social Worker just to talk and see if she could help. She is an awesome woman. We talked for an hour or two. And it hasn't changed anything except the idea *that I feel I can go to her… if I ever need to.*

Becky is giving me so much love and support at home. I have gained a lot of strength and with her, I always have.

I got back to work and began getting into a swing, not like crazy just enough to get by. My heart and mind are not 100 percent. I sleep in the daytime. I work basically 4pm until 6 or 7 am. Most of the time

I was asleep on Sept 11th 2001 and my wife woke me up to show me the news. I sat there and couldn't believe my eyes. It was devastating. I *figured the world was coming to an end.*

66
Working with Grease

Based on these events we have an entirely new way of performing our duties at work. Extreme Vigilance...The Hospital is right next to a mall. I was outside smoking, and I could hear sounds in the parking lot, it was very dark when the lights are out in that area it is total darkness between the Mall and the Hospital .I knew a cargo van had parked in the lot, they had minimal lighting in the truck and it was turned away so *I had no visibility*. I could hear pipes clanging together; it was like staging or something. With a heightened sense of alarm, I called the local Police and asked if *an event was going to take place at the Mall* they said "No" I told them what was happening. *That was my responsibility*. We monitor the Police on a scanner

I heard one Officer say "why doesn't Security go and ask them what their doing?" I thought WHAT? Maybe, it's *because it's not our problem asshole, you have a gun so stick it in your ass and go shoot yourself"*

The dispatcher must have had the same sense as I did because, every cruiser in the city showed up. Come to find out. It was a set up for bicycle helmet safety program *sponsored by that Police Department.* Just doing my part trying to be vigilant

The Department of Corrections sent me a letter it read *Dear Sir You were scheduled to begin the training academy in October, we regret to inform you that due to the events of September 11th the academy has been cancelled indefinitely.*

Well I am glad I didn't quit my job. *Oh wait I did,* my boss is letting me hang on until I start the academy. Oops, I told my boss… he informed me that I already quit and all sorts of changes were made. I have to go…

He gave me two more weeks to find a job. I applied everywhere. A Security company was *hiring like crazy to fill in Airport Security jobs.*

The regular airport coverage had all been fired. And the TSA will be taking over it's a temp job but it pays well so I took it.

I began training with a guy named Chris at American Airlines main check point.

Our supervisor is a Spanish woman named Rosa. I have to say "What?" a lot because she speaks with very broken English.

"Grease? Grease?" I could hear her saying "Grease" finally… Chris turned and said" I love the *way she says my name its music to my ears*. I just laughed.

Most of the people training with us are either Spanish or Italian they all have great tans, Grease and I have "pale faces" We are not in the "in crowd." We are isolated …So he is training me and we hang out at lunch. The guy is dam good at his job.

He sees *everything*. I feel like, I am learning from the best. He wasn't even distracted at any of the *celebrities coming through and we saw a lot of them*. And just so "as it was known that we don't discriminate" we check anything that doesn't look right even Pilots, Celebrities, People that wont make eye contact. People with hats even Military personnel.

All the employees park in Chelsea and they *have a shuttle every 2o minutes*. I am on the bus at 4:15am, I start at the checkpoint at 4:30am sharp we go through the entire security process and get scanned just like passengers once we clear.

We get a briefing on the days concerns. And new policies, etc. By 5: am we are open for business. *You are very busy at all times. You can't be distracted*, if you have to pee, stop drinking coffee! You must pay attention to all of the people that pass you.

When someone "taps" you, you're supposed to look at the person that tapped and go where they point. If it's out of the area you have a 15 minute break and *you can pee*. I love that time. I pee, then I have a smoke or two then I head back go through the security screening and go to the supervisor she then sends me to a position. I will stay there until I am tapped out.

Lunch is the best it's usually around noontime and it's a half hour, at this pace *that feels like a long time*. Before you know it, the shift is over and you take the shuttle to your car.

I talk with Chris on the bus. He told me he is in a band. I know him as a suit and tie person and he acts very responsible. *I figured the band is a contemporary thing*. I told him I would see him play Friday. To my surprise.....

He had torn clothes, earrings, tattoos all over, (covered at work with his suit and tie.) He *sang with a screaming rage* He did stage dives... he is the *front man in a popular heavy metal local band.* Wow, I am surprised. I play drums, but not too good. My older son at home plays too. I would love to let him see these guys.

I couldn't wait to tell my son; Chris offered to let us go to his practices. In time we were going often it was a treat. I have been working at the airport for just over seven months. Chris and I are friends for the most part. The TSA is considering for me to stay on and become a checkpoint supervisor. A job offer like this doesn't come by that easy. I wonder how long.. I could realistically keep this kind of pace without being over my head. I could never forgive myself if I were the cause of any type of disaster. So I am not too sure about staying on at that capacity.

I got home one day and had a message. It was from the Campus Police Chief at a local State Hospital, He wants to interview me. We set up the date and time. The interview took place later that week. I sat with the Chief and two Sergeants. One of them liked me *and one didn't.*

The Chief liked me too, so it was two to one and I got the job. I was grateful because it's very close to what I have always wanted. And I no longer have the worry of staying at the airport with such incredible responsibilities that could mean life or death for so many people all at one time. I know my own limits.

67
Quasi Cop

I gave notice at the Airport. When they know your leaving *you are done*. I knew that so I waited a week.

The Chief had some *uniforms that fit me and some supplies like badges, a duty belt, handcuffs and accessories.* I had to purchase my Rockies (Boots) and in a few months the entire department will get a uniform allowance so that should bring me up to date. One of the Campus Police Officers is from Lynn his name is Clayton, He looked at me real funny and said *"Your brother's name is Jimmy, Huh?"* I said "Yes it is why?" He told me he knew him and had bad experiences. I replied "Me too" I told him I have a restraining order it got so bad. *He didn't seem to care.* As far as this guy is concerned. I am Jimmy's brother and I am a piece of shit too. *He will work very hard to prove it.* Oh Boy here we go... I waited all my life to get a cop job. I actually have a *quasi cop job* and it comes with more strings attached. The Department has licensed and unlicensed officers. The difference is academy training, *Licensed Officers can make arrests.*

Our uniforms are Identical to the Mass State Police. My arm patch says *Massachusetts Police* and at the bottom it says D.P.H. *Department of public health.* We drive around in a marked police car with blue lights, we respond to emergencies on and off Campus. We deliver court papers, Investigate crimes etc. As long as a certain number of the department is licensed, we are covered. At some point, I may have to go to the academy… so I must stay in good athletic health.

Tim is the sergeant that likes me; he is a no bullshit kind of guy. He can tell an asshole when he sees one *and Clayton is an asshole*. Tim is in agreement. Clayton asks a lot of people about me. He wants to know as much as he can. This guy thinks he's a real cop. He's not even licensed and he would never pass an academy. He is a punk in a uniform.

Most of the other guys are really good people. It's important to be in good with your fellow employees here. We have detox centers, kid jail, shelters and drunken driving programs. If something goes wrong we are the first to respond and we need to feel *someone has our back.*

I try to be friendly with Clayton. He and the other *Sergeant* were mental health workers and they transitioned into the Department because they had "State time" The time on the books... Even then, the Department was called *Security*. They became Security guards and now they are cops. Based on time... Between the hospital, the airport and life itself, I have *ten times the experience as these guys put together*. I am not so stupid, that I tell them, I just do what I am told, and try to learn when I can. We learn anything pertaining to the State Laws and the Policies of the facility we give out tickets, We initiate Traffic stops. Respond to emergencies, I really like this job and I hope it leads to bigger and better things.

My sister Debbie decided to move back to Mass. after Linda died. She has a boyfriend, and his family lives near Springfield. They came to the area and live in a small town. She is only an hour and a half away now. On a day off, Becky and I took the kids out to see her. It was nice. She is living in a ranch on 5acres of land and it looks fresh and clean and the houses are far apart. Becky really likes it too. But we are thinking if we ever move we will head to New Hampshire, just over the line so we are *close enough yet still in the country.*

Even though life seems tough right now, Becky and I are simple and easy going and we picture a quiet comfort somewhere else….

After talking with Debbie I begin to think about John some more. I wonder where he is. I haven't seen him in six years. I wonder what he would think about me having a job with a Police uniform. Dad would love it! Its crazy, when Dad first died, I would go to the phone and start to dial Dad's number to ask if he heard from John or to tell him something… Anything. And then as I did. I would *realize he is gone*. It was a hard habit to break.

At this point, I maintain telephone conversations with my daughter. And my son came out to the house for a day. He fit right in with us. It was like he was born in the house. Becky treated him with love, *like he was her child*. I was very proud. He had a great time. But we still don't talk much.

After my son passed away, Becky lost her Nan and Stephanie died from an asthma attack and Grampy McGee passed away. It's been a very tough time and we try to hang on to our dreams. I want all of my children in my life and Becky feels the same she feels sad for me, But she feels worst for *my children*.

She loves me I think she is most *proud of me as a Dad and realizes the distance for my children and I is tragic*

My oldest son was hostile for a while, he told me their number was always in the book, and I could have found them and tried to be in their lives. When I tried to tell him things about the past, he shut me right off and said it doesn't matter. He doesn't want to hear about it. I figure in time, he may get to know me and realize, I have good intentions

Jimmy has been getting his name in the papers for arrests and drugs. Since Dad died he *has no control*. We were going to the court every year to renew the order. The last time I went, the Judge saw Jimmy and his behavior and decided to make it *a lifetime restraining order*. That's the only thing protecting my family from *the grief he can cause*. He is petrified of jail. I am getting use to my job and I like it very much. Becky is proud of me. I would love for Dad or John to see me. Dad bitched about cops but he would change his tune for me. He would probably ask me to be in uniform and he would take me visiting relatives and his friends just to show *one of his kids are alright*.

My cousin Gail called and said Joe is in the hospital all she said was *he is jaundice*. My sister Amy is not doing too good either she is in the hospital and having breathing trouble. Wow it's always something. It's only been 11 months since my son and my other sister died. I hope they are going to be ok. I'll visit later today.

At the hospital, Joe was in a bed he looked pretty yellow. I said "Joe what's going on?" He said "I woke up this morning with a big lump in my stomach and *lemon head*." then he chuckled. You could tell he is nervous, but he still has a sense of humor. I asked what the doctors say about it. They told him he has a problem in his liver and they *can't do much because he drinks*. They are doing some tests and they will have better information. He has to stay *sober six months* before they can help him with a transplant if it's needed.

I didn't stay long… Amy is in another room. I wanted to see her. I knew, I would be with her for more time, so I saw Joe first. Amy was hooked up to all sorts of machines for her breathing. I guess she has COPD and some other trouble she just looks horrible, she couldn't talk because of the machinery, so I just sat in with her for an hour or so.

I got home to Becky *she just can't believe the things that have gone on in the past few years.*

We are ok we have each other. In a week it will be the anniversary of my son's death. I will spend the time with my wife and kids at home. I can't go to New Hampshire it's just not in me.

I have been spending a lot of time thinking about my son. Amy and Joe are on my mind but *my son is almost all I think about. Becky understands and she is supportive.* My kids at home are doing great. Becky and I began talking about all the people we lost in the past. Becky was devastated over losing her Nan; she had not experienced losing someone so close. I can't believe what the fighting with courts and other agencies and working all the hours has taken away… as far as our *valuable life time*

Times change and I have always known how precious life is. But, I really haven't spent any time with my own family. The only quality time my youngest son and I have is breakfast and a nap. That's not fair to him or me for all that matter.

My oldest and middle sons see me at dinner once a week.

They need me. I need them. I need for them to know. I love them and want them to be in my life every day. The boys know we have had a lot to deal with, and Becky and I face it and fix it, we always find a way. Even now we struggle with the bills, actually more, because I get less pay and have to count on overtime. We are a family and we have to *focus on what's right under our noses.*

68
It just keeps coming

On the anniversary of my son's death I went to work, I was quiet and spent so much time just thinking about him, and my kids in New Hampshire. I wonder how their doing today. I will call on my lunch break. I blame Marie... I remember when I was 18... I would hold a razor to my wrist, and then I would realize, if I slipped it was over. I never thought of it before Marie or after. That woman killed my son and ruined any chance I had at being a father to him. I can't turn back time and show my son my world; a world of hope and dreams and moving forward through the toughest of challenges. The sound of laughter is in my life somehow every day. He could have that too. I cant remember a day that went by in the lives of my family.. where everyone got at least a minute of one to one time, and it always concluded with...

I Love You! And everyone gave me a hug. I am fueled by that love.

The day is a tough one, Sgt.Tim knows what's up and he likes to talk to me as a friend, and his input does help. At lunch, I called my daughter; she is also having a tough day probably a lot *tougher than I am*. She told me her mother is always at the grave and my older son is feeling very mixed emotions about everything in his life. He wants to move forward and this is something he responds to but he keeps too much inside. He won't talk about it. *I told her I love you and she said she loved me too*. That is really something. *My baby girl just told me she loves me for the first time in her life*. I was so glad to hear it. She is really my little girl wow it's so hard to believe. My spirit is lifted somewhat. I am devastated about my son. I am sick over it. But at the same time, a prayer *of mine was just answered*. I have pictures in my mind of her as a little girl looking out a window at the world and wondering what *her* future holds.

Ten minutes before the end of my shift, Becky called in a panic. She told me Elaine called her and said that Jimmy has taken a massive overdose. He's in the trauma room at Lynn Hospital. I told her I am alright, and I am going there before I get home. And that I will call her. My sergeant Tim heard me and told me to get the hell out of here. I raced to Lynn.

I saw Elaine standing out front with her sister. She said "He doesn't look good." I figured of course he doesn't look good.

The ER doc was one that I knew. He also worked at the hospital where I used to work at. He said" Brian is this your brother?" " Yeah, He is" I replied "I have to tell you, *he took enough lithium to kill two horses" Brian I am sorry but he isn't going to make it.* We pumped his stomach, but who knows how long it was before he got here. He has been in and out of cardiac arrest several times. We are waiting for him to stabilize long enough, to bring him to the ICU. *I am very sorry he's not going to make it.*

I waited with Elaine and her sister. I watched the staff bring Jimmy to the elevator, he still had color and reactions to stimulations like the meds, sounds and the world. The doctor knew me, and he was a straight shooter. Jimmy's life is ending right now, before my eyes. I stopped the nurse and said "*Jimmy, I forgive you, I hope you can forgive me*" His eyes twitched a lot. Like they did when he was screaming in a rage His body remained lifeless. The elevator went up two levels and took no more than 40 seconds.

I ran ahead of the elevator, and when the doors opened, I noticed his face had blue coloration and the twitching stopped. He was technically alive... but he was gone.

He died in that 40 second ride.

I bit my tongue so many times. I figured he was the big brother, if I could have found the patience to talk in a way he could understand, he would have listened just like he did with Dad. Why does this have to make sense to me now? I am way too late.

I know Jimmy is gone... but they still have life activity and they will keep him on machines

Years before.... the day Jimmy told me to go right, and he went straight ahead. I wanted to say NO! Not a chance, but he is *the big brother* and he knew better, so I kept my mouth shut. I took a right and he just kept going. He seemed to know where he was heading. And he knew where he wanted me to go.

I turned and saw Elaine and her sister... Elaine was pretending he was here and pretending to hold on to some kind of hope.

I saw more effort when she said happy birthday. Stop pretending, you suck, and have nothing to prove to anyone. Especially me! I notice she isn't trying to confide in me, her hate is far too deep for that. Did you cry at Dads funeral? I bet you did. Dad knew you were fucking your boss, long before you confessed. Do you even know what love is? Not a chance! Your own kids should get some brains and write you off. I told them, I had to go home and see Becky. I will return tomorrow. *I always had a feeling Jimmy would die young. The only relief I have… is that*
No one got a notch in their belt at the cost of his life. I have my reasons for my bad feelings… I would NOT want to see his death shine as a medal on anyone.

I went home and gave Becky the details of the night's events. She was obviously upset. She looks at me with strange eyes. She won't say it, but why am I not breaking down again? She feels the same about Jimmy as I do. She also knows he is my Brother. I explained some of the emotions I have good and bad. If tears should come they will just happen when they are ready.

The next morning, I went to the hospital. As I arrived, I could see Elaine, Gil, Pete, Marie, Debbie and the Police. Oh boy is this a crime scene? I found out Jimmy has two children with Maries sister. Everyone wants to establish who has what for rights.

I showed the Officer my badge; this will hopefully establish a separation. *I am not one of these people.* Elaine said "Debbie wants to take Jimmy's kids," I guess the mother left them with Jimmy. Marie also wants the kids.. *of course she does..* her support is going to end someday. Elaine's daughter wants the kids.

I just said "I want no part of this Officer, *I am here to say goodbye to my brother.*" The officer spoke with everyone and warned them… That if there are any issues in the Hospital. They will all be arrested. Jimmy would be flattered to know they were all arrested on his behalf. The "who is who" and who did who in this group. I really don't care; it's a mess I haven't seen in years. The Cop called the ICU to let me know that he *has warned them*. I thanked him and hung up. Dad would be proud.

I watched the cop tell Elaine to *shut up* in front of Marie. It was sweet to see the look on their faces. They have no powers here.

Timing is everything, I stood back while Debbie said her goodbyes, and the group came in quietly, as the group watched from outside the room. Jimmy happened to *code* again, this time all the bells and whistles started going off. The nursing staff pulled Debbie away, *and tried to revive him to no avail. He expired,*

Somebody in the group, blamed Debbie for *"giving him a heart attack"* That's why he died

Debbie has just created a name for herself in the eyes of this group, They said she is the cause of his death. Jimmy's kids will hear it that way. These people are always so dramatic. I am so relieved to be away from these people. Aside of my adult children I will have no connection to them. I can associate with the children and not the mother. It's all getting better. This is the way it should be. *My relationship with my kids should be ours* and the rest of these assholes should have no input. They made all the rules before. That has just changed.

Knowing these people and all of the past… I have no intentions of showing up for his funeral. The police Officer told me *the city will have officers present* based on the history that they are aware of…. I guess Jimmy would be proud. He is somewhat of a local legend in the eyes of small time shit bags. There going to have to roll all their Joints with red papers. *Rolling out the red carpet*

The story he would tell would include a *twenty one gun salute.*

Once he screamed about snow amounts. After I said "I heard were going to get 6-10 inches in just a few hours. He turned and shouted "**were getting over a foot! It's a fucking Nor Easter!** Gee, ok Jimmy, ok, relax; I had no idea it was such a dramatic thing. We ended up with 5 inches so we were both wrong. I wasn't going to talk anymore with him about it. *Some day it will melt anyway.* Jimmy had a son and daughter with his wife. They will be there. He has two sons with Marie's sister, they will also be there. That's the saddest part

The funeral director said that Jimmy's body has to go to Boston and then to a funeral home. When he gets there, I have to identify his body. I am the next of kin.

He also mentioned that he spoke with John. I wondered how John knew, I still haven't seen him. I didn't even ask. I just want this behind me. I still have my sister and cousin in intensive care.

John isn't going to show up. I guess he's not in the area. He probably read the paper or someone knows where he is and told him what happened, and that someone won't say anything to me. *I am angry that he hasn't called.* People know that.

Jimmy is a veteran just like Dad was and they paid for Dads funeral, they will cover Jimmy's too. He had a girlfriend... she was "no prize." She said *"Well Jimmy moved Mountains in life imagine what he can do now!"*

Last time I checked.... all of the mountains in the world were still in place. I imagine he *can no longer affect the landscape* now.

I guess I suck badly for saying that. But *he was saddened to see that I wasn't on deaths door.* So, I have to speak from my heart and say it's always tragic when someone dies. Jimmy has only become *someone* to me.

He stopped being my brother a long time ago. I wish it was different, I tried many times. Maybe I was one of his Mountains. *I have certainly been moved.*

A while back the lug nuts on my car where loose. John thought it was Jimmy, I had a leak of brake fluid and think it was the cause. I didn't know anything about cars at the time. I can't remember why I had the leak. It is just another thing for me to keep in my mind. That was one thing that can be questioned. The day he asked if I had cancer was unquestionably disappointing to him when he knew I was fine. John can have his opinion, I have mine. Either way we both agree he wanted to see me hurt.

My neighbor is an old friend of the family, " Jessie" He was a friend of Dad, We saw so much of him we called him a cousin. *Jessie is a biker*; he is a badass to some and a good guy to others. He liked me and offered to go with me to identify Jimmy. We got there and Jimmy was in an *actual wooden box*. He wasn't cleaned up. They are going to cremate his remains.

Strangely enough the look on his face was that *of a sarcastic smirk*, Similar to the kind he would make when he said *"Ill get you back mother fucker"* As he planned cutting your cable TV or something.

He had a black mark on the side of his head. Jessie and I just stood there looking in disbelief, I guess.

We got outside and Jessie turned to me and asked *"How did he get the hole in his head?"* Jessie knew he died, just not how he died. I thought for a second and said "Oh the black mark on his head, that was charcoal from *when they pumped his stomach."*

Jessie took a deep breath and said *"Oh I thought he shot himself"*

The funeral is tomorrow and I will watch Debbie's kids. She's going, not me. I will think of Jimmy, and in my heart… I will be there. I expect nothing good can come from it. I called my Boss and told him that I will be in the next day. He told me to take all the time I need. Since I started working here I have accumulated a number of days on the books and I have bereavement leave.

The next day was bright and sunny, the kind of day, I choose to visit Moms grave. I looked up often and wondered what's out there. Debbie returned a couple of hours later she told me it was the *scariest thing she had ever been through.*

The feel of the entire event was extremely stressful. She didn't even want to talk about it. I have a good imagination. It's nothing I haven't seen. All I know is that this can be put behind me and I will try to move forward. Let everyone fight over his ashes or survivors benefits and anything else; keep me out of it. Those people are insane. I am going to see Amy and Joe. Anne called and informed me that Joe can get a procedure using part of her liver and he may be just fine. That's good to hear.

Amy is in bad shape. She has all types of machinery to help her breath she has IVs and she is unable to talk. I just stay and sit quietly. Joe heard about Jimmy and he's all freaked out. I spent the rest of the day at home with my family we just tried to have a quiet day, my son had his friends over Jessie came by for a few beers. I want to look to a future. I was prepared to return to work. I got another alarming call from Elaine. She told me *Amy just died in the hospital*. Something to do with her lungs, I really don't know.

This cannot be happening. My son died last year, four days later my sister died. A year to the day my brother died, and my other sister died four days later how is it possible? …. Joe actually died a week after…

Less than twenty years ago, I had such a large family we had to rent a hall for Christmas and Easter, Now, *They are almost all gone.*

My sergeant Tim came to the house to see how I was. He is a friend more than a coworker. Tim stuck around and gave me plenty of support. *Numbness is setting in….*

69
Precious moments

I went back to work. I wanted to focus on our lives, my job and our future. Things began to normalize, winter came in and brought along the snow and ice.

We decided to get a dog from the shelter. He is a lab / shepherd mix. He picked us, we didn't pick him. I walked by the cages and he just started dancing *and jumping around like crazy*, I asked if we could see him. They took him out and he jumped all over the place whimpering *as if he hadn't seen me in forever*. He hadn't, He got so excited he was dripping out pee sprinkles everywhere. I held him away for a second he came right back and sprinkled some more, Becky said well *he marked you, you're his Dad now,* His name *was Fonzie*; He is still a puppy his new name will be Hunter, or as we say in Lynn "Hunta" From that minute on he became "one of us"

We play so much with Hunter.. he is a great extension of the family

Bad things can happen for good reasons?.....

My son and I took Hunter outside so he could do his duties and run for a few minutes. I walked carefully across the snow and ice. I had a large coffee cup in my hand. I hit a very icy spot and slipped backwards. *My head and my cup crashed against the ice at the same time. I heard the shatter.* And I touched my head wondering if it just broke. It was not bleeding but I had a big lump. I took my son and the dog inside quickly. In case I passed out. *I wanted them safe inside.* The bump was pretty big I decided to get checked. At the Hospital they took an X-ray the Doctor told me my head is fine but when they find something they have to let me know. He said "You have Ankylosing Spondylitis" I said "Ankle biting spider-itus?" What the heck is that? He said "It affects joints in the spine and the sacroilium in the pelvis, causing eventual fusion of the spine." I said "so basically I'm old right?" He said "Yeah your old"

The doctor said "to put it in simple terms it's basically arthritis." I told him I feel great and could run a mile and a half in twelve minutes. He told me that's great. Exercise is the best thing for it. You'll have inflammation periods.

He also told me some people never have problems, other people end up in wheel chairs. For some reason….I figure, I won't have any trouble for about two years. I should start looking at our life and how it would be easy enough for Becky to provide for us if she has to…. *Ankle biting spider-itus huh?*

Hmm, Well until I have a problem, I'm not telling anyone. Ill let Becky know. If work wants to send me to the academy, this will put the brakes on it. I have seen some cops that have settled with time. All I need is that license. I can settle with time anywhere then.

Feeling great, I continued to work. Trying to avoid Clayton, Even though Jimmy is gone, I am still his brother. And that must mean I am bad news. If I am, he will prove it. In his mind…. I am very bad news

The apple doesn't fall far from the tree, is what he tells other people. And everything he says ends with "Ya know, ya know," He says it in the same tone as Eyore from Winnie the Pooh, "It'll never work ya know.

I never fell from a tree. What a dick…. this asshole *could* show me some respect.

He went all over the Campus, trying to get other people to see a more negative side of me. He probably has Bi Polar, or something that hasn't been diagnosed yet. I can't understand why he has to search for these problems. I have had his back a few times already. And I have nothing to prove. He likes to come off as a tough guy. The only thing I worry about is the snowball affect. Like I had.. when I, was doing Security. If he is liked by enough people it can and will happen. I daydream about vocalizing my real opinions...

The day *I screamed at Pete for holding the gun to my head*. I released so much stress I was like a new man. Just shouting it out! *If I actually just got nose to nose and screamed in his face. He would never fuck with me again*. That's all it would take. I choose to avoid him instead.

I have always known, that without any trouble from anybody else. Life can be tough. I have to touch on older people again. They look back and reflect on all the good times and Precious Moments. Not shit like this….. Lucky for me, I have my wife and children, Precious moments just happen.

When we aren't thinking about bills
or lost loved ones and work and anything
that distracts from the true pleasures in life.
You can't plan those moments you can't buy
them. *They just happen*, and if you're lucky
enough to notice, you can put them in your
pocket and look back at them forever. I do
and it helps me maintain a good attitude

I looked at my son one day and said
"Daddy Loves you, He replied "I You too,
Da tee da," It sounded like a song to me.
And, I will never forget it. He is much
bigger now, and I won't hear it that way
again. But.. as a precious moment… I will
always hear it as clear as the day it was
spoken. Clay should focus on his kids and
maybe less cop stuff. This man has grown
kids, That should have created so many
"precious moments" that he should have that
happy humble feeling that his life is good.
But from the equipment he buys, you can
tell he wants to be a real city cop. That's his
focus…*His actions show me he would
NEVER pass an actual interview*. His
common sense factor is way out there. Ya
knoooow

I could never educate him as to his
prejudice. He has me judged as *Jimmy*, and
it will not change. I do wonder why I have
to know him.

Why can't I just have applied, got my job and worked with people that have an actual mission and do my best to excel? Who threw this fifty year old nut case into my mix? Someone up there really likes me. I seem to meet one like him everywhere I go.

I have never gone out of my way to bother anyone. I have also never thrown the first punch. I actually try to bring humor to everyone I meet. Some of my humor can be offensive, but it is brought on with good intentions. Simply to hear someone laugh or at least make a smile

I am very professional in my role at work. All humor is left on the back burner. I just wish there was a way to make MORONS like him find another hobby other than me. Get a life…. C'mon would somebody knock some sense into this loser? It's the only way he will ever learn. I could just quit and give up and he will no longer be a thorn in my side. That is not what I want at all……

We got a call to the Juvenile prison. They had a person out of control. I was assigned "Car-*1*" Clay was assigned *Portable 2*, He is on foot patrol, if needed he can back me up in another car.

We arrived at the same time. *Clay said "You play good cop and Ill play bad cop" I just looked at him and thought what?* We could hear screams of anger. It sounded like a grown man. I thought it was staff. I entered the area to find what looked like a professional wrestler... He was shouting all sorts of profanities and threats. He had the face of a ten year old child. He was actually fourteen. He pulled fire alarms threatened to kill people and threw objects. I slowly approached him and said "Hi" the room became silent and he just looked at me. I said "I'm Brian are you ok?" He started screaming again, some staff members began telling Clay a story. I approached him carefully and said" I can listen to you if you talk to me, you don't have to yell, I am going to treat you with nothing but respect, and I want the same thing in return"

He started to become a lot more reasonable. But, I could see he figured, I might be a push over, so he began to set up "an attention seeking game scenario." I knew.. I only had to buy time. A State crisis team is on the way. The staffing here wasn't enough to deal with a crisis involving him. Clay stayed as far from this kid as he could. I noticed it and decided to put him on "Front Street." Just because... Karma for him

He wanted to play *good cop bad cop*, I can see the report in my head, and how he came and saved my ass. I told him the kid wouldn't talk to anyone but him. I will take over the initial report with staff and he can restore peace with this irate young man. I saw all the color leave Clays face and he began stuttering trying to find a way out of it. I knew the kid just wanted a "moment in the sun" at this point, and well Clay could be his sunshine. And to give Clay a small treat… I told the kid he could *confide in* Clay, and if he wanted me to I would *partially close the door* so he wouldn't think anyone was eavesdropping. Alone with an angry bear…

Clay got the bonus in this deal. He wanted to be a big shot and now he can be.

Within seconds, I could hear the conversation begin to escalate. I waited until it seemed to be close to violence. Just then Clay called my name, like I was his Daddy, I walked… almost… as fast as I could… and I asked the kid "Hey what's your deal? You told me you would be fine, as long as we were here and staff wouldn't bother you, do you want us to leave? I can bring back my Sergeant" He replied "No it's just this guy is talking stupid and he seems like trouble, I want to talk with you"

Just then the crisis team arrived and peace is officially restored. Later…
Clay said " That kid was a fuckin punk, I should have given him some shit, but I was trying to be cool with him" "Yeah ok Clay, Go hand cuff yourself to a radiator or something." I thought.

All anyone really wants is the respect of other people. Clay wants it, but he can't return it. I try to respect everyone I meet, until they abuse that privilege. We are all human and everyone has a story. I approach people the same way I have, since I was five years old.

Eighty percent of the time… I find the respect I gave, wasn't deserved by the recipient. Now that I have a uniform, that has the word POLICE on the patch. Everyone I meet shows respect before I even open my mouth. People have opened doors and call me sir. Everyone apologizes if they bump into me or if I bump into them. It actually got to the point where it was sickening. I could probably have pissed on someone's shoe and they would have said" Oh sorry, my shoe was in your way, here let me wipe it off for you." *I was flattered when the return respect was equal to the respect I gave.* That's the way the world should be. *Respect given for the respect received.* It's a simple concept.

The respect given to me now was not mine. It was respect for the uniform and it was given in fear. POLICE POWERS the powers of arrest. Cops have access to information that *can and will be held against you!* Don't rub this guy the wrong way!

When I worked at the Hospital doing Security, I witnessed real life tragedies that were not mine to suffer from. It was the world of People around me. I remember talking to a guy that had a cut on his finger and he needed a few stitches. No body knew he was also having chest pains. *He was dead fifteen minutes after he asked to get some stitches.*

I have seen people that I knew where assholes… and they were *better than everyone else*, until they were looking for medical help. Now they were so humble and polite.. Why not just live that way to begin with? If lightning struck between them and I… I believe we have EQUAL chances of survival… people sure can suck!

I am doing a great job with my approach to any situation at work. Excluding the asshole I work with…. *He doesn't have my respect and now, he never will.* I know he will never have my back, or have an instinct to act protective on my behalf if it's ever needed. He may also be the only one that can provide me with CPR, if I ever needed it in his presence.

With that in mind, I still aim to show some respect. He doesn't deserve any, but I have to cover my ass a little. Knowing that I am really alone in any situation here, I try to be careful at all times. We are present when irate drug addicts are removed from programs. We deliver bad news to all sorts of people. We are the front line in many hazardous situations.

I have always had positive results in these situations. Really, because of the respect I give…. It's that simple "Kill em with kindness"

When I think about it, I realize that he is my only obstacle and I should let it go. I am at a place in life that I have always wanted to be. I find he has dragged me into a mind consuming situation with his child like behavior.. That can cause me to react in ways that I don't want to.

I have to wonder WHY… In all these years have people just gone OUT of the way to make trouble for me… As If, I treated people like the shitbags that they are. But I don't. I sometimes wish my nature was more like Jimmy or John. People fuck with them too. However… they make people regret it! At least at home, I can find that comfort and peace that we are all entitled to. Well sort of….

70
Two family

Becky and I always talk about living in the country; we have since our first trip to the White Mountains. We have been going each year and its part of our life and the things we love about it. I think about our lives now and I don't feel so good about being in Lynn. All of my family is gone for the most part. Debbie is the only one I talk to. I saw her life style and it's peaceful. The housing market is good right now.

The guys that I do like at work all live just over the Border in and around Hudson or Nashua. I asked Becky if she wanted to start thinking about selling. We could have the country; pay off the arrears, the regular support will go down. We could have room for the dog to run and it gives us a new start. All of the life we had so much trouble with… can be put behind us. She became very excited. We started looking and we saw many houses we liked. I told Debbie, and she said "You work for the State and you can transfer anywhere in the State, *Move here… its New Hampshire enough.*" I really liked her area, but we have our hearts set on New Hampshire.

She always pushes us to try Western or Central Mass. I finally said" If you see a house like yours in our price range we'll look at it.

She lives in a split level ranch on five acres. I like the split level ranch style a lot. We put our house on the market, Debbie told us about a house we should see. She sounded very excited. We drove to the area. It wasn't a split level ranch, and it doesn't look like what I picture as our dream house. It is nice and has four acres. And the best part is the fact that it's a single family.

I haven't begun to touch on the trouble we have had with the tenant. He dates back to the first Hospital job I had. At Mount Pleasant. He was a nurse's aid. Back then When ever he heard me talking…. he got the attitude that I was just some punk kid.

When we looked at the house fifteen years later we discovered he is *the section eight tenant*. His tone changed he saw me as a "buyer" and he said "*Gee Bri, My wife has bad hips and we love the neighborhood it's a first floor its really helpful if you let us stay when you buy the house.*" I figured he seems to have mellowed in his old age.

I decided it was no problem.

The rent is only $417.00 his portion is $117.00 a month. I was misinformed that I can request a higher rent. He has four rooms on the first floor on the outskirts of town. Comparative apartments are $675.00 and up.

The previous land lord made him park down the street. He keeps all of his tools in his van. He fixes up houses for work and has expensive tools. I told him he could park in the driveway. I said he could use the entire basement for storage. I figure… if I am good to him he will return the respect.

The first day after we closed he said "Hey I am worried about the other land lord I think he will break in can you change the locks?" (I just bought new barrels and paint and cleaning stuff and I was pretty tapped.) I said "sure" I bought two heavy duty locks at $70.00 ea. I installed them. Front and back. He came out and saw me and said" What about my door?" I said "Hey Bob if the guy gets in the first door it doesn't matter if you have a new lock on the inside. I just spent $140.00 that I wasn't expecting." And the barrels were $40.00 each the previous owner took them too totaling $300.00 to walk in the door.

After I installed the locks, I decided to view the basement and get the status of things that I might have overlooked. In the area that Bob leaves his things, I saw ten brand new lock assemblies just like the ones I just replaced. He fixes houses for real estate companies. *What the fuck is this asshole doing?* I know he is on Section eight, I know he fucks with the system. I hope he doesn't think I am some rich slum lord or an entity of some sort. I just gave this guy the whole basement, off street parking and he busts my balls over locks he *already owns that he can replace* and just ask me to take it off the rent or something. *I just spent my food money for that.* Not a good start, in time

I realized I made a serious mistake keeping him there.

I was unable to get the rent I wanted. I fought with section eight a lot. He was always late with his portion. *He paid his portion of rent in change once; it was in a wine bottle.* He had his daughters move in and my water bill went up $300.00 a quarter. He told section eight his daughters *visit to help his wife.* I had no proof. Like mail or something, please c'mon. How about they are shitbags and they don't get mail. I had a small pool for my son.

He reported that the pool doesn't have a permit. The city inspector came in and told me to get my son out and empty it now. Bob sat in the window smiling.

He complained about any update that he was aware of that his apartment didn't have yet. It was a very nice place... fresh paint, updated with immaculate landscaping. When I de-leaded he convinced me that his grand daughter is always here and she could get sick. It was $9500.00 to do that portion. I didn't have to, but I wouldn't want the child to have lead poisoning and feel I was the blame. He used to bang on my ceiling when my kids played in the living room. My mortgage was $1875.00 a month he contributed $117.00 who owns this fucking place him or I? Three years of fighting the legal process, He lived under me for six years. I finally got to a point where the legal process wasn't helping. Cousin Jessie convinced him to *leave the day after I asked for his assistance*. Fear created respect. For the most part... On his way out he emptied garbage barrels on the floor, and the cat box, Awhile back he told me a trick he knew of where he *caught cockroaches in a jar with cereal. He emptied it in someone's house*. He played that trick on me as well. Then he used contractors glue to secure the windows closed.

71
Pay up Grampa

I got good news today… *I was just told I am a grandpa.* The family in New Hampshire doesn't call me and keep me informed about anything. I actually initiate the calls. *I am just a financial resource.* I asked my son why he doesn't call anymore. He used to and he came to the house. He told me he doesn't need a father. His actual wording was…

"I already have a father, you better not be complaining about the support that's your responsibility. *You need to understand your role. It can be a role of friendship at best. But you need to earn that friendship.* You don't demand that I call you! Pay your support… and in time, I may want a friendship with you.

I replied "Well I am at least *half of the foundation of you established hereditably*. You may not think you need a father. But it's nice to know you have one. Call me if you ever change your mind."

My daughter stopped calling and I can't get in touch with her on the phone. I decided to go to the college website. She hasn't been a student for over a year. After some search words and other peoples face book pages and various site viewing

I discovered she had a child. And that I have been paying a woman over eighteen with her own child, Child support for at least a year more than I should have. It took two more months to prove it. That just confirms what I bitched about for years...

Everyone wants to tap the resources when they can. I had all my social security quarters for life in at the age of 32, I am sure that was probably eighteen years early.

All I know is that Becky and I can
finally have the life we have work so hard
for. Its all ours now, And yes we will take
the house in Massachusetts. We will even
buy our dog his *own baby*. A beagle, they
can run on four acres.

Becky and I are just as happy as we
were when we met. Let's get started and
have the life we want! We sold our house
and bought the new house. We got the
beagle a few days before we left. He is tiny
but he is built with such a muscle tone I
want to call him Rocky. Becky picked him
up and he began wiggling all over his little
tail was spinning around and he snorted like
a pig. Becky said "*You're not a beagle
you're a piglet.*" We began calling him
Piggy, Pig, or Piglet. He answers to them all.
Hunter has a nick name too…. he got big
and my son calls him Moose,

OK boys lets go, *like two little ducklings the dogs followed Becky's voice without even having to look up.*

We walked out the front door. I happened to look up and say "Look at this place?" My son said "think we can catch frogs?" I said "yeah it's Froggy out". Instantly with all the trouble behind us gave me a sense of comfort, this place is beautiful, with plenty of land and woods, I wouldn't call it the woods *it's the forest*, it's like a wall of trees right from the edge of the property. We even have a *brook in our yard now.*

(We like going to the brook to catch frogs. My fun was watching my children. It was a challenge, in the wild, watching, waiting one move and it was a free for all, the art of catching one without getting wet. Someone always ended up in the slimy green gunk, Or with some very wet sneakers, that was usually our cue to head back to the house.)

Becky loves this place so much. She is putting up bird feeders and wind chimes, the previous owners told us, a mother deer and her babies can be seen in the yard.

Becky likes to look around for animal tracks, she has already invited every bird, I've ever seen to the place, she knows the right foods their looking for. She buys it, so she can attract them.

What a difference. We go to the store and there are no lines. The speed limit on the road just outside our driveway is 45mph. There is one traffic light in the Town. I try to adjust my speed so it's usually green, as I approach it…. Most of the time it works, This is what it feels like being in the country.

The air seems to have the fragrance of clean linen. The Peace and quiet with only the sounds of nature *Tree frogs at night can be pretty noisy little things.* I have never seen so many stars there's even clusters of them, it looks like overspray, At least one or two shooting stars go by each night, that's during the time that your watching.

I keep asking "Becky what do you think?" She says "I love it; I can't wait to get my Mother and Father out for a week to enjoy it with us. Becky puts the linens out on the line because she loves the smell on them when she takes them in.

We decided to buy a big swing set.
The industrial kind *it looks tiny in the yard.*
The yard is so big I can fit two city blocks in
it from Lynn. We don't even use a leash
with the dogs they run free and tire
themselves without even leaving the place.
Sometimes Pig goes just beyond the
property

Piggy is in his element. He's thinks
he is vicious once he gets a smell. All you
can hear is woof, woof, and woof as he runs
in circles with his nose to the ground. He
actually has raw marks on his face, from
pushing his snout down so hard. His ears are
long for a beagle; He has tripped over them
once or twice.

Hunter is a well mannered
gentleman; I sometimes say he has more
integrity *than most humans I know.* He
keeps piglet in check. Piggy isn't afraid of
anything in the woods; However, he is very
concerned… if Hunter puts him in place
from time to time.

Piggy has a nose for trouble, I
watched a squirrel once walk around a tree,
up another tree, across the yard one way and
back another. He finally ran into the woods.
I let pig out, and he followed the exact same
path, barking all the way.

Piggy has made a name for himself. A neighbor called and asked me to keep my beagle on my property, because Piggy stands on the guy's car and barks at him. *I think he was just telling him where his cat is.* Another neighbor called and said your beagle keeps looking in my basement windows. I told the neighbor with the basement windows to just yell "PIG" at him and he should stop. The guy did, and I watched, Piggy ran off looking back. He must have thought *"Oh shit they recognized me"*

Once, Becky and I were standing at the back of the house, Hunter ran up he just started barking like he meant it. Hunter doesn't do that. I joked and said" *What Timmy's stuck in the well?*" he barked louder, I thought what if he is telling me something? I said "Show me" and we ran, as we did, we found piggy limping back, with a very serious wound in his leg. Hunter was trying to get help. He's the best. We got piggy all fixed up. He wasn't happy with the leg protection and the head funnel. In fact he was pissed. We have no idea what happened.

He had already escaped from the leashes and the chest harness when we first arrived. So he either has to stay in, or we have to pray that he's ok.

In time he was back out. One day he came home looking fine, I thought he was calm and cool. I happened to see a large red bump in his leg. I got closer and realized it was his testicle. He had ripped the skin opened somehow and *his balls dropped down and out.*

The vet has to remove them; she said *"if we wait he will eat them."* I am surprised he didn't.

The removal of his balls never slowed him down. He still lifts his leg almost over his body to pee. *In his mind they are really large.* Every now and then he runs through the yard with a half of a rabbit or something. He seems to remind me of someone I just can't place it. His bark shouts *"I'm right and everybody's wrong"*

Hunter is really smart, he wants to show us he will protect us… so he stands tall and looks like authority. When they hear a sound, they bark and run to the woods. Hunter stops at the edge, while piggy runs in as fast as can *ready to take on anything.* Hunter waits there, seemingly in case something goes wrong, or is it because something is so big he didn't want to meet it? Piggy doesn't seem to care either way.

They usually hang around the yard or travel on adventures with us. As long as Piggy keeps his nose to the ground we should be fine.

73
Country Living

We are blessed with very good boys. They all do very well in school. They have no trouble getting As and Bs.

My oldest son "at home" My Tiger earns the right to advanced programs all the time. My second son is right behind him. My youngest is just starting; He is well on his way. His teacher told us she would *love to have a classroom full of him in multiples.*

As to the emotional considerations it is easy enough for us to take the drive. So they can maintain past relationships. The idea that Lynn has a *bad wrap* I think its home Becky does too. Anything *unfamiliar can be frightening.* The first time I was in Worcester, I was worried for a minute here and there. If Lynn was as bad as it's made out to be. I am sure it would be shut down somehow.

Just a few weeks before we left my oldest son was robbed in front of a convenience store; a couple of assholes punched him and took his money.

A week later… In front of convenience store further down, a couple of assholes shot a kid in the stomach and took his money.

That was enough to decide a better life for them can be found away from the City bullshit. Even if this Town has a couple of assholes it can be monitored closer. Our boys are adapting quite well. They are finding friends, my two younger boys like the adventures in the woods and going to the Brook. We like to have a fire in the yard. My middle son watches it and says" Wow the fire is always the same, yet its constantly changing and doesn't get boring like TV can" Usually I sit by the fire with my younger boys and the dogs. Becky isn't too impressed by the fire. I call her out and she sits in the window shaking her head no.

I really don't know why she doesn't like the fire. She probably doesn't like the idea of bugs flying around, but the smoke keeps them away. My oldest son.. got the idea to bring his friends from Lynn to the house for a weekend get together. It was a real good time. It's nice to see normalization and happiness. As we plant our roots in the ground here. we had no idea it could get so bad, now, we don't see much in the way of craziness. We have the chance to live the *American dream*.

We control what happens in our lives, without everyone else stepping in determining our direction. The house is newer so lead isn't an issue, child support is done, and mostly everyone we know is in general good health. It's all good. And It's about time!

Becky found work as a cake decorator in a nice shop. Her boss is a good guy and the women she works with are easy going. She is making friends too. I still work close to Boston. I am waiting for an opening closer to us. But to do the transfer I have to stay in Department of Public Health. "DPH," There have been similar openings in DMH, DMR; I would have to quit the job and hope to be the best candidate to be rehired. I don't mind the ride. It is an hour and a half each way. It's also a job that I love to do.

At home… I am busy working around the yard. We got a lawn tractor and it takes hours to mow the lawn. Its so big…. if I used a hand held It would take two days. It is worth it the yard looks like a golf course when it's done. Our driveway is a tenth of a mile long. It's lined with evergreens. Next year Becky wants to string them all with lights. Or should I say she wants me to string them. Nah that's not true. She has already done the house herself.

The house has a wood stove in the basement. I thought it was for decoration but it actually works. I cleaned the chimney and got it working so I am about to learn about wood. The outside fires are great but I can't believe the heat this thing puts out. I have a new hobby. My sister's boyfriend was born around here. He told me the things I need to make life easier.

Most important is a pickup truck, then a wheel barrow, a lawn tractor, an eight pound maul and a chainsaw. I never liked chainsaws, it always looked like the chain could break and cut your head off. I bought a small one at first and tried it. It was safer than I expected. If you like hats, a baseball cap is good. Sometimes horse flies like to dive into your hair, while you work outside. There are horses and cows on our street, the property lines are separated by stones, thousands of them. It feels like you can pan for gold in the brook.

In Lynn, Jessie and I were looking at Maps; He found a very old map. There is a rumor that a lost treasure *still remains in or around Pirates rock* in Lynn woods. We went back and forth with both maps, and based on the original location of the treasure. It is now known as "Happy Valley" golf course.

I would say that the treasure might have funded the Golf Course. I wont be panning for gold, I think, if it was here at some point, it sure is gone by now. *It just feels like you should be panning.* Maybe it's the kid in me and the sense of adventure I like… that keeps me thinking this way. I am very busy with the chain saw,

You learn fast, On my first attempt to cut down a tree. I cut the wrong side and the tree bit down on my saw. It wouldn't let go. *The tree tilted in the same direction of the cut.* It should have been cut on the other side. No problem, I have a pickup truck. I decided to tie rope to the tree and the truck and pull off the weight, the saw should fall right out. The tree was all set to pull, I had the truck in 4wd and went slowly pulling and digging the tires in the ground, back and *forth digging deeper* and finally after about ten minutes, I realized the tree wasn't moving. I opened the door and realized I wasn't getting my truck out either; I dug myself in half way up the tires. Becky watched the whole thing. She tried not to laugh, But c'mon. I am out a chainsaw and a pickup truck.

I wanted those things… and it's the tree, *I wanted to get rid of.* It didn't look too good. I left them both there until I could develop a new strategy.

Calling a tow truck would be too embarrassing; I bought sand and tire ramps and chains. It took three weeks….

I finally called a tow truck. And I went and got a larger chainsaw and that tree came crashing down. I succeeded in cutting down my first tree. It wasn't easy I tell ya. I have to get a new transmission for my truck too. I am a country boy now. *Where's my hat*?

Becky's parents came out to see the house. They love it. Becky's mother misses her daughter and the Boys. I guess she is upset that we moved so far away. I wish it was closer. But this is what we've been dreaming of all our lives.

If we had dreams of staying in Lynn We would have never left. I would like to build an in law apartment or something. But they want to stay in Lynn. This does create a bit of trouble. I know Becky talks to her Mother every day and she still gets a little home sick. I do too. We go back to Lynn for a day trip here and there and it feels good.

I think saying goodbye on the phone starts to get them both upset. I really don't want to return. Becky says she wants to stay here too. The boys are adapting very well.

We have mixed emotions. At times Becky doesn't seem very happy. When I ask her what's wrong she says she's just tired. I know she doesn't like to make me worry. I think it's more than that.

Is she really homesick? If she is, we'll sell the house and move back. I love this place, but I love her more. *Her happiness is the most important thing to me.* My happiness *is her and the boys*.

It's a long way to a Dunks or a mall. That can be draining at times when you're used to everything being right there. We do go out and do things. We have a good time then. However, When were home and in the routine she seems sad.

I keep getting "blown off" when I ask what's wrong;. I know she worries about my drive. I wish I knew what's bothering her.

We have coffee in the morning. She is usually in good spirits. As lunchtime comes around, she seems to get tired. I am beginning to think she's probably getting depressed. I said "Are you ok? She replied "Yeah, I think the country air makes me tired".

I remember feeling that way for the first week or so. I thought it was from the move. "I hope you're not getting depressed" I try to talk about the good things.

Look at the differences in our lives now, we have some money in the bank, we have half the Mortgage we used to have. The kids seem really happy, the dogs love it here. I know you miss your Parents at times. What's actually bothering you?" I asked. She just looked at me and said. "There's nothing bothering me I am just a bit tired"

I thought about it and realized her ride to work was no more than 5 minutes in Lynn. Its twenty minutes away here. They may also work her buns off. I know that she talks to her mother a lot on the phone.

It's all mentally draining. We can move back if that will make the difference. We went through so much. It's mostly due to my past. *I never wanted her to suffer.* This should be what makes her happy. Unless it's too late and all the happiness in her was sucked out over the past ten or so years. I have a lot more work to do. We have never talked about divorce or anything.

She had that option before and she was more than shocked at the notion. She fell apart crying at the nerve of the Lawyer suggesting it.

Even now, just hearing about divorces, and couples in trouble pisses her off. She usually comments "People suck! *Why did they bother getting married in the first place? You take the good with the bad"*

I know relationships usually start off on a high note and within months you can tell its not all roses. People escape the reality of their lives and create a whole new reality. Its not always fun and games.

I don't think there's such a thing as perfect in a Marriage. I mean mine seems perfect for me. Look at all the trouble *Becky has had to deal with*. It wasn't perfect for her. I have always known how lucky I am and I have always felt bad that she isn't as lucky. She walked into a nightmare. She loves me and stuck through it. She said she has everything she ever wanted. She still wants a baby girl; she said she's been thinking about it.

My son spends time with a friend up the street, Heather is the boys Mother, Her and Becky hit it off right away.

Heather is married to Bill, They are very nice people. She believes in her Family as much as Becky does ours. We have been invited to the lake with them and we did some water skiing and cookouts and things. I work different hours so I don't spend any one to one time with Bill, like Becky does with Heather so they have more of a friendship.

It's good for Becky to have her own connections here. It helps with homesickness. Every time we go to Lynn, on the return trip we say "Ah so close and yet so far" Aside of the *tired feeling* I see in Becky, She seems to be happy here. Her and Heather are really becoming close enough, that if we do move back now. Becky will miss her friend an awful lot. And that could make her homesick for this place.

Becky bought a wooden sign that says "*Grow where you are planted*" she wants to put it near the garden somehow. The garden is as big as three city buses parked side by side. Next year she will figure the right spot to put it in

She has specific things she likes to see, and it should to go just the way she pictures it. At the front of the yard there was a rock… it didn't mean anything to me.

She quizzed me about the possibilities of moving it up and in a different position. It was very large. I told her I could move it a little with the plow. After, I positioned it the way she wanted. She painted flowers and the house number on it. Then she added a planter tipped over and plants as if it *spilled everywhere*. That's how she pictured it ahead of time.

I never even noticed the rock before. Now, it's the first thing I see before I reach the house. It's good because *the house is easy to pass*. I've done that so many times. She has her Ideas; and she does a lot around here. I guess maybe she does so much it makes her that tired. I feel a lot of energy because all the work I have done in the past is at a minimum now. I enjoy the yard work and I don't think of it as work. However, It can do a number on your muscles.

My son and I cut logs from old trees and we chop them into fire wood. We do that a few hours each week and try to get more each time. We have oil heat and we don't need wood; we just like what were doing.

Heather called me at work and said "Becky fainted," *she hasn't been herself for a few days*, and Heather thinks she should go to the Hospital. I told her... I would meet her there. I got to the Hospital and Becky was in the Emergency room. She had IVs and a bag of blood. The doctor said *"she has lost a lot of blood."* I asked "How?" He told me her menstrual cycle was ongoing. It went longer than it should. They took all kinds of tests. Everything came back *fine*.

One test indicated *a hint* to a problem with her liver. She had stabilized and she was able to go home. The doctor said she should get an appointment with her Doctor to check for *underlying problems*. She had one appointment and the Doctor told us she has high iron content. *Becky was taking iron pills*. Due to her cycle she figured she needed it.

The Doctor can't find any other indications of a problem. He gave her some medication and told her to look for changes or new symptoms. Heather quizzes her daily.

Becky seemed unchanged the rest of August and September, One day while I was at work Heather called me because she was concerned and she told me that Becky spends *most of the day sleeping on the couch*, I noticed the house doesn't seem so clean and the kids have been eating a lot of microwave food. Becky still works, but she does call in once or twice a week. *I still work eighty miles away.* I can't transfer yet, I am beginning to think, I should change jobs and fix cars again, so I can be *close to home*.

Becky is sick and I need to be ready for an emergency, my family needs me.

The next day at work…. made my decision for me. My assignment was in Car-1, at the beginning of my shift Tim handed me some court papers. He told me a woman in one of the programs has her children with her. She was arrested last week for DUI.

Her ex-husband got an order to take *temporary custody of his kids*. I have to find a way to do this gracefully.

I went to the program and asked to speak with the young woman and a program staff member. I explained all about the order and what has to be done. I also informed the woman that it is temporary and if she stays in the program she will have staff and program assets to assist her *in their return*.

With a staff member and the Mother we approached the children. We explained in cautious detail. What has to be done. The oldest child was her son, He was a big kid, but he only was eleven. The next a sister was nine and the youngest sister was about six.

I spoke with the kids I focused on the son. He expressed anger at his father. I said "You are the oldest. *This order is temporary....* Just make sure that you look after your sisters, and be happy you are all together. Sometimes parents get angry at each other. That doesn't mean they don't love you. They just have to work things out better, and when their feelings change, they act in ways that are not as what everyone wants to see. Everyone is upset, just try *to be strong and stick together*."

They all seem a little more at ease. I know I sure wasn't. *Who am I? Walking in with a piece of paper and taking someone's kids away?*

I thank God for what I have

The minute I returned to the
Campus, I went to dispatch to write the
report. I didn't want to dwell on that all
shift. I just need to put it behind me. Tom
asked about Becky, and if I was ok. I said
"yeah fine" I dreaded bumping into that
mother. I feel terrible as they were all crying
and they gave each other one really big
family hug. We do that

I remember the day that began, we
were on the couch watching TV, Becky was
on one side, I was on the other and my
oldest son at home was in the middle. I think
he was four at the time. We both turned in
to kiss him at the same time. He panicked
and cried,

He got double whammies…. I guess
he was so into the TV program he never saw
us coming. We started hugging him and we
said "*OH someone needs family hugs*" and
Family hugs were born for us.

About 7pm I saw the woman outside
of her program, She smiled and said "*thank
you for caring*; you were very nice about the
way you did your job." I just smiled back
and wished her luck. *I don't feel any better.*

About 9pm an individual ran up to the car and informed me that there was an accident on the main street. I responded, as I approached the scene, I could see a woman walking around with a head wound, And another guy standing in the road... he appeared *confused*. Another man was trapped in one of the cars. I saw flames at the dashboard. I called into dispatch.

("*Car-1 to dispatch....*" Dispatch go ahead car-1,".... *Dispatch we have a serious motor vehicle accident, with a person trapped and fire is showing. we'll need at least two emergency ambulances and their going to need the Jaws of Life to get this guy out.*" What's your location Car-1?.. *Just in front of the main entrance.* Car-1 everything is rolling. I have Portable two to assist you.)

The injured woman had been in the vehicle with the trapped man. She got out when I arrived, *She tried to climb back in* as I emptied my fire extinguisher on the dashboard as best I could. Flames were still showing. I knew the Fire Department will arrive in less than a minute. I held her back. She wanted to be with him. *I figured he may not make it.* I can't have two dead bodies on my hands.

I told her... I'd stay with him in the vehicle until the Fire Department arrives.

He was an older man. He was crying. I held his hand and told him I will stay with him until they arrive.

For a good thirty seconds. All I could think was "What the fuck am I doing sitting here?"

I have a wife and children at home that need me. Now, more than ever I have to get out of this car safe, and then I will resign on the spot.

I remained on the scene until med flight arrived. It took two Jaws of Life to get the guy out. I don't know if he survived. At the end of my shift… I made my report. I asked my Sergeant how much time I had on the books. He said about 2 weeks.

I told him to use that as my two week notice…. I can't do this right now.

75
It`s my problem now

The next day… I began searching on the internet. I saw an opening for a rotating Manager to work in a popular Muffler shop franchise. One man owned about seven of these shops. He needed a Manager to fill in at all shops to give his regular managers a day off. I realize… I will be working around cars again and I should settle with that.

He promised good pay and benefits. All the shops were close enough that I could be less than an hour away in case of an emergency. *Except one*, it *was eighty miles away*. I could fill in there in an Emergency. I started working for him learning the process for each location. It was nice to change locations everyday. I had a freshness going store to store. I never expected to be around cars again so quickly.

The owner soon proved to be a complete asshole.

His greed was worse than anything I ever saw. He did so many things that pissed me off. It was all related to his greed. The worst was when a young girl came to the shop. She needed brakes, one wheel cylinder was leaking. *I could do this job and have a conscience for about $200.00* and the rear brakes would be like new. The front still had time.

The owner was present he looked at the same girl and the same car. He looked pissed off at me, and he gave her a new estimate for over $1100.00 Dollars. He told her she needed many extra parts *He will throw in a free oil change.* She told him "she doesn't have enough money" he told her *she must have a grandmother or someone that can wire the money.* She called her grandmother and she was crying so badly she almost vomited.

When he saw this… he said *"you're all upset about* your car, it's not your problem anymore. Stop crying the car is my problem now so you should not worry anymore"

I wanted to say "she is upset about the fucking you just gave her you cockroach, Not the fucking car" And YOU know it! You manipulative piece of shit.

Her boyfriend showed up and the owner said "You need to buy your girl a drink she is all upset about her car, But I told her... *Its my problem now*" ...

If I were the boyfriend, I would have " Pulled a *Jimmy* on him" and *that* would be *his problem now*. He did so many other things I wouldn't know where to begin. I decided to leave. I will not be an accomplice to his crimes. I *need* to be local for work

76
Beers after work

I found another advertisement for a Muffler shop in Worcester. The shop needed a Manager. I was hired, but the Area supervisor told me *to fire all the staff* and start new.

I am not firing anyone, I figured, until I see a reason. There were broken windows and trash all over the lot, weeds and broken down cars. *This place looks like Aunt Ruth's house, but it smells better.*

The crew consisted of Seth the assistant Manager and Gary was a tech. Seth looked at me as if, I was some Company guy that would *push him out.* Gary shows up when he feels like it. He'll probably have to go. The first day I just watched the way the shop ran. Seth was disgruntled.

Gary came in and said "Hey new blood huh?" Gary had a scruffy look about him. He had cracked glasses and a scruffy beard, his greasy hair is just past his ears, Dirty uniforms and filthy hands.

I think he has two teeth. *He looks like a circus hobo clown.* Seth is clean and he has a good appearance he gets along with everyone that comes through the door. When an asshole comes in he handles it with gentle firmness.

So far Becky is ok. She isn't feeling better but she hasn't had a crisis of any kind. Changing jobs has created a tighter money situation and the insurance that I had is gone now. About two weeks into the Job they guys began feeling better about me. I cleaned the place up and fixed the windows. I am trying to sell jobs for them so we can make incentive money. Gary always has a story; his most recent is that he had to move because his place had rats. Seth and I started laughing Seth said *"Now that you moved the place doesn't have rats anymore."* Then we joked and started calling him "Gary the rat" Gary is a good mechanic if you keep an eye on him and prompt him from time to time. Seth works steady and slow. He does the company jobs by day and side jobs by night.

I figure all of his tools are here and they cost thousands of dollars. He can work on a friend or relatives car. I guess the company thought all the jobs were side jobs. That's why they wanted him fired. We started to focus right away and our sales are already up.

I am allowed an extra guy based on our sales progress. We hired a part time guy for the light work *Manny* is his name. He used to always hang around and help out anyway. He likes Seth and so do many other people. Seth has many visitors

Our customer base is established from *oil change coupons.* All though we are full service Most of the marketing people came from *Supermarkets and figure Volume equals sales.* To me... Quality and discount pricing equal sales, I cut the price almost in half and the company still has great profits and that has increased our sales, Its common sense.

Just drop your fucking prices and they will buy your product. People shop around. This location is on Park Ave with a lot of competition

It's been three weeks and we have a comfort level with each other. My opinion is that Seth is a great guy he is honest and genuine. Manny is the same. *Nobody here should have been fired they should just be appreciated for who they are.*

The previous Manager was the problem. I have worked with assholes and these guys are far from that.

Gary has a heart of gold. But his motivations are focused on coffee and cigarettes and Beers after work. "Beaz afta wurk" We all seem to becoming tight with each other. Even the Rat, As Seth says "He may be a Rat, but he's our Rat". Gary doesn't like being called a Rat because street folks, think it means he talks too much. Nah he's just a filthy critter is all. Kind of like Piglet without a bath, Gary's hair style looks like Piggys long ears.

Slowly, we all cleaned up the shop in heavy duty style. One small area at a time it's looking much better. Customer Satisfaction is beginning to show. We are a team and it feels good, *just like I belong here*. I am beginning to give Seth a little insight about what's going on at home. That way he has a heads up in case of an Emergency. He is the Assistant Manager and he would have to cover for me. I am starting to hear more about his personal life as well. And the more I learn the more *I know the guy is honest and has integrity*. The market supervisor thought he was very dishonest. It seems to me it's all going to work out well with these guys. Becky calls me at work and I give her some details of the day and clue her in on the guys. She knows I like it and she feels good about that. She figured I was angry about leaving the State.

I will not have insurance for another two months so I hope she stays healthy. We still don't know what happened.

She has been taking the new Medications and *she stopped with Iron pills*. But she's still tired most of the time. Even when she feels at her worst, she takes it, and doesn't let me know how bad she feels.

I look for things like that to keep her smiling and feeling better. The weather is turning its December now so the snow and cold keep her from leaving the house too much. She doesn't like the idea of not controlling how she feels in General.

77
Aggressive treatment

On December 9th I got home at the usual time. Becky didn't look good at all. She is jaundiced and having difficulty breathing. I told her I should call 911. She said "No Ill be fine if I can just lay down for awhile" For about ten seconds... I was going to agree with that.

I called 911. The ambulance and some Police arrived. They gave her oxygen and it gave her minimal relief and she was taken to the local hospital. They had to send her to Umass in Worcester. *She needs more aggressive treatment.* Upon arrival the Doctor could see she is yellow and has water build up all over. He assumed she had alcoholic's hepatitis. He said "*When was your last drink?*" I remember we had a drink on Halloween, so I told him. He said "your wife can't be placed any list for a liver until she is free of alcohol for six months." I said "*she doesn't drink. She had one on Halloween.*"

They tested for Tylenol and alcohol they couldn't find any immediate evidence of either one.

The doctor had a team of other Doctors working on various concerns relating to Becky's health. They had to remove water from around her heart. Her kidneys have almost stopped working. She needs dialysis The Doctor said "Your wife has liver failure. And some indications lead towards alcohol and some indications lead towards Hemochromatosis

At this point they have to rule against the Hemochromatosis based on her age. The illness causes an overload of iron to store in the organs. A woman her age has regular cycles that prevent that kind of buildup. An *older woman could have this problem*. I tried to explain about the Iron pills. But they were thinking more towards alcohol. I try to tell them what kind of person she is, but based on what they see. It would be unethical to give someone a liver that would possibly drink it into damage again. I keep telling them but they won't listen.

They removed the fluid from around her heart and began dialysis, she seems a lot better. She is very afraid now. The doctors are really not being very polite to her.

They are going to keep her in a room near the ICU. In the event that she has a crisis they can rush her to the right place.

I waited until she was comfortable and had a regular room. Then, I raced home to the boys. I told them she may be there awhile. And we will have to start working together around the house. I can cook the meals and the boys can clean up a little. In the morning I will leave early and see her before work. My oldest son has the morning covered with the routine and buses. I made lunches when I got up, and got their clothes so they should have it easy getting out.

Based on what the doctors are saying, Becky will be in the Hospital and remain in a room near the ICU. At work Seth is really there for me. He has everything covered if I need to leave or if I am on the phone. I am very grateful, that I have been able to acquire my position at this location. *I am minutes away from the Hospital*. I was placed here about a month ago. And I was told to fire Seth. Already he is proving to be an incredible asset to my personal life. I have enough money to leave the boys money to order out. My youngest son just turned eight years old. He needs to maintain. My two older boys are sticking with the routine.

I am very lucky to have such wonderful children. Becky needs me now more than she ever has. We are in this together. I have to focus all my energy towards her. She has been through a lot in life. And she is strong. Let alone the faith she has. *Her will to survive is very strong.*

All day while I am at work…I try to get updates and I look for opportunities to go see her. Seth makes that easy. The guys at work are doing double duty because they want to. *It is because they care.* I am very lucky to have these guys in my life right now. It's hard to believe they were total strangers a month ago now they are working their butts off *to help me every day.* And its amazing that I am so close to the Hospital

When I see Becky, her demeanor seems unemotional but concerned, as if she did something and feels guilty. I have always asked her to take vitamins and eat better. But that's not why she's in this place. *The iron pills were something she thought were helping.* I try to coach her and lift her spirit. She seems to think she is being punished for something she has done. *The attitude I see, when the Doctors talk to her, only adds to that.* I pulled one aside and gave him a piece of my mind for a minute or so. I hope they lighten up.

Every day I get a *slightly updated* report. The doctors think her kidneys are trying to work. They will stop dialysis to see. I think maybe they should keep it going the kidneys could use the help. *But I am no Doctor.* Now that she is this sick she can pick up any illness in the air. And she can get infections. She is getting an infection now, so they are adding antibiotics. She has no appetite, so they are pushing fluids. She asks how the Christmas tree looks. I tell her it doesn't look as good as it did *when she put it up*. This is her way of saying she wants to come home. She asks about the kids and the dogs and the house. I tell her it's ok and not to worry. The kids will be able to come up to see her on the Weekend.

I am hoping this gives her something to look forward to, instead of feeling worst that they aren't with her. I have always told my kids the truth. I have always tried to ease painful truths. But my oldest son is always researching whatever I tell him. He knows she is in serious trouble.

I haven't spoken with her parents as much as I do now. I give them daily updates. They can see her on the weekends too. They hospital staff are beginning to recognize me and they put an effort forward to address any questions and concerns I have.

I haven't told anyone that I have some experience in this setting. They see me as some guy that fixes cars.

Becky is winning the hearts of a few people here and they are becoming friendly and kind. She needs that right now. Your emotional state is a great part of a chance for recovery. The weekend has arrived. I knew Becky's parents were going to spend all of Saturday with her. I will bring the kids up Saturday night and well go back Sunday. If she has to remain hospitalized this will be the routine. I go up before, during and after work.

She has good and bad days, on the days that she had a good day and we had a good visit, I feel recharged and feel a lot like I did when we met and I would race to her work to see her. I notice when I leave after an evening visit. I am already looking forward to the next morning visit.

I found myself singing songs on the way to see her the next morning. I miss her and she really is missing home. She has never been alone in her life. That's the hardest part for her right now. It became very tough for everyone by Christmas and my middle child has a birthday the first week of January, This was more painful for her.

She stopped eating and refuses meds. She is *begging to come home*. She is also becoming confused at times. The doctors say this is all part of the illness, ammonia is on her brain. She went from dialysis three times a week to everyday.

The first week of January the doctor pulled me aside and said "She isn't going to survive. I just looked at him and thought "do you have any Idea what we have been through?" We make it, I said "I think she's a fighter and she will make it." He shook his head and walked away. With the machines in place she is unchanged…. without the machines she would be gone.

My children listen to my updates and check online to put all the information they have together. They like the fact that Becky and I have been so positive. They are waiting to see as well. Now that she has stopped eating. We are all worried. At home the food we have is just filler, I have been to the smaller stores and I buy as needed. I have never shopped by myself for all the groceries before. Any cooking I've done has been limited to burgers and things.

The nurses told me to encourage her to eat or she will need a feeding tube. If she gets that she won't be able to communicate. Her infections are back to back. Just when they beat one she gets another. January is a long month of that. I get my strength from Becky and the kids. Seth has been there more than I can imagine. He is probably one of the greatest people I have ever met. He hasn't asked for anything in return for helping me. Our sales are still up and I think he's proud to work with me, and he likes knowing he is this appreciated.

Now that the staff have told me about the feeding tube I am prepared this can get worst quickly.

I went to see her and they told me she needs more intensive therapy. They are taking her to the ICU.

This is not a good sign at all. Becky communicates with me and she says she is keeping hope and wants to get better. She says she just doesn't want to eat. I told her she has to or she will continue to get sicker. She knows but she just can't. Nurses are telling me it's the illness. Becky has water build up, and this can give her motion sickness. She needs physical therapy to try and use her extremities.

She has always had a strong will, and I see it, even if they don't. The idea that she is here and is missing her children and life events has brought her way down. She feels like she has failed them. She wants to get better. If not for herself… for us.

This feeling of failure is depressing her…. Her friends from Lynn have been coming to see her. That does lift her spirit. Becky asked a nurse *if anyone has ever been as sick as she is and survived.*

The nurse said "Yes, and he is here today, another nurse told him about you and he wants to visit with you if that's ok." Becky smiled and said yes. He is an older man; he and his wife come here often to see the people that saved him. I got a call from his wife.

She told me not to give up hope, because you will have days were you want to but don't, *its hope and faith that kept them strong and they won.* I told her, I agree and that's all I have. She told me, I can call them, if I ever need support and they will check in on Becky. It's a good feeling being in a place where you don't know anyone and people want to help.

My boys have done so well at home. We always told them when things get tough we need to be a team. When I get home the house is clean, quiet and homework is done and everyone is waiting to hear what happened today. I tell them about the bad days, but I try to *underscore the better moments*. Franks blessing at our Wedding came half way true *are little ones are no trouble at all*. The ICU staff is very good when it comes to communication. If things change either way they call.

Tonight they called and said "since I left Becky has been showing signs of improvement in some areas. Kidney function and she has requested some juice." Small things, but they are good signs. I think the visit Becky had today gave her a very good lift. People showing a little hope can go a long way. It is giving her hope and strength.

The hospital staff tells me that Becky has been free of any crises for a couple of days and she shows a lot of signs of improvement. But for someone in her position she can go backward or forward at any moment. I went to her room and she was smiling at me as I approached. My smile was felt from ear to ear.

I usually watch TV with her and we talk and then I head home. If she is asleep I stay a little less.

Tonight the staff gave me a recliner instead of a straight chair. As we watched TV, I got very comfortable. When I tried to get up, I made an old man sound; 'argh' then I pushed myself up. I looked at her and she said "Oh my God" she had a very concerned look on her face. I said "What?" She said *"This is kicking both our asses"* I smiled and said "I love you" And I am fine. *I think that was the greatest thing anyone has ever said to me. This is my wife and this is our problem.* To know she really feels that way.....

She just gave me the strength of ten men to have higher hope and to be stronger at home and work. I love my wife so much and she loves me just the same. If she can stay like she is right now she will be perfectly fine. I expect some tough days but today she has really come around.

It's going to be Valentines Day in a few days and she is doing well.

I still haven't done any regular food shopping.

We get what we need, I cannot find an hour or two for big shopping my day starts at 5am, and I am out the door at 6am, I see Becky for a half hour or so. Then I work all day; I am able to leave to see Becky for a half hour or so. I officially leave work at 7pm. I see Becky until about 830pm, then I head home usually by 9:30pm, I try to have time with my boys. My youngest son usually falls asleep around 9pm. I begin laundry or prep for the next day, and I fall asleep around 12 or so. It's been the routine. To squeeze an hour in for food shopping is very tough. On Sundays, I have some time to catch up on what's been missed at home throughout the week. The Boys want to see Becky. We spend much of the day at the Hospital

On Valentine's Day Becky is a little down; her illness is turning back and forth. It seems when she has dialysis she perks up. It helps filter her blood. She is at a point where she needs it. This is always a tough day. The day itself is an emotional one. We talked about past Valentines days.

On our tenth Valentines day, I happened to see a singing Quartet at Boston Market in Salem. I asked if they could go to her work later that night. They were perfect gentlemen they gave me the address to mail the payment and promised they would show. This was a verbal transaction. *I didn't know them and they didn't know me.* I also wanted her to have flowers and balloons. I went to the flower shop and prepaid so I knew that would happen.

As it turned out… a clown showed up with the flowers and balloons at the same time as the Quartet. She was Prom Queen at her work that night.

This is a nice memory to help her today.

Administration and the team of doctors want to have a family meeting regarding all the aspects of Becky's condition and treatment.

The team holds the same position that they held the day she arrived. It can be one reason or the other as to a cause.

Nothing there has changed. We are a few days before March. This will be almost four months that she's been here.

They discussed how the illness works and they are very surprised that she is hanging on. Not many people can make it this long in her condition. The only cure is a transplant and if it's successful it will take a year or so of physical therapy to learn how to walk and live normal again.

At this point Becky is getting "open windows" when she is free of infections and other concerns. The windows are not open long enough to be able to handle an organ transplant. Becky has to stay free of troubles for more than 24hrs.

At that time, they can place her on the list and hope that an organ is available. The windows are really very small. If the conditions are right they will place her at the top of the list.

To me this is a sign of hope. The team looked like they were giving us bad news.

A year of physical therapy to me is something we can do, if Becky had to deal with my 'ankle biting spider-itus'. She wouldn't even think, she would just do what is needed. I can certainly deal with anything she needs.

Becky's mother, father and sister were present they feel that hope too. Now it's in the hands of Becky's hope and strength.... she is the strongest person I know...

All she has to do is have a couple good days in a row. I think she has the chance of doing that. We wait with hope and excitement *when we find she is on an upswing*.

Everyday is an incredible challenge. It's crazy she does so well one day and turns completely down the next. It's like being very healthy and being horribly Ill within hours and then changing back it's just terrible what she's going through. I try to give her hope and lift her spirit and when I see how hard she fights I feel guilty as if she is trying for me

Sometimes she is so confused she doesn't recognize me. Her confusion is something that comes up a lot now. One day she thought I was an orderly. She asked me to help her escape another day. And when I couldn't she broke down and look terribly frightened. This was the ONLY time she seemed to be frightened... Thankfully

It hurts so bad to see her like this. I remember the other woman telling me there will be times when you want to give up hope and let go. But you have to hang on and she will feel it and try to fight harder. I am trying to give her that hope, but I wonder if she feels it or knows it's me.

She told me she has to get ready for her reception. I asked her what she was talking about and she got frustrated as if I have no clue. Her dialysis was on and off.

Now it looks to be 24/7 and today she has a new feeding tube. She can't vocalize anymore. Our communication is done with me talking and I watch her eyes. She is conscious and responsive.

March started off very badly. However, Becky is on an upswing again. Her feeding tube is removed. She can talk, but she doesn't have much to say. The hospital staff report any changes good or bad even tiny details like her temp changing one degree. Everything is critical. It looks as if her window is coming. My spirit is climbing again. Becky is holding on, she has been too sick for too long and some people say *why is she fighting so hard.* A lot of people can't believe how strong she is. I know she loves life and wants to grow old; this is her time…. that's why.

The Doctors now have considered this to be more in the way of Hemochromatosis. The only things keeping her back are loss of open windows. She has been here four months. And now she has a chance at recovering.

Sunday the 20th was a nice visit, Becky had energy and interacted with us, and she had a few laughs and didn't appear confused or uncomfortable.

Monday the 21st she developed a slight infection. Her spirit is fine, she is a little nervous.

Tuesday the 22nd Becky showed signs of improvement. She is tired when I see her, but she is conscious and hopeful.

Wednesday 23rd Becky continued to improve and fight her most recent infection. She told me that she feels defeated. I told her she is almost ready to get on the list and they move the sickest people to the top.

Thursday 24th Becky continues to maintain, the hospital called today and told me that Becky is finally on the list. *And she is at the top of the list*.

The organ transplant team spoke directly to me. They added that over the weekend an organ should arrive and by Sunday or Monday, Becky will get the transplant.

This is the greatest news I have heard…. I called everyone and I went right to the hospital to see how Becky feels about the news. It looks like were almost there.

When I arrived I noticed Becky had a slight smile but she looked exhausted. I ask her what they said "about the good news." Just to feel her response..

She was informed but she told me she just feels defeated. I asked her to hang on a couple of days. If she went this far she should feel close to defeated. But she is winning. I told her we can see the finish line just ahead. I know she has the power to fight and have her life back.

Sunday is Easter, Becky's parents usually spend Saturday with her, and I take the boys up Sundays. Her parents will see her all day Saturday then they will spend the night at our house. And we will all spend Easter with her, unless the transplant is going to take place.

Friday, I went to see her as usual, I feel a whole new energy, she seems so tired but she knows the transplant will take place. She is a little scared of the surgery. I tried to comfort her, and I told her I will be right here for her. She seems better; we held hands almost the entire visit. Friday night I returned and she was sleeping. The nursing staff told me she was up all day. In the ICU that's unusual. *I think she is very nervous.*

Saturday morning I went to see her *she is in good spirits*, I told her, Ill see her after work. Her Mother and Father will spend the day with her.

They did, and they had an awesome visit. Becky was wide awake and full of life. She laughed and joked and remained awake the entire time. The nursing staff told me she didn't seem nervous at all. She is asleep and the nursing staff added that I should let her sleep, that visit sure took a lot out of her. I got home and her parents looked very happy. They said Becky was great today. It was a time to feel better and relax a little. They told me I should go out with my friends I haven't in so long and they are here to watch the kids. I couldn't, but they convinced me that it will be fine and I deserve to enjoy a couple of beers for a change.

I decided they are right. I called Seth. He and His fiancé decided to meet me for some food and beers.

We had some laughs; I told them how excited I am. I told them how grateful I am for his friendship. And it just felt good to have a normal night without worry and in the Morning… It will be Easter and I will see Becky… she is hours away from a new life. It feels so good not to have all the worry. I only had a few beers I don't want to be drunk and drive that's all I need right now.

I headed home and when I arrived I saw a note on the door. Call hospital ASAP. I walked in and my son said "Nanny and Grampy are at the Hospital you have to call right away." He didn't look happy at all. This isn't good. I called the ICU the Nurse said they are having a crisis with a patient and a Doctor will call back in a few minutes.

(I think the patient she is talking about is Becky. All night I was within five minutes away from the hospital. I could have gone there if they called my cell phone. Now, I am 45minutes away and I have had beers. I think I should just go. Just then the phone rang. I answered and it was the Doctor.)

As the phone rang, I looked at the clock. Its 12:10 am I answered and the Doctor identified himself as the doctor *that is trying to give Becky emergency care.*

He told me that Becky has had an extreme downward spiral and she is in respiratory and cardiac failure. *She is not going to survive.* He asked if I wanted him to administer medication to ease her pain and help her go with less suffering.

I told him that her parents just saw her and she was fine. She is getting a transplant. He told me that sometimes when someone is this ill, they can have a burst of life and spirit just before the end. I began to panic.... He told me her parents were with her.

I wasn't listening to him, I pleaded for him to give me better answers, I had him on the phone long enough.... that her parents waited as she passed away... and they came back to my house and they told me she is gone. They were with her....

I hung up and began saying this cant be real, I just couldn't believe it.

I just can't believe she is gone, it's impossible. She fought so hard. She didn't drink or smoke or anything. She was on the Donor list, she cut her hair for cancer patients, and she helped anyone that needed help. She saved box tops for the Kidney foundation; she saved can tops for another charity. She fucking fed birds. She never asked for anything… She was fine today she was perfect and ready to live again.

I drink, smoke, and drive like an asshole sometimes Why the fuck is this happening? It can't be real. I sat down staring at nothing… feeling angry, numb and thinking it has to be impossible. I didn't sleep I just sat in disbelief.…

79
She would be proud

I have to tell my younger boys.
Before…, they open their Easter baskets. I
can't picture them celebrating a Holiday as
we prepare for this.

My oldest son told me he expected
the worst and he has prepared them. He read
a lot about the details as I gave them to him
and I had much more hope than everyone
else. They will be ok.

I sat them down and tried to say
*"Moms not sick anymore, but as I said that,
my youngest son lit up with a huge smile. I
said softly, No she's gone honey and I am so
sorry, she fought so hard and she wanted to
be here with us. If there's a heaven,
something big must be going on because she
was taken on the Holiest day. We held each
other and cried.*

We fell apart. I just can't believe it. Every fuckin day was a roller coaster, just like our lives have been and we always made it. (Did I lose hope for a minute? I think I might have. If I did, it was only for one minute. I remember when she was confused, she didn't recognize me. I left feeling *alone that night*.) I talked myself back into reality and that she is only confused. I know she will have less confusion and know who I am. And the next day she did. I just can't believe this. *It can't be real.*

Her mother was very strong for us. She gave my boys so much love on Easter more than usual. Her father is just as strong. You can see he just wants to run away or something. I don't think anyone can believe this. My boys seem so strong but they are hurting so bad. It just doesn't seem real. My mother left her children this way John's wife left her children this way and now Becky. It can't be real.

That morning was just as horrible as anyone can imagine. Becky's mother slowly turned the day around for the boys. They were able to have a sense of family. She held us all together. I was able to talk with Becky's Mom and Dad alone.

I told them I was glad that they were able to be with her when she went. Becky's mother talked with her and they held hands, they talked about when Becky was a little girl and as they talked they were walking in the story they were sharing.

Becky and her mother walked all the way from the hospital and right to her mother's house holding hands, as they passed stores and familiar land marks Becky pointed them all out. When she arrived at the house she went to her room and said" Its just like I remember" And that's when she let go of her Mothers hand and closed her eyes.

I know in Becky's fight to survive she wanted to go home to her children and feel safe. Now she was able go home to her childhood and her mother had everything to do with guiding her there. *She was supposed to take Becky home.*

I never said goodbye, I always told Becky I never would.

Monday, we prepare for her funeral and not a liver transplant. The funeral director is a kind heart. He took time with us and view pictures and listened to stories of who Becky was. I could tell he was fond of what he was hearing.

Mr. Morill is a gentleman. He tried very hard to ease the pain.

He pulled me to the side and said "*I have been doing this for a long time, every few years someone comes through that fought a very hard fight. And your wife's fight is probably the toughest one I have seen.*"

His statement made me proud to hear that she was that strong. However, I have seen her since she passed, and I can tell she should not have held on so long. Now, I wish she didn't fight so hard. I can see the Doctor was right. I wish she let go sooner. I feel so bad for her, Now more than ever. It wasn't fair that she became sick. It was really unfair to push her to fight. I am going to carry this as guilt. I can see now she had no chance back in December. Arrangements are made and the funeral will be Tomorrow.

The next day… The procession past the house; On the way from the funeral home to the church. Mr. Morill Had the flower car Stop in front of the house for a solid 60 seconds. All the cars followed behind. Just waited and realized, *Becky wanted to go home so many times.* It was a wonderful act of respect for her.

Becky's father, her uncle and cousin; along with me and the boys carried the casket. My youngest son walked in the front with his hands touching the casket.

She *carried* them into life... they will *carry her* to her resting place.

They are brave and she would be very proud. The Priest spoke about her in a way that seems like he knew her. He mentioned the sounds of wind chimes and asked us to try to have sweet memories of her when *we could hear those sounds*.

80
We can do this

As we try and pick up the pieces and *try to move on*. As they say… I realize… I have to work hard to maintain. We have bills and the kids only have me to rely on now. *I can't let them down*. I am going to work harder than ever so they don't have to worry about anything. I will start with Groceries.

I have never actually gone food shopping. I checked the cabinets and remembered things we used to have.

Confectioneries sugar, maraschino cherries, meats, milk, bread, vegetables, Bathroom supplies, Coffee, tea, I made an incredible list. I got everything I could imagine.

At the checkout… I could feel my body shaking. I am not sure of what I was supposed to do.

Becky used coupons, she always told me about double coupons, and two for one deals, but you have to look at the unit prices.

I was confused and upset. I don't know what half of this stuff is even for. The cashier totaled it up and said

"That will be $ 347.59, is that all we can help you with today?"

I knew it was going to be a lot of money. I wasn't concerned with that; I figured some weeks it will be high. I was on the verge of tears as I said" I don't know I've never done this before, my wife usually does"

I left with my groceries, and I could feel my entire body shaking.
It is a different life now….

I wanted the house to feel warmer than it has. We put the heat at 72 to 75. Becky and I were not big on cupcakes and soda. But *I wanted the boys to have some comfort*. I stockpiled those things. I also wanted them to keep taking vitamins and eat right. Every dinner will have meat, potatoes and vegetables. I can make a great spaghetti sauce with meatballs.

We can do this. You take what God gives you. Eight years earlier, I had asked to *keep me here for my children*, I had no Idea it was going to be like this.

It is what I asked for and here I am.

I guess during the time Becky was in the hospital… my boys had time to adjust to the differences, I am just beginning that now. Becky wanted the boys to have things like a pool and a trampoline. I am going to try to get those things before summer.

I developed a solid routine, up at 5am get the boys up at 6am get clothes out make lunches, and head out to work. I work until 7pm I get home around 8pm. I make dinner and we eat by 9pm. I think it's not so healthy for the kids. I try to make dinner for tomorrow, today… and the kids can heat it up before I get home. They prefer to wait and eat with me.

It's late and my youngest is losing sleep. They usually have plenty to eat before I get home its just not healthy stuff. I do anything I can… to stay busy, By May I purchased a trampoline.

August I purchased a pool. We were outside at night with lights installing it. It took 14hrs to put up and 5 days to fill.

Just days before they went back to school they were able to use it. Next year they don't have to wait at all…

For months…. I can't think of anything but Becky. And I stay busy it puts so much into my mind that I am able to get through each day. I can see that my kids are doing their job and they are able to function.

People suggest counseling. I told them I spoke with a counselor once in my life and it was fine. But I think it was the same as talking about it with anyone you can trust.

I have been talking to Seth almost daily about it. And that has helped. At home we all talk about it. My oldest son has had a girlfriend the entire time and they talk about it. My older son talks to my younger sons and so do I, *I know time is a healer*. That's what they say. *And we have been able to move on in time from all sorts of bullshit in our lives*. I stop sometimes and cry…. I think that's a good thing to do. It helps letting things out.

Becky's family will take over the holidays and that should seem normal. One of Becky's friends asked if we should move back to Lynn now. I just ask why?

I have Becky's sign out here and it says *grow where your planted* even though this place doesn't feel so good anymore.

I think it was for Becky, Not me. It's her house. I decided to paint all the rooms brighter and in striking colors, to have a different feel.

We still go to the Lynn area and we still love Border Café and Bisuteki. We make a trip as often as we can. We drove all the way to Lynn just to have Mino`s suvlaki dinner. I love that, and their homemade salad dressing. I think it was worth the 160 mile round trip. I am still skinny as a rail. I wish I could make the trip more often. I love Lynn and miss it. *But this is home now and my kids have established close friends.*

I have two or three friends that visit from Lynn and I have two or three friends from here. As long as they have what they need they can heal right here. I keep so busy time is my healer. I do her job and mine now. I am getting better at cooking. Its *Nothing like hers* but I can cook and sometimes I get creative. For example….My kids love chicken, I love beef. You can cook both and add thick peppers and onions and teriyaki sauce, pour it over rice and every ones happy. I am learning a lot about things like that

81
Enjoy my Award

I am getting better at shopping I
haven't had a bill that high since. I can do
the two for ones and check unit prices. I
have coupons but, I always forget them.
Now I know why women have pocket books.
I just stay busy doing the laundry, cooking,
cleaning, cutting grass, working on the pool,
even sewing my kid's clothes; I don't want
them to worry about anything. My youngest
son worries about me constantly. If I sneeze
he runs over and asks if I am ok. He is afraid
of losing me now.

Working all day and going home to
all the domestic stuff. Is an awful lot to
handle but as far back as I can remember, I
have always had a lot on my plate. There are
times I want to stop and take a break. But
my children have needs.

I am here for them and this is what I can do, our sales at work are very good, and continuing to rise. My oldest son is getting his license, so I got him a car. I know he will take my younger boys around too. And I *replaced almost everything in the car* with new parts. It's giving me the sense that they are safer that way. It's a used car, but it's like new. I personally feel that *there isn't a car in the world worth more than a few thousand dollars*; they all suck when you get inside and underneath, and see what they are made of. We joke when we cut old parts off and as we throw the scrap parts away we say that they will come back someday as a beer can or something.

We are busy enough to hire another guy, Matt, he's young but he has ambition he wants to learn, aside of saying "Ah Dude" all the time he seems ok.

I am ready to teach if he's ready to learn. I just hope after I teach him what he needs to know, that he stays… it's a lot to train someone the right way. While doing my usual duties… I am the only Manager with a *filthy white shirt* but it gets the job done and done right. *No comebacks*, that's what we strive for. Customer satisfaction…

My Market supervisor informed us that a couple of shops were fined for oil spills and cleanliness issues. We have a lot extra cleaning to do to meet the standards

We also have to refresh $80,000.00 worth of small parts in order with new packaging and find a way to remove every drop of oil. It's hard when you do so many oil changes but we will do it. Being this busy keeps my mind occupied

Becky's birthday was tough to handle it's always been in line with Thanksgiving, Christmas was very hard. Aside of very late dinner everything at home is ok.

At work this new project is overwhelming. We are focused on complying with all the new company rules. My boss wants at least ten oil changes a day. If we focus on oil changes at $9.99 with coupon we will not be hitting sales like we were. If that's what he wants that's what he gets. Seth and Matt know the job that I do in the office and I know their job so we all work together. It's been eleven months since Becky passed and I haven't stopped since. At work I am getting angry as well as the difficulty I have just coping with my own issues.

On February 20th the mailman brought in a large package.

I opened it and it was this stores first "*Customer Satisfaction*" award. We did that. My Market manger came in just minutes later. I took him around and asked what he thought of the place his response was "ah it's ok."

The Market Manager just down played all the extra work I've done? I could feel stinging in my hand as I pictured myself *slapping his face*. He stood at the counter and gently touched the award as he told me my sales and car counts are down. I wanted a reason to leave and I just said "*Are you trying to fire me Jack?*" He shook his head and said "Yeah I'm afraid so." I shook his hand and said "Thank you, enjoy my award, and have a good day"

82
A Reunion

I left. Feeling as though the only reason, I ended up here, was because something greater than anything I know, planned it ahead of time. I know people have all sorts of opinions on religion. *Maybe there was something so big Becky had to be taken, All, I know is the Pope was taken a week later.*

When my son died, my sister went about a week later, and when my brother died, my other sister went about a week later and Joey went right after that.

Were they all back to back to assist each other in some way? I don't know, all I know is, I needed to be down the street from that Hospital before Becky even went there. And now I don't need to be there…. I am not hurt for being fired;

I am hurt for working so hard the past year. When I took the corrections tests, the fingerprint guy, had to touch my hands to do the prints. He commented *"wow those are working hands." They always were.* I had enough money in the bank now to get by a couple of Months. Time to stop and review life...

I decided I will try to *separate myself* from Becky. I don't know how, but Time will be my healer. If I sit and think about my life I guess

Maybe I can find a direction that will make sense to me, and let me enjoy life with my kids; they haven't had any of my time in a while.

Without a plan, I wake up in the morning and get the kids ready and I spend the remainder of the day on the couch, I watch crazy talk shows and what ever else seems unreal and allows me to wonder. I had a plan with Becky, Now I am "on hold"

A day can turn into a week and a month before you know it. Several months past, In recent months.... I had done my food shopping mostly at a store near work.

Now, that I am home…. I decided to take a left and head to the stores around here. *That's how Becky and I did it. She did the shopping at times I went along*

The last time we went that way we were able to *see brand new baby cows*. Becky asked me to stop and we looked at them. It was funny to see the babies.

This was my first time going that way since. Those babies are grown, not fully, but they are much larger. You can see *they are the same babies*. I never know when thoughts of Becky will overwhelm me and I never expected to see those cows.

I could feel Becky hitting my arm and say "Oh look honey." I raced home trying not to think, finally when I got home, I took a bag out of the car and ran in the house I *asked my kids to get the rest* I can't and I fell *apart as if she just left again.* I know I need to get better. How?... I look around and see all of what we have was for her.

A few days later… while I was watching crazy talk shows the phone rang, I picked up and it was John He said "Hey Bri" I said "hey how's life?" He said "It's good; how are you?"

I told him about Becky and brought him up to date. I haven't seen him in ten years. We discussed maybe meeting up sometime, I really haven't seen him and I figured why not? He found me in the phone book. He was surprised that I moved from Lynn. *He hasn't even met my youngest son yet.* We were close until his wife died.

I understand what he was going through but, I did things differently and I will not understand why he did things the way he did. I guess he tried to escape his reality. I want to as well at times. But my kids didn't ask to be here. And I did. *That's my motivation.*

I stay home most of the time leaving only to get things for the house. I have no desire to socialize. I get lonely but you take what *God gives you.* When Becky and I saw the movie *Ghost* I turned to her and said "If I ever passed away would you move on?" She said "No way, would you?" I said "Not a chance"

My sister tells me that I still have a lot of life ahead of me and I should move on. I just don't feel I would like anyone else. And I promised Becky, that I wouldn't. The truth is here and I have to accept it.

I also said "I wouldn't take another day for myself; my sister said "The boys need a normal home situation and a woman is going to complete that. I told her we are a normal home situation. It's *quiet and comfortable and its feels like the safest place on earth to us*, what more can you ask for? We *have already had what many people dream of*. I can deal with being lonely at times.

Sometimes I crank up heavy metal, and hours later, Soft rock or mix music. My ups and downs with the emotion are felt through music, It can be a *distraction from the loneliness*, And helps me express my emotions most of them are anger right now

I realize I miss her when people come by to see me. I don't feel as lonely. Our old friends come by, the friends we had together and when they leave I feel horrible. *I show that I am doing fine, while they are here*. But I feel like they view me as a broken half of something that was so complete.

When they leave I sink so low it takes a day or two to rise up and get on track. My *here and now isn't much of anything*.

What the fuck is counseling going to do? It will allow me to talk about how I feel, and maybe they will try to prescribe a Medicine of some sort, sorry, I don't do pills and I like to have my mind in tact good or bad it's my thoughts and feelings, I can control. I like my beers. I still wait until around seven at night before I have any. Even then its only two or three

John has been calling often and we talk about the past present and future; we are beginning to develop another relationship. It's been ten years and he thought I was still *pissed* because when Dad died and he wasn't around,

He also left his girls with their grandmother. He had insurance money left from Cheryl and used it for *drugs and booze*. I had no insurance for Becky, not even health insurance. If that's what could have happened *I have no regrets there*. I don't think I could have felt good at all, spending any money received from her passing anyway. It would have helped with the kids I hope they go to college and it would have made things easier, But It just isn't right to me. *I still think elbow grease is what pays the bills*. John is going to come out to the house for a reunion of sorts. He has a girlfriend "Jan" she is an older Asian woman.

I told him he could bring her along. I have told my boys stories about when I was younger, and some stories about John mostly adventurous things. And when John and I met after he got out of jail.

My youngest was eager to meet John. He loves everyone. My other sons were curious and looking forward to see if it helps me pick myself up and get ready to move on in life. My oldest son thought I was doing fine *as long as I stayed working*. But my own mental well being *was not so fine*. I am at a point in life where we should be planning our children's future as a man and his wife. I feel as if half of my soul was taken away.

Working all the time isn't doing it for me. I feel doomed and awkward

I don't feel like a person that belongs anywhere, *just walking through life searching for something*. Not even knowing what that something is.

At times I feel like my rocket landed in a fiery crash, and I somehow survived, and I have to *search for a life that I have never known* in a place I've never been. I have my children with me; I want to be all I can to them.

I just have to *find me*. I met up with John and his new girl in the next town. It's very confusing when you're on these country roads, so I will direct them to the house. It was funny seeing him; he used to have long hair and a beard, now he resembles Dad.

That is *only* a compliment if you know and love Dad. His girl seems very sweet, she is shy. The dogs came out barking at the stranger's car. I forgot John was attacked by a dog when we were younger. *I told him they are just big babies.*

He almost believed me. He was cautious, I know they bark for a minute but they are just checking and want to be noticed, after a quick sniff to the crotch, and your ok to pass. It's the same routine every time with them. I started telling him stories about the dogs especially Piggy. He laughs about it, and he seems to see the look in pig's eyes and feel its all true, "*Pigs up to no good I tell ya*" he said

John was very surprised to see what we have done. Moving to the country, the house is beautiful. If it were in Lynn, I would have to spend a million dollars or more for what we have here. He really can't believe it.

We have created such a life for us in the ten years that he hasn't seen me. *We made dreams come true.* It's a long way from the projects. He loved seeing the kids. Especially my youngest John never knew he existed. My middle son is a solid mass of muscle; my oldest is taller than me. He just can't get over what he sees. They were *skinny little babies* when he left.

I made the *sauce and meatballs*. He said it was better than Elaine's, we had beers by the fire, and he drove the tractor all around with a huge smile, singing the Green acres song. He just can't believe it. I told him it was all for Becky and the boys. I love it here, just *not as much as she did*.

Matt and Seth came by to meet him; they also like the fire and beers. We all had a great time. John had prepared to stay at a hotel in the next town. But we have plenty of room. We drank beers until daylight. John and my youngest son spent a lot of time in the pool. They love the water. We were laughing and goofing around. This is what the toys and yard, are meant for. Nothing beats loud music and beers by the fire. My kids get upset when; I let loose drinking so much. I am not an angry drunk, I actually get silly. But they know it's just not a good habit, and when I am alone, I stop at three beers.

When I am with anyone else I have many beers. At this moment life feels *"the way it should"* John and I made a plan to get together again next weekend this time he will leave his girl home. She is very sweet. But I think he wants one to one time.

After his visit…. my boys and I talked about him and the fun. They were glad to see I still have someone that's been in my life since I can remember, but they weren't happy about the beers. We were a bunch of drunk guys partying I can see their point. It did feel good to me. And I have some new spirit. I have always had beers when I am with John it's *just what we did.* I already know we will have just as much. When he returns If were going to be carefree and just enjoy the time.

I told my boys I will try to play it cool next time. My boys view me as an upstanding man. And when they see that…. is embarrasses them and they feel. I have lowered myself. To something I am not. I try to tell them it's ok to let loose sometimes as long *as nobody gets hurt.* John arrived as planned; we did up the fire and started with some beers. We left the music and friends behind this time.

We talked about the old days and bars we hung around in. He asked about the bars here I told him there's one in town and I have only been there once, my drinking is done at home.

I am all my kids have and I don't want to fuck it up drinking and driving. He agreed but he disagrees, He asked if we could go down and check it out I figured yeah... if we had to.... *we can walk back*. I figured for one or two beers is fine

As we entered, *I realized these are the same people that were here last time.* People aren't big on fancy clothes and make up in this town. John was shocked. He wondered where the good looking women went. I laughed and said "This is it" He replied "These people are *carnie folks* and this is a *carnie bar* is the carnival in town?"

There is one blonde woman that checks me out from time to time at the Post office. She was there and I said "Hi" politely

I am not looking for a woman. It is almost two years now, I can't think of anyone, but Becky. This blonde woman is the first person I've even looked back at.

We had two beers, John isn't used to the laid back attitude, he expected a sports bar with nicer looking women around the kind with *make up and tight clothes*. Hot chicks don't compete here. Just carnie folks…. There is usually only a couple of woman and a lot of men

He began getting belligerent, so I decided its time to go. He likes the land and the house but *he doesn't like the lifestyle*. It's slow and steady. He has an apartment in Salem near Lynn and he is a Bartender, The Bartender here could open beers, he wanted to be impressed *by her skills* and he wasn't. I told him to chill out. I remember now the things I didn't like about him. For starters, I didn't want my kids worried about drinking, *and here we are*. I wanted to stay home by the fire, *and here we are*. I can't stand when people try to belittle other people, *and here we are*. We got back to the house in a less hostile environment. He has nothing to trigger his attitude He *hates* most people and he has an *acidic tongue* the rest of his visit was slightly stressful but we were able to salvage some cheer the rest of time.

Now that he is in my life… we do communicate on a regular basis.

He wants to visit for weekends often, after what I saw today.

I realize as long as he stays away
from "hard stuff" it could be ok   He loves
Vodka... To me... It's pure Poison. One shot
and he "transforms" Into the *acid that*
frequently spills from his tongue

I have new worries anyway,

83
Weakening

The bills are piling up and my money has dwindled. I have no real connections in this little town. I find many people *rely on odd jobs*. I have had the opportunity to work a few. But the ones available are with people that disappear when you need your paycheck. You can work your ass off for them but they can't pay you. Seems like... I am in hot water.

I can find similar jobs to what I had. *In my state of mind* I have created negative reasoning, the problem to me... is that they are far away and they have long hours. Working 10 hrs and a 1hr drive twice a day is a bit much. I have worked over 40hrs for 27yrs... *An easy 40hrs locally would be fine.*

A job in this area for anything with my experience doesn't pay a lot. I am knowledgeable in so many things. I am *qualified* in car repair. I don't think my back can't handle that much more. I would be doing the same thing I did when I was twenty.

When I began saving money, it was to try and put my kids through college. Now I have spent almost all of it.

I feel like I gave up or I just don't care enough any more. I am slowly beginning to accept that I may be losing everything. Some days it makes me physically ill other days I feel like it doesn't matter. I am in a place I have never been and I cannot find "me"

The bills are suffering. And I can't seem to motivate my self like I always have. I feel like *I have also been defeated.* Not to undermine what Becky had said,

But I really feel like I lost myself and I can't find the spark. My thoughts have been geared towards making sure my kids have their *basic needs*. It feels like all the goals I wanted to meet in life. Are a thing of the past ….

I have no goals on my own. I just meet each day as it comes and do what's needed that day. Right now I want to do things at my pace. A snail's pace… I don't know why

84
Brush with goodness

I guess when I saw actual progress with my most recent employer and an *award*. I knew how hard *I worked for that*. I was proud, Customers often came in to compliment the store and us guys, they showed appreciation every day, many of them stopped in just to chat and see how the shop was doing. They even brought treats. You could tell they really liked the place and it was a comfort to them. "My *Mechanic*" Is what we were often referred to as. They would say *"Oh I'll just take it to my Mechanic"* In seconds some Jack Ass, showed me that *all of my efforts never even mattered*.

I began to spend so much time thinking of past employers and past horrible experiences and I remember things that I had all but forgotten about, like my time at Meineke He put me through *years of hell* it seemed like it was for his enjoyment. I worked very hard and fast every day... He was an excellent business man. However, His human side was nasty.

Once, when we had a slow period at the shop I asked if I could drive down the street to get a coffee. He said "If you punch out to get a coffee, stay out and *lose the days pay*!" Half an hour later he had his office girl get them *a coffee*. He pushed the intercom button that made a loud noise in the garage

I looked up to see him hold up a hot coffee nice and high and he smiled as he sipped it. *That day it was raw and cold and all the bay doors were open. I just wanted to warm up.*

He would do things like that all the time. He constantly referred to us as monkeys. He retired with tons of money. I left that job filled with resentment. I wonder if standing on his concrete floors all those years, contributed to my back trouble. If I saw him now, *I would probably spit in his face... that man took my best working years*. And treated me like a lower life form the entire time.

I always thought *hard work and honesty were the way to success* and you would be appreciated for all of your efforts. I had a strong work ethic. But these greedy mother fuckers have chipped away at it over the course of my working life. I don't give a fuck about them.

I cared so much, I faced cold raw weather with snow and water dripping all over me, as oil and transmission fluid would drip down my face. I would hurry up and finish because more people are waiting. All for ten dollars an hour... 60 hrs each week

The owner got about $6000.00 for my efforts each week, and treated me like shit. You try to do the right thing, *and people see it as weakness*. I know when I was in high spirits; I could do two cars in the amount of time it takes to do one. *He lost out* when ever he *dragged me down*. But that's business, He had his reasons

I have been out of work too long now. I am worried about losing the house and facing shut offs. I care... but not enough to fight hard to change things. I feel numbness. And some anger, I feel like *I am on hold*. I can't shake it. I know we need to eat and we need the basics.

I saw an ad for a painter and I decided Ill try it. I can be left alone and work at my pace.

The ad was placed by a guy named Ralph. I contacted him and we were to meet at a house the next day. I showed up on time and he arrived about ten minutes later. Usually, *I am the one ten minutes late.*

We agreed on eleven dollars hour cash under the table.

I know I can produce; I learned in Georgia and I just did my entire house. I just hope he can produce. I worked a few days and began to realize this guy is a half witted moron. He has no common sense, He seems to make up stories a lot and he just doesn't seem very bright at all. I find myself covering his ass.

The house we were working in belongs to a real estate agent named Roberta, Ralph would constantly say "Oh boy, Roberta will be pissed if *that's not right*, and Roberta will be pissed if *we do this*, Roberta will be pissed *about that*, He made it seem to me Roberta pisses and moans about *everything*.

The house also had a refrigerator with magnetic calendar. Sporting her photograph she was a short African American woman and she had a very *angry* look in the photo. It supported his claims to her *attitude*.

The way Ralph spoke of her was beginning to *piss me off*. Maybe she doesn't like anyone. Maybe she has a serious attitude problem. Maybe she thinks she's better than everyone.

Ralph would schedule projects in the house for me. And he would stop me in the middle. He would redirect me and tell me Roberta wants *this* done now, if it isn't done before *that* she will be pissed. Do that after, she wants *this*, she wants *that*. This Roberta is really getting on my nerves. Every time, I walk by her picture. I get even more pissed, as if she is watching me and *bitching at me* as I work.

Ralph told me to clean up good today... Roberta is coming by to see the progress. Great, I thought, I get to meet the bitch today. *It's all I need.* Well, if she gives me any shit, I can walk out. And I will certainly give *her* a piece of my mind.

Later that day…I could hear the door, and I didn't want to scare anyone by surprise. I said "Hello" Then I heard a soft spoken response "*Hello*" I walked out into the room that she was in; she stood looking all around and looked right at me.

That very second, I could feel a sense of warmth come over me. She had a *pleasant smile and her eyes projected a deep kindness.*

She said "I would have been here earlier, but my husband has a doctors appointment he is sick with Cancer" *I apologized*, and told her about Becky, We talked for about ten minutes.

I could feel myself stopped, as if I were on the church steps surrounded by police cars.

The conversation was caring and kind. She concluded with "*I don't think I came by, to see the house, I believe, I came by to meet you*" I gave her a hug and I said "Thank you and God Bless"

The feeling I have been given from this encounter has given me a burst of energy, *I left that day with a feeling of excitement that something wonderful had just happened.*

The ride home is about forty five minutes. The entire time, I thought about her. The feeling was great. *I imagined that somehow an Angel had taken her wing and brushed it across my chest.*

The feeling had magic and it was a gift. I was ecstatic and relaxed at the same time. *It was the opposite of my anxiety attack*, but with the same *intensity*.

This is the first time; I felt this good since Becky was here.

I couldn't wait to get home to tell my sons. I wanted to tell everyone. *I was touched by an Angel.* It's not going to get me into church every week, *but it is giving my life back.* The good feeling... The one that I have when I love life... I just saw it, she showed it to me. This was not in my mind. *This was real and I never saw it coming.* In fact, *I was prepared for quite the opposite,*

Ralph is a slacker, and he puts this woman through a lot of crap with his laziness and lies. I hope she was *as bitchy as he said she was to him.* He still owes me money, but I stopped working for him a few days later.

Life itself can guide me in directions *at times when it's needed.* I was directed to her *for that intervention.*

Ralph was just the sign at the turn. With new hope, I want to try and save myself and become as motivated as I always was. My spirit is lifted. I can try to proceed with my goals. They are to try to make the lives of my children better. I am what they have as an asset. *I don't want that asset to be a dead end.* I see that now.

Thanks Roberta you're the best! I will keep this experience with me and never forget it. I would love to tell people *if you ever get a chance to have an encounter this amazing you need to embrace it and keep it with you. Let the feeling carry you to find your hope and strength. You are not always alone.*

I remember her looking around and saying "I told that Ralph, I wanted it done *this way*, I told that Ralph, I wanted him to *clean the place*, and so on. John was with me at the time… he likes Roberta… especially for the way she *complained about Ralph.*

He was laughing his ass off and pretended to be her and he said "I *tow dat Raff,* Well *tell that Raff, to take a Baff, and wash his nasty Aff.* "(Ralph also had a bad habit of displaying his hairy ass crack when he worked.)

With a new feeling of hope, I am ready to try. I will look in the automotive area, it will probably have to be a bit far and under conditions that suck. At least, I have the experience and back to do it. I searched around Worcester. I have some contacts there.

A few days later... I found a muffler shop. It is an attached three car garage. On the side of a house, it doesn't look it... but it's an official business. The owner offered a pay rate that could pull me out of this hole.

As soon as I started, I could see he was impressed with my *experience*. He approached me and said "I see you've done this before"

I started in 1986, He started in 1996. So yeah, I've done *this before*.

He wouldn't let me do the "engine *stud jobs*" he figured only *he* was capable. He made that *clear*. I watched him break them and then, He would yell and turn to me and say "See I am glad *I* did that and not *you*, if you did it... I would have been *really pissed*" *I would remember some of the toothpicks I removed. He couldn't do that.*

I realize many people can come to work at a shop claiming to have so much experience and then they prove to be complete idiots at times.

I figured oh boy here we go again. It is his shop and he has to feel confident that the job is done right. So I let it roll off my back.

It's all *custom pipe bending*, and a lot of *welding*. It's a busy shop. His prices are great and the work is just as good as ours was at Saugus Meineke. No comebacks. He takes great pride in his shop. He *seems* a little overbearing, but in general a *good guy*.

85
Your job is your life!

When he hired me... I told him about the distance and I was concerned because I know I have a very *bad habit* of being *ten minutes late*. At first he said "well, we do start at 7:30am so try to be on time." I said "I would."

I didn't tell him, but... I often wonder if it's because of when I lived with Ruth and Ed. They never liked having us around so if we had to be anywhere they always sent us very early and we stood in all types of weather, wearing thin clothing and I remember often being cold and wet as I waited. Early birds trying to "catch that worm"

The shop opens at 7:30am He has three techs… that's me, and two other guys. The guys like to show up at 7:20am, they have worked with him for five years or so and they all live within 15minutes of the place. It is a routine that they have established over time. I live about forty five minutes away from the place. I feel successful when I arrive at 7:30am. My average time to arrive is more like 7:35am or so.

And since they have been here almost *20 minutes* it can create some disharmony. Even at 7:30am I already seem to be ten minutes late.

I am not sure if my lack of punctuality or a *jealous tech* created the beginnings of some hostility However, I am feeling that negative vibe. Of course one of the techs has made it clear that he doesn't like me. He watches my every move

The boss pulled me aside and said "Dude your ten minutes late everyday, the other *guys have no trouble getting here. And they are starting to complain. I need you on time or I have to let you go*"

I understand what its like to wait for someone so I don't blame him. I told him about my situation and that I am doing my job and my wife's. I said "everyday something has to be done or rechecked, *before I leave in the morning*, I have three kids that have to get ready before I leave. The boss responded by saying " *Dude you have no idea, When I notice its 7:30 and your not here, My heart begins to pound in my chest and I get nervous because I have customers waiting*"

After that "warning" I began to see things go downhill fast.

If, I went to the bathroom he would knock loudly on the door and remind me that he has customers calling about the cars. My son calls my cell phone everyday when he gets home just to check in… the call lasts less than a minute. He mentioned that I am always on my cell phone. If it keeps up I will have to leave it home. *He has a blue tooth stuck to his head and talks all day.* But he is the boss… I guess that makes all the difference.

Funny he talks strongly about God and family, *His God and his family*

I can understand about punctuality… the truth is… at his place a half hour would not make a difference. All of his customers drop the cars off for the day. He gets *pissed if their in after 7:30am as well.* He feels very strong about punctuality. He always says " Drop your car off at 7:30am and plan on leaving it for the day, When it is done we will call you."

All of the customers are scheduled. He takes in a specific amount of cars daily. No one can expect to arrive at 8am or later and plan on a repair for that day.

I told him "I will do all my cars everyday, if I do them in ten hours or nine hours and fifty minutes they will all get done."

I also call from my cell phone so he doesn't worry and he knows I am almost there. Or, if I am stuck at the exit The Holy Cross exit can be a breeze or a nightmare you never know until your one mile before it. At that point there is no turning back. I have sat there for a half hour at times. I am not looking for sympathy only understanding...

The guys all have wives and children at home. The guys all tell me " My wife does all the crap at home I just get up and leave for work." I don't have that luxury anymore and I want the *quality* of my *kids home life* to remain as it was… so I do Becky's job to the best of my ability. When I am *ten minutes late,* I do work much faster *so the boss isn't pissed.* He actually benefits this way.

He said "*All you have to do is leave ten minutes early; I tried to tell him it's not that easy. In fact, I am dressed and on the road at 6:40am.* He is just waking up. His wife does all that has to be done at home.

He has so much *all around* support from his family, a Mother, Brothers, a Wife and children. I have my children

I see it's a control issue, this job may not last very long, he will not be flexible he is a type A personality. He told me he used to do drugs and be an *asshole*, but his wife stopped him when she was going to leave him. They were just dating then, he was 20. Since then, he has built this business and *helped so many people* and he just goes on about how wonderful he is. He eventually fired me. However, months later, I returned. I did try. But to no avail, I found my self ten and fifteen minutes late.

He said "*Dude your always the last one in and the first one to leave.* I explained again,

I do all of the cars that you give to me, I do them quickly, I have to go home and do the *same job your wife does*. I am both parents to my children. He responded by saying "you tell me you are trying to save your house and that you have problems Dude everybody has problems but let me tell you..... Your house is not important!"

Your job is the most important thing this is your LIFE!

A job is obviously incredibly important However, his job is not *my life*. I didn't even get angry… I didn't even want to think of anything that could possibly *hurt* this guy. He claims to have this great *faith in God and Family*.

He just proved to me that *he doesn't*. I have seen so many times. That it all comes back and *I feel for him*, because he hasn't *experienced any life yet*. I left and realized, I may lose my home, I may hit rock bottom. *But I do have faith in my children and myself. That is what's most important. It doesn't matter if we live in a house or apartment.*

I worked off and on for him for two years, I noticed he was always happy and bouncing around he has a lot of the energy… I have that too when *things are going good for me*

He has all of his family and friends and plenty of money and a nice home and he has his health and family's health. He is extremely fortunate.

I know he couldn't last 24hrs in my shoes. But that doesn't matter. *They are my shoes.*

He would say "Dude why can't you just be happy? you seem down sometimes" I tell him *I am happy* (In my thoughts... I am thinking gee I don't know maybe, I have things to worry about, things you could never imagine. He knows about all of my troubles. He regards them as trivial) *His business is his life* not much else matters

86
See the real you

One day a coworker's father came in and the Coworker became a bit testy. My boss said to me *"Well his Father used to give him beatings when he was a kid. So I am going to let him have the rest of the day off, could you pick up the slack?"* I said "Sure I know what he feels like"

The Boss said *"What?! You have NO Idea what he went through!" You think you have problems, He went through a lot with those beatings ok, so think of other people, and their problems, sometimes not just yourself, you aren't the only one with problems."*

That made me imagine somehow letting *him live in my mind and heart for one day*. But then, I stopped myself and worried that *it could be so terrible for him to feel like me*, and as if I wished it on him, I would feel some bad Karma.

His ignorance is his freedom

However……The day that he said "my house and life meant shit and his business was my life" that ended it. I just had to go…

I went back to my couch and crazy talk shows; I tried to *find the feeling*, and what I could do to save my family from, losing everything. Or where to go and what to do

Should I just stop worrying and get an apartment? I talk to John every day. We joke about *a potential family curse.*

I have not forgotten about Roberta. And that somehow, gives me an inner peace. I have begun to except the fact that I will most likely lose the house and everything that goes with it. Strangely I have a sense that its o.k. And I should first begin to love myself and remember how to live… everything else should follow and I can build new dreams

John calls to check in and see how things are. He does worry about me. His health has become a very big concern from years of self abuse. We do have each other to cheer us up. *We often talk about the old days*. Especially Ruth and Ed, John often feels like he abandoned us. I know if he stayed, he would have been killed. John tells me stories of when I was born, He says "Bri I got to tell ya, when you came home, Oh you were perfect, you looked so handsome and you had those pretty eyes and you were just so quiet and happy all the time. Mom would say Shh the baby is sleeping, so I would tip toe past you, *don't wake the baby*. You were just so cool, Man, I knew right then and there, this wonderful little baby Brian he is just amazing. When you came home you weren't Moms baby, you were our baby."

John also told me that when Jimmy came home he was crying all the time, he screamed for his own way, all the time. John couldn't remember a time when Jimmy was nice or quiet. He didn't want another baby around.

But, I showed up and he loved it. If he stuck around Ruth and Ed's house to see my first beating, that would have given him an instinct to protect me and he would have been killed in the process. *John doesn't take as much shit as I do.* He would have attacked Ed with a sharp object or something.

We talk about our Dad, He was a Korean War Vet and one time we saw him pull out his own tooth, no problem. We laughed, because it's not something people just do. *But it was the radiation; he was on the test sight. He told us the bomb went off and he felt a surge of heat and then he felt a surge of cold go through his entire body.*

He died from Cancer, My Mother did as well, my sister Linda found out she had Cancer before she died. My sister Amy had lung disease, Jimmy had head trouble, and John has many health issues and I thank God everyday, for each one given to me. *Everyday you get a new one.*

I was informed that the Government gives money to survivors of the Korean War to Veterans and their families. If they have had *one* of the listed of types of Cancer; Relating to the testing... *Dad had most of all the types listed.*

You know how I feel, about taking money for someone that died. Elaine probably already did anyway. *Legally, she was his wife and that entitled her to it*. I hear she has a new husband, and he is loaded with cash, so she found her dream guy. Good luck to him.

I worry over money now. I never *loved* money… but I realize that green paper is a driving force. If I want my children to live an easier life I have to show them how important it is. *They have to have some greed, I guess*. It's too bad.

Based on the way things are going, I think the *money system has to be changed*. I have earned so much money in my life time, Yet, I am losing everything and I worked for I eventually lost the house in foreclosure.. We got a small but cozy apartment

When Becky was around, we had a plan to get these things to enjoy in our lifetime and to leave for our children. *Giving them something, as a gift of our love*

Hoping that it can make their lives happier and easier I feel as though, I let her down and more so I let them down. I try to look past all the horror and move forward and find that energy again. It's very tough.

Sometimes, I wonder if there's any fight left in me. I look at my boys everyday, and I am so thankful that I have them in my life. You figure this would be my motivation. It is however, my spirit gets shattered when I try and fall down. At this point in time I am feeling a little better I am no longer worrying about the house

John and I talk all the time. We talk about the entire Marie situation; we really just rehash the memories. John knows *I was so lucky to have a bush to hide in and I saved my own life covering her mouth.* During the time Becky was in the ICU MY daughter called, She asked how I was doing I told her not so well,

She asked if I had $1000.00 I could send her. I told her no, I'm sorry but Becky's in the ICU and it doesn't look good. I only have my pay coming in.

She said "Mom's all upset too, her fiancé came home and found her sleeping with his best friend, so he drove his motorcycle into a tree and killed himself"

Wow, sounds familiar? I told John about the past conversations with my son, John agrees *their minds were poisoned*, and I will never have a place in their hearts.

If I had some money to give my daughter, she may call... every now and then.

John told me he saw Elaine and she looks like she is a rich woman. *Her kids look like shit.*

Being a bartender he sees a lot of the people we knew when we were growing up in Lynn. It figures if *you want a reunion hit the Lynn bars.* John talks about his kids and my kids we are proud of our kids we want them to be better than us

He keeps telling me I can fight to fix all of my money problems, he knows, I will find a way. I am glad he knows I sure don't. I can't find a job that pays without documentation proving my experience. I have no degree *I have enough experience,* to fill almost 250 pages of real life experience now that's a resume. Well, money isn't everything, I can start fresh. This tiny apartment feels a little like a stepping stone.

I just want to find the starting line, and position myself just right, so I can run with it and begin my life in a way that feels normal and comfortable.

Every day, shouldn't be so full of worry. It's my time, I have these talks with John and he keeps trying to guide me to a place in my life, where I find the drive and motivation.

He talks about it so I can see what I have faced, and made it. He wants me to see these things. He told me when he thinks about me, he feels like he can do anything just knowing, I am his example.

I feel these things in spurts. It helps when someone that knows you has your back. I have carried a lot of guilt and that has held me down. *It's not easy when you're in it.* I have to step outside of myself sometimes and just see *the real in me.* That same person, that Becky wanted to spend all of her life with. I think because she isn't here. I feel like nobody else will ever see the real in me. She was my biggest motivation. She's been gone for four years now

I did try to date a couple of times. I saw the blonde from the bar for about a week. I was riddled with guilt. I promised Becky that I wouldn't do that. But then again, I am human and I wanted to be married all my life and I am still alive.

I have wasted so much time just sitting here trying to find me again.

I sat back and quietly thought for awhile about good things. As they say….. it can always get worst. With that in mind I realized….I was very lucky to have the help when I needed it.

My children have always been my Angels right here on earth; Becky was my angel here on earth, without any doubt. Stephanie was my angel here on earth. My youngest son was my angel and pulled me right back into life, Seth, Matt, and family friends were my Angels when Becky was sick. Roberta was the Angel to give me that gentle push. The push that allowed me to start to see the real in me again

If you are lucky enough to have a chance to be touched in this way you need to embrace the feeling and know how special it is. You never know *what form your angels will take or even when they arrive. But help is always here.* Even the bus driver for my son, gave so much to us. In the way of help when it was needed, she is another Angel. Heather and Bill have been so kind and such warm friends. Angels

I could go on and on Becky has had so many wonderful friends. That just cared and went out of their *way to give comfort*. My friends,

My in laws have continued to give the sense of family. The more I look around, I sure do have *a lot going for me*. Even Piglet loves me, *He's got a funny way of showing it*. Hunter would take a bullet for me. I realize now it's time for me to let go of all the things that *have held me back*.

Losing Becky was the toughest challenge I have faced on my own. I asked for this time here on earth. Because I love my life *I asked to stay for my children*, Because, I want them to love this life. I needed to hit rock bottom and I sure have.

With the help of my children, faith, and many other people, I will climb out from this *pile of rubble* that I have let collapse around me.

John called the other day and we started talking about way back when I was a baby again. He said *"oh remember when Dad had to look for our puppy in the snow?"* I said "ah not really"

He said "Oh yeah the dog was white and Mom was upset because she couldn't find him Dad went out for two hours looking in a blizzard when he got back he found the dog was sleeping under your bed."

I laughed and I said "I remember bits and pieces here and there but that's about it." He said "nah c'mon you must remember all kinds of stuff from when Mom was here" I said "John I was only like five… I remember the ice cream truck, and oh wait a minute, I remember one day as clear as anything…. It went just like this…

OK boys lets go, like three little ducklings we followed Moms voice without even having to look up. We walked out the front door. I happened to look up and say "Hey what is this stuff?" Jimmy said "its fog" John added yeah it's 'Froggy' out. Instantly the humor and the experience we had with frogs gave me a sense of comfort,

(*We like going to the brook to catch frogs. My fun was watching my brothers. It was a challenge, in the wild, watching, waiting one move and it was a free for all, the art of catching one without getting wet. Someone always ended up in the slimy green gunk, Or with some very wet sneakers, That was usually our cue to head home.*)